Custom, Law and the Colonial State in Northeast India

AF766723

This volume presents a multidimensional analysis of the current operational law – both constitutional and customary – in Northeast India. It looks at how colonialism redesigned and redefined extant customary practices, leaving a permanent legacy on the legal governance and societal structure of the post-colonial Indian state.

The book interrogates "law" through a broad spectrum of issues including gender, partition, the legacy of colonial structures, and religion as a form of resistance against land grabbing and censorship. It delineates a distinct historical process of the evolution of law and custom and focuses on the intimate links between law and the dynamics of state, ethnicity, and governance.

As a unique contribution, the book offers new insights into how and why the continuity of colonial law within a democratic framework perpetuates deep-rooted problems in governance and the psyche of the people. It will be indispensable for students and researchers of history, law, anthropology, legal anthropology, sociology, Indian politics, and South Asian studies.

Nandini Bhattacharyya Panda is currently project Director in Indian Council of Historical Research, New Delhi, India. She is also the Distinguished Fellow of Asian Confluence, Meghalaya. A historian and Sanskritist, her book *Appropriation and Invention of Tradition: The English East India Company and Hindu Law in Early Colonial Bengal* (2012) was a seminal contribution to modern Indian history. She has also lectured on Hindu Law, Northeast India, and other subjects in leading national and international universities, such as University of Cambridge, UK, Penn Law School at the University of Pennsylvania, Dhaka University, Bangladesh, among others. She has been working on the Eastern Himalayas including Nepal and Northeast India since 2006. She has published books, articles, and made a documentary film in 2016 on the Lepcha community of the Eastern Himalayas under the title: The Lepcha Community of the Darjeeling and Kalimpong Hills: Quest for the Roots.

Custom, Law and the Colonial State in Northeast India

Dynamics and Challenges for the Postcolonial State

Edited by Nandini Bhattacharyya Panda

Routledge
Taylor & Francis Group
LONDON AND NEW YORK

First published 2025
by Routledge
4 Park Square, Milton Park, Abingdon, Oxon OX14 4RN

and by Routledge
605 Third Avenue, New York, NY 10158

Routledge is an imprint of the Taylor & Francis Group, an informa business

© 2025 selection and editorial matter, Nandini Bhattacharyya Panda; individual chapters, the contributors

The right of Nandini Bhattacharyya Panda to be identified as the author of the editorial material, and of the authors for their individual chapters, has been asserted in accordance with sections 77 and 78 of the Copyright, Designs and Patents Act 1988.

All rights reserved. No part of this book may be reprinted or reproduced or utilised in any form or by any electronic, mechanical, or other means, now known or hereafter invented, including photocopying and recording, or in any information storage or retrieval system, without permission in writing from the publishers.

Trademark notice: Product or corporate names may be trademarks or registered trademarks, and are used only for identification and explanation without intent to infringe.

British Library Cataloguing-in-Publication Data
A catalogue record for this book is available from the British Library

ISBN: 978-1-032-40479-0 (hbk)
ISBN: 978-1-032-88818-7 (pbk)
ISBN: 978-1-003-53979-7 (ebk)

DOI: 10.4324/9781003539797

Typeset in Sabon
by SPi Technologies India Pvt Ltd (Straive)

This volume is dedicated to the memory of late Shri Shakti Sinha, former Director of Prime Ministers Museum and Library (formerly Nehru Memorial Museum and Library)

Contents

Contributors

Kaushik Thakur Bhuyan was awarded the Indian Council of Social Science Research (ICSSR) Doctoral fellowship (2017–2019) to work on his thesis titled *"History and Cinema: Ideologies, Sensibilities and Popular Culture in Assam (1935–1995)"* from North Eastern Hill University (NEHU), Shillong. His specialization is the History of Modern India with interest in history of cinema/popular culture, social history, historiography, and history of culture. He was a recipient of the IRIS Indo-Japan Program and a visiting fellow of the Embassy of India to Ministry of Foreign Affairs (MOFA) Japan, January 2020. He is currently serving as an assistant professor at the Department of History at Pandit Deendayal Upadhyaya Adarsha Mahavidyalaya (PDUAM), Dalgaon, Assam, India.

Erik de Maaker (PhD Leiden University, 2006) is Associate Professor at the Institute of Cultural Anthropology and Development Sociology of Leiden University. His thematic focus is on the social constitution of values, objects, and places, and their relevance in terms of ethnicity, indigeneity, heritage, environment, and religion, mainly in upland South and Southeast Asia. Current research focuses on how appreciations of heritage can inform notions of sustainability in both local and globalized contexts. He is author of the monograph *Reworking Culture: Relatedness, Rites, and Resources in Garo Hills, North-East India* (OUP, 2022) and co-editor of *Environmental Humanities in the New Himalayas: Symbiotic Indigeneity, Commoning, Sustainability* (Routledge 2021), *Audiovisual and Digital Ethnography: A Practical and Theoretical Guide* (Routledge 2021), and *Media, Indigeneity and Nation in South Asia* (Routledge 2019). He is an author prolifically published in journals such as *Asian Ethnography, South Asia*, *Visual Anthropology*, and the *Journal of Borderland Studies*, and he is also an award-winning visual anthropologist. He is a track leader of the Heritage and Identity track of the Leiden-Delft-Erasmus Centre for Global Heritage and Development.

Binayak Dutta teaches history at the North-Eastern Hill University, Shillong. He was formerly with the Assam University and Visiting Fellow, OKD Institute of Social Change and Development, an ICSSR Institute,

Guwahati. He is currently also a Senior Honorary Fellow at Asian Confluence, a think tank working on Northeast India.

Theyiesinuo Keditsu (PhD) is Assistant Professor at the Department of English, Kohima College, Kohima, Nagaland. She has published two books of poetry, *Sopfünuo* and *Wake* and a children's book *Ukepenuopfü: An Angami Folktale Reimagined* and contributed to a number of anthologies and journals such as *South Asian Review*, *FemAsia*, and anthologies like *The Many that I Am* (Zubaan), *Yaari: An Anthology on Friendship by Women and Queer Folx* (Yoda Press). She advocates for the revival of indigenous Naga textiles and women's narratives through her popular Instagram avatar @mekhalamama. The impact of her textile and fashion activism has been recognized and featured in Roots & Leisure, Verve, Voice of Fashion, Indian Express, Huffington Post, National News UAE, and, most recently, Vogue India. She serves as a trustee on the boards of the Dr K & T Keditsu Foundation and The Highland Institute. She is a member of Rattle and Hum Music Society and the Nagaland State Audit Advisory Board (NSAAB). She has served on the Board of Undergraduate Studies (BUGS), Nagaland University as well as the Board of Studies of the Faculty of Arts and Culture, Martin Luther Christian University (MLCU).

Cecile A. Mawlong is a professor at the Department of History, North-Eastern Hill University. She specializes in archaeology and prehistory, state formations, material culture and gender relations in Khasi-Jaintia Hills. She has been a teacher at the North–Eastern Hill University, Shillong, for more than three decades and has widely published in national and international journals. She is a member of a number of national learned bodies and is an editor and author of eminence. Her latest book is *Interrogating the Past: A Study of Gender and megalithic Tradition in Khasi – Jaintia Society* (2022).

M. Amarjeet Singh is Professor at the Centre for North East Studies and Policy Research, Jamia Millia Islamia, New Delhi, where he teaches postgraduate courses on society and politics of India's North East, armed conflict and migration. He has previously worked with the Institute for Defence Studies and Analyses, New Delhi, and the National Institute of Advanced Studies, Bengaluru. He has conducted studies sponsored by several agencies. He has written on conflict studies, identity politics, and migration studies in widely circulated journals such as *Journal of Asian Public Policy, Small Wars & Insurgencies, Commonwealth & Comparative Politics, Strategic Analysis*, and *Economic & Political Weekly*. He has written and edited several books including *Identity, Contestation and Development in Northeast India*, Oxon and New Delhi: Routledge (2016); *Northeast India and India's Act East Policy: Identifying the Priorities*, Oxon: Routledge (2019), *Understanding Urbanisation in*

Northeast India: Issues and Challenges, Oxon: Routledge (2020), and *Political Autonomy and Democratic Governance*, Oxon: Routledge (2022).

Tanka B. Subba is Visiting Professor at the Department of Humanities & Social Sciences, Indian Institute of Technology, Gandhinagar and Ombudsperson of Darjeeling Hills University. He retired as a Professor of Anthropology, North-Eastern Hill University (NEHU), Shillong, India in April 2022. Earlier, from 2012 to 2017, he served as the second Vice-Chancellor of Sikkim University. He received awards like the Homi Bhabha Fellowship (Mumbai), Dr. Panchanan Mitra Lectureship and R.P. Chanda Centenary Medal for 2015 (Asiatic Society, Kolkata), DAAD Guest professorship at the Free University of Berlin, and Baden-Wuerttemberg Fellowship at the South Asian Institute, Heidelberg University. He served as a member of the Advisory Boards of the National Museum of Mankind, Anthropological Survey of India and the INTACH. He has authored and edited 18 books and published over 80 articles on various issues related to the Eastern Himalayas. His recent publications include, as Sectional Editor for Northeast India and Bangladesh, *Brill's Encyclopedia of the Religions of the Indigenous People of South Asia* (Brill, 2021 Gen. Ed. Marine Carrin) and, as Co-Editor, *The Routledge Companion to Northeast India* (Routledge, 2022, Lead Editor Jelle J.P. Wouters). His forthcoming book, edited with Ben Campbell and Mary Cameron is titled *The Routledge International Handbook of Himalayan Environments, Developments, and Wellbeings.*

Virginius Xaxa is currently a visiting professor at the Institute of Human Development (IHD) New Delhi. He was Professor of Eminence and Bharat Ratna Gopinath Bordoloi Chair Professor at Tezpur University. He was a professor and Deputy Director at the Tata Institute of Social Sciences, Guwahati. He has taught Sociology at the Delhi School of Economics, University of Delhi and the North-Eastern Hill University, Shillong. He is the author and editor of a number of books and the Chairman of the High-Level Committee on Socio-Economic, Health and Educational Status of Tribal Communities in India, Government of India (2014).

Acknowledgments

This book is the product of a collaborative international conference between Prime Ministers Memorial Museum and Library (formerly Nehru Memorial Museum and Library when the conference was organized), New Delhi and North Eastern Hill University, Shillong, Meghalaya. The conference was held in June 2019. I convey my deep gratitude to the late Shri Shakti Sinha, former Director of PMLL (NMLL) who agreed, inspired, and encouraged me to hold this conference. He attended the conference in Shillong despite his busy schedule and listened to the deliberations with engaged interest and exchanged views.

I am indebted to Dr Narendra Shukla, Head of Research and Publication Division PMLL (NMLL) who extended his help and support to make this conference possible and successful. I am extremely grateful Mr Iqbal Ahmed for organizing the logistics and making the event a success. I am thankful to Mr Rajnish Ranjan, Ms. Haimanti Dey, and many other staff and members of PMLL (NMLL) who extended their help toward organizing the event.

I convey my gratitude to the authorities of North Eastern Hill University for extending the best possible support. I am grateful to Professor Desmond Kharmaphlang who helped me out of the way in the initial stage and introduced me to Dr Binayak Dutta. Binayak Dutta from the Department of History became the co-convener of the conference on behalf of NEHU. Binayak and his colleagues and students worked hard to make the event smooth and successful. I am thankful to all the members of the History Department, especially Professor Ruata Rengsi, the then Head of the Department of History.

I convey my heartfelt gratitude to the participants who kindly agreed to participate in the conference and contribute articles.

I am deeply indebted to Dr Shashank Sekhar Sinha, Publishing Director, Routledge, for his patience, encouragement, and support. He patiently waited for almost four years and constantly encouraged me during a critical time to finish the volume. I am happy that I could finally accomplish the job. I convey my sincere thanks to Anvitaa Bajaj who accommodated all the problems while I was editing the volume, especially my technical inadequacies.

Subhankar Bhattacharya, my brother extended every possible logistic and technical help while I was in the process of preparing the final manuscript. Chandrani, my sister created the space enabling me to continue uninterrupted work.

Finally, I was able to finish the volume while I was staying with Ahona, my daughter in Claremont. She left her study and writing desk during her semester with full-fledged teaching so that I could finish the work.

Introduction

Globally, the historic process of colonization fundamentally affected the structures of a given society. Colonization process led to the transfiguration of the notion of community, cultural expression, world view of the people, and most importantly the existing political structures of which law is the most crucial component. Likewise, the experiences of colonialism are vast and varied in India in different layers of society and categories of native subjects as recorded in extant documents.

Legal governance, not merely the military operations, solemnized the symbol of British sovereignty in the Indian soil. Since the foundational phase of the British Empire in India, legal governance in order to deploy the instruments for legitimate subordination of the native subjects remained the most pressing engagement of these colonial officials. It was not an easy task for them given the heterogeneous and pluralistic nature of the subject people in terms of ethnic composition, religion, culture, and language.

"Law" therefore evolved in colonial India through complex civilizational encounter. The British arrived in a territory marked by ethnically and culturally heterogeneous character with linguistic diversity. The colonial rulers tried to formulate pragmatic structures in the loosely defined territory called India for different social groups to implement legal administration in different regions. The legal governance of the British Empire produced broadly three sets of "law" – (a) Hindu law, (b) Muhammedan "law," and (c) tribal "customary law" and became integral components of colonial governance in India. The legal structure in the postcolonial state varied in different geographical region and culturally framed to address the administrative "expediency" of for governing ethnic communities. The postcolonial Indian state therefore inherited the legacy of an uneven legal structure from the colonial governance which still poses serious concern, more so in the border regions such as India's Northeast frontier. In this larger historical context, the essays in the present volume interrogate how "custom and law" remain a crucial site of significant dynamics as well as serious challenges for both the state and the people living in the region.

Diverse in ethnicity and culture, rich in terms of natural resources, and human and geo-political aspects, Northeast India poses pressing challenges

DOI: 10.4324/9781003539797-1

to the Indian state. Since independence, there has been continuous dialogue at the level of policy, political negotiations, academic discourses, and civic activism to understand and address the issues. The endeavor however yields hardly much success as yet. The entire region still remains within a twilight zone of hope and dystopia. Northeast India therefore is a focal point of engagement of the postcolonial state since the early days.

India's Northeastern "frontier" poses multiple challenges to the postcolonial state combined with significant dynamics on account of its rich natural and human resources. The large stretch of international border enclosed by Bangladesh, Bhutan, China, and Myanmar is indeed a pressing concern and serious strategic and diplomatic challenges for the government. The challenges have been further aggravated by two significant factors: economic backwardness, "underdevelopment" as denoted by the early postcolonial state, and ethno-state estrangement. Scholars were and still are actively engaged in locating the root of the "backwardness" and the major sites of "estrangement" and "alienation" from the mainland political-economic scenario. The present volume does not however directly engage in tracing political economy of the "durable disorder" in the Northeast – as defined by Sanjib Baruah. It turns its gaze at the face of "law" – "law" that underpinned the colonial state formation leaving a strong afterlife till date. Colonial law molded the life, livelihood, and world view of the native subjects of the British Raj, and current "law" is the direct product of the colonial past. In this larger context, this volume interrogates "law" with all its edges in producing multifaceted impacts on the socio-economic and political structures. The book examines "law" as the source of dynamic forces as well as challenging factors during the postcolonial period and at the same time a contested site for resource and labor, relationships of power and authority. It looks into "law" to locate the sites of morality, cultural imagination, and a formidable source of the current discontent that often relates to what is called the "Northeast problem."

The volume approaches the issues from the basic premise that "law" forms a crucial site during the colonial period and more so after independence. Through "law" the colonial and postcolonial states engage with the tribal and non-tribal communities in the realm of identity politics, cultural contestation, and the issues of authority and morality. "Law" in this study however does not refer to a set of homogeneous entities of codified rules and regulations. "Law" in Northeast India refers to both constitutional "law" of the state, administered through formal courts of justice, and customary "law," administered through village councils of the tribal communities. "Law," as currently operational in the Northeast – both constitutional and customary – is not a product of postcolonial legislative enactments. It is the legacy of the colonial state which the independent Indian state inherited and formally endorsed subsequently after some cosmetic and certain structural changes. There were many crucial missing links in the passage of devolution of colonial "law" on to the postcolonial legal governance in the Northeast that had been glossed over and legitimized in the early days of independent India. Such twilight areas still remain and create hopes and dystopia among the people in the contemporary period. The essays in this volume touch upon certain significant issues relating to economy, politics, and culture which are integrally connected with "law."

Colonization of Northeast India since the middle of the nineteenth century started a new epoch in the cultural and material life in the Northeast. "Law" played multifarious role toward culturalization of the entire region including its geography, history, culture, ethnicity, and politics. In the African context, a large volume of literature has been produced toward the making of customary law in Africa during the colonial period. A corpus of discourses examines how the making of customary law had been produced through the encounter of the colonial rulers and native subjects that shaped and determined the contemporary socio-political structures in many African countries. Such analytical insights are absent in the Indian context while looking at the postcolonial socio-legal dynamics. The instrumentality and centrality of "law" have hardly been addressed in the existing studies and also policy formulations in relation to the Northeast since the initial years of independence. One of the great ironies of the post-independence history of India is that the major policy structures, especially the legal one, remained firmly ensconced within the colonial framework. The history and passage of colonial legal formation have hardly been questioned in the postcolonial literature and policy formulations in Northeast India. The colonial structure had been largely retained albeit with minor modifications. The policy formulations essentially focused on backwardness and developmental package. The tradition still continues although the laws relating to the National Register of Citizens (NRC) and Citizenship Amendment Bill (CAA) which had been brought into force over a few decades culminated in complex turmoil in 2019.

There was no territorial definition called Northeast India before the advent of the British. The politics and production of Northeast India were integrally connected with the borderization and legal colonization of the territory now called Northeast India. The entire region loosely emerged as the Northeast "frontier" of the British mainland through colonial sovereignty articulated through "Regulations" and "Enactments." Also, the territoriality which was structured by "law" defined the otherness of the region as "frontier" or the periphery of mainland India. In the colonial discourses, the region emerged as a "dark" cultural space – a "primitive" space inhabited by "numerous savage races" and "barbaric" people, the land of "headhunters" and the cultural contraflow against modernity and civilization. "Law" and "Land" remained a violently contested site throughout the passage of colonial rule. The afterlife of the colonial legal structures and its direct bearing on the ethnic imagination and the ethno-state conflict during the contemporary time are yet to be scrutinized in depth. The essays in this volume interrogate some of the critical locations of conflict that emerge through the historical passage of colonization and its afterlife.

The colonial legal formation in the Northeast "frontier" had been driven primarily by the following imperatives: (a) control over resources – land, revenue, water, mineral, and others; (b) legitimate subordination of the native subjects; (c) establishment of civilizational supremacy over the subject people; and (d) territorial and commercial expansion beyond the "frontier." It is evident therefore from the extant colonial archive that legal governance remained a pressing engagement since the initial era of the military conquest of the Northeast. The Special Acts such as AFSPA (Armed Forces Special Powers Act) – an Ordinance pronounced by the President of India in 1958 followed by many other Acts and Ordinances, especially relating to counter-insurgency, are crucial sites of conflict. Close scrutiny of those Acts and Ordinances however remains beyond the purview of this volume. This volume essentially focuses on custom and law as framed within colonial socio-political contexts and the teasing impact of the colonial legacy.

A few submissions may be posited here as the volume discusses both constitutional but more of "customary law" from varied angles. Customary law is an established category in the postcolonial legal terminology – especially in relation to the tribes. This is also an inherited term from colonial legal governance. The colonial administrators generically referred to the "custom" of the native subject as "customary law." In this context, one may pertinently ask the question of whether custom and customary law connote the same definition. "Law" is a purely western concept – evolved through cultural/civilizational trajectory over centuries. It is difficult to trace a similar word with all its qualities (as understood and professed by the British) in any pre-colonial discursive genre in the Indian soil. Hence, one may ask whether the indigenous communities had "customary law" before the British came. The present author has already studied (to be published shortly) the colonial legal formation in the Northeast. One may therefore ask whether the customary law governed during the colonial period had already existed which were structured, reified, and ready for use by an imperial power such as the British who cherished the ulterior agenda of grabbing land and expropriating resources. Custom is flexible and the term connotes usual, generally accepted and long-established ways of behaving or doing things or distinctive practices and conventions of a group of people in a given locality. "Law" is structured and formally instituted to be the integral apparatus of a state. The British repeatedly proclaimed that they retained the traditional "customary law" for the indigenous communities in order to assert moral rule in the newly acquired territory. The colonial archive makes it clearly evident that the British sovereign interpreted and represented the indigenous custom as customary law and coalesced them within the contested hierarchy of colonial regulations/code and customary law. Perhaps there lies the crucial missing link – the historical passage of transformation from custom to customary law. The ambivalent domain or the contested hierarchy between state law and customary law of the tribal communities thus remains till date as the vital sources of conflict. Most of the essays in this volume do not directly address the issues of the conflict between code and customary law, although a few papers do focus on the ethnic anxiety and political turmoil.

There are myriad discourses on the customary law of different communities in Northeast India, especially from within the communities. But there is an urgent necessity to trace how the customary law of different indigenous communities had been shaped by the disruptive forces unleashed by the colonization process – forces leading to displacement from land and forest, life and livelihood, folklore and memory, migration, and cultural homogenization. The areas mentioned above are hardly addressed with rigor and depth. It is generally assumed that "customary law" of various communities has been an immutable entity despite political, economic, social, and cultural transmutation. Perhaps it is necessary to interrogate current customary law as a product of an evolutionary process keeping in mind that the process had been initiated during the colonial period. In other words, the instrumentality of customary law should be understood by situating the current conflicts in a historical perspective. Few essays in this volume throw some lights toward understanding the elements of instrumentality.

In current geopolitical, administrative, and academic definition, Northeast India constituting eight states – Assam, Manipur, Meghalaya, Mizoram, Nagaland, Arunachal Pradesh, Tripura, and Sikkim – is the site of both dynamics and challenges. Rich in natural and human resources, the regions are formidable sources of the dynamic potential to substantially develop as a strong economy that in turn contributes to national development on the whole. The entire region provides a vibrant source of water, energy, oil, natural gas, minerals, plantation crops, horticultural products, and medicinal plants and is also an exotic tourist destination. The region offers the diplomatic corridor to India's South and Southeastern neighbors. In reality, Northeast India is viewed as a backward region in terms of socio-economic and human development index. It is perceived as a source of threat against national security and integration posing multiple challenges for the Indian state.

The dynamics as well as challenges as encountered in this region are varied and critical. The major challenges as defined from the mainland discourse are mainly on account of "difference" and "disparity" in terms of geography, economy, polity, society, culture, and most importantly the ethnic composition. There are around two hundred and twenty communities in the entire Northeast and each group has a separate dialect along with separate customary practices or customary law.

It is already mentioned that "Law," as currently operational in the Northeast – both constitutional and customary – is not a product of postcolonial legislative enactments. It is the legacy of the colonial state and the postcolonial Indian state formally endorsed the colonial "law" within a democratic framework. The endorsement had been accomplished on the basis of the assumption or "faith" on the colonial masters that they retained and continued the indigenous custom/"law" for tribal and non-tribal communities. The colonial legal structure had been constructed with the motivation to expropriate resources and sustain hegemony over the people through the power of arms. The colonial "law" thereby marked gross discontinuity from the pre-colonial past. Customary law in postcolonial Northeast evolves on the basis of colonial legal mechanism. The essays in this volume have addressed some of the issues that emerged from this discontinuity – further determined and shaped through political event, current ethnic imagination, politics of identity, ethno-state relationship, and the conflicts over vested economic interests. The ideological and operational overtures are indeed intimately connected with fragmented accomplishment and partial failures of the formerly Look East and the current Act East Policy.

Social scientists and policy research analysts draw from a vast array of themes under discussion including development policies, neighborhood policy, regional cooperation, ethnic politics, militancy, insurgency, identity movements, human development, land and agriculture, and ecology/environment. The studies also focus on the history of military encounters, insurgency, peace and conflict before and after independence, ecology, economic backwardness, ethno-state relationship under postcolonial state, "sub-nationalism," and territorial movements, folklore among others. "Customary law" constitutes an important area of research as an integral part of ethnographic study and identity politics. It is also a part of necessary exercise to streamline "customary law" to be dispensed under Autonomous District Councils in Fifth/Sixth Schedule areas and this has become a site of ethnic discord. The academics and social activists have situated "law" within the framework of a contested hierarchy between "code" and "custom." "Custom" is not treated not as "law" *per se* or a discrete field of inquiry to understand the historic passage of social transformation; instead as a site of identity and part of the total cultural system. Within a larger socio-political background, Sanjib Baruah and Samir Kumar Das, among others, have offered significant insights that aid our holistic understanding of the various strands at play in persistent ethnic conflict, violence, and confrontation in view of the incongruity between the ethnic homeland model and the actually existing political economy of the region. Despite the merits of their work, however, the scholars do not analyze the workings of "law" within the context of ethno-political studies.

In a short article published in 1995[1] (*The North-East and the Indian State: Paradoxes of a Periphery*), B.K. Roy Burman – the eminent anthropologist and ideologue in the policy research on the tribal population in India – posited a brief critique in a larger perspective. He pointed out that the "starting point of authentic democracy" should be an "outright rejection of Austinian legal epistemology which informs the judiciary and land resource-based policy planning." Roy Burman however argued that despite political will, the policy did not take any new turns due to the "dubious" attitude of bureaucracy. Interestingly, he defined the Sixth Schedule of the Indian Constitution in a different vein, contending that the "rhetoric of self-management of the tribals has proved to be nothing but a political toy." What Roy Buman indirectly referred to is the inadequacy of the lopsided developmental approach and the inexorable link between the current legal structure and continuous ethno-political turmoil.

Walter Fernandes and Melvil Pereira – both eminent scholars from Northeast India – have made significant contributions by looking at customary law from the standpoint of the uneasy interface and contestation between state law and customary law, inter-ethnic dynamics and the subversion of class and gender in the practicing "custom." This area of study is primarily concerned with political, sociological, and moral perspectives on "law" in the context of identity conflict and tribal autonomy. The scholars have initiated dialogue addressing bureaucrats and policymakers in order to explore the feasibility of codifying "uniform customary law" or the "statutory recognition of customary law" as a likely solution to the current imbroglio. A recent publication on *Legal Pluralism and Indian Democracy: Tribal Conflict Resolution Systems in Northeast India*, edited by Melvil Pereira, Bitopi Dutta, and Binita Kakati[2] however analyzed the functioning of constitutionally recognized dual conflict resolution systems – legal courts and Autonomous District Councils – which is defined in the Northeast as "legal pluralism." It addresses the debates over the Uniform Civil Code while analyzing multifaceted aspects relating to the conflict resolution system in the Northeastern region. The book is divided into two parts, with the first part discussing the theoretical aspect of customary-law-based conflict resolution system – its usefulness and its limitations. The second part focuses on discrete case studies. This book is a valuable addition in terms of understanding the interface between "state" law and "customary" law, the theoretical context of "legal pluralism" and its implications, customary and human rights issues and customary law as a shield or instrument to either protect or subvert women's rights. The study, however, has been undertaken largely in light of the role of current "law" as a conflict resolution system. It barely touches upon the historical passage of colonial legal formation which is inexorably linked with the current contestations and conflicts in the troubled areas such as militarization, ethno-state estrangement, thwarted socio-economic development, inter-ethnic and intra-ethnic conflict, and related issues.

The essays in this volume interrogate "law" from a broad spectrum of issues including gender, partition, the legacy of the colonial structures, religion as a form of resistance against land grabbing, and censorship. Each paper delineates a distinct historical process of the evolution of law and custom and focuses on the intimate link between law and dynamics of state, ethnicity, and governance. The essays are not presented within a predisposed theoretical framework already operational in the narrative or in action-oriented strategies. Instead, this volume proposes multiple frameworks for understanding law and society in the Northeast.

Virginius Xaxa sets the tune of discussion by examining the historical knots toward understanding the colonial dynamics of formulating and administering tribal law and its afterlife. Focusing on Northeast India Xaxa stretches his gaze to a larger canvas of making of tribal law by the colonial rulers and its long-term implications for the tribal communities. He explained the fundamental distinction between law and custom. Xaxa elaborated that custom and law are generally contrasted with each other and associated with different types of society. The former is treated as the characterizing feature of traditional society and the latter with modern society. Thus, the transition from traditional to modern society is viewed as opening up an interface between the two. Xaxa traces the root of the transitions in the colonial – in the case of North East India, as in other parts of India. Much of India under colonial rule came to be governed by a law introduced by the colonial state. Notwithstanding this, as he argued, there were certain parts of India, which were excluded from the reach of such laws unless the executive authority thought otherwise with a provision of modification. In doing so, the colonial state allowed such areas to be governed by customs and traditions. Groups and communities delineated as tribes inhabited such areas. In his paper, Xaxa explores the reason/reasons as to why the colonial state had the policy to exclude tribal regions from the reach of the act framed by the colonial state. What implications had this policy been on tribes on the one hand and India as a whole on the other? It also examines the kind of customs, the colonial administration infringed, and the mechanisms through which they were done. He further examines the mechanisms deployed by the postcolonial state for addressing these issues.

Xaxa's paper delves into the nature and type of administration in tribal areas in colonial India, in particular the interface between statutory and customary law and the implications such arrangement had on tribal communities in Northeast India. The essay is organized into five sections. The first section is concerned with meanings and concepts of law and customs and their general features. The second provides a synoptic view of the history of the region and its transformation from the notion of mere geographical territory to an embryonic form of the politico-administrative structure resulting in a form of northeasterner consciousness. The third discusses the general approach of the colonial state toward the administration of tribal people and tribal areas. The fourth examines the interface between law and custom in the colonial period. The fifth and final section engages with the national discourse on such arrangement and argues positively as it has ensured the people in the region in securing their land, territory, and identity.

Xaxa's essay raises the point that the colonial policy of the British Empire restricted interaction and exchange between tribes and non-tribes and thereby posed obstacles to forging larger national solidarity and the Indian national consciousness. In his view, the policy of isolation might have jeopardized the development in the sphere of either infrastructure or economic, political, and social such as education and health. In the essay, Xaxa addressed the debate about whether colonial tribal policy thwarted the political consciousness and formation of their identity as being part of India and put forward his own observation.

Xaxa argues that colonial tribal policy protected the tribes not only demographically but also from exploitation from people from outside in the sense of alienation of land, forest, and other resources from tribes to non-tribes. This was largely due to the opening of the partially excluded areas for trade and commerce through the extension of roads, railways, and other means of communication. The result was large-scale migration of people from the plains into tribal areas and appropriation of their land and other resources through deceit, forging of documents, credit indebtedness, intimidations, etc. The shrinking landholding and landlessness pushed them out of their own territory for work and livelihood elsewhere. Xaxa argued that the tribes have become a numerical minority in their own territory. It is precisely because of this safeguard that tribes especially in the excluded and partially excluded areas of Northeast India were able to safeguard their resources under their control as well as able to protect their language, culture, and identity. It is this that facilitated the provision of the special constitutional arrangement in postindependent India, which provides space for people to govern themselves on matters granted under the constitutional arrangement. This has enabled them to safeguard and protect their interests as well as develop according to their own genius. It is this control over resources as well as their distinct language, which has been a stimulant to their social and cultural development. He argues that there has not been such a policy of protection under the British, it is unlikely that the postindependent India would have extended such provision of self-governance to tribal people of Northeast India.

T.B. Subba's essay is situated in the context of constricting the power and space of women in the current customary law. He interrogates the status of women as evolved and articulated in the customary law and the conflicting arguments about women's status in the customary law in Northeast India. He reflected upon the dominant assumptions in the writings on the tribal societies of Northeast India that they are gender equal while some writings go to the extent of claiming that women among them enjoy a much higher status than the women in caste societies. Subba further added that simultaneously it is frequently argued that tribal customary laws perpetuate gender inequality in favor of men.

Subba specifically referred to the researches conducted by the Law Research Institute (LRI), established in 1977 in Guwahati. LRI had been documenting the customary laws and practices of the tribes of the region for almost four decades now. Under this scheme, 200 tribes were proposed to be covered with the help of one research team for each state of the region working under the overall supervision of the Chief Justice of Gauhati High Court (Sethi 2015). Subba argues in his paper that although the mandate of the LRI was only documentation, it paved the way for codification of the customary practices. He explained that while customary laws are flexible and underwent periodic revisions, but the documentation almost froze them. Following their codification, they have assumed the force of law in the state of Mizoram whereas in Nagaland, Naga customary laws are recognized under Article371 (A) of the Constitution of India.

Flexibility, as Subba argues, can be a double-edged sword, as it can also be misused. For instance, it is alleged that in Nagaland, customary laws are so interpreted by Naga men as to deprive Naga women of their political rights, in particular, the 33 percent seat reservation in the urban local body elections in 2016. Even the role of Nagaland state has come under a scanner in this regard in view of its ambivalent position with regard to the reservation for women.

Subba elaborated on the differences between custom and customary law in their legal application. He pointed to the identifiable boundary between custom and customary law, except that the punishment for a breach of a customary law is generally more stringent than it is for the breach of a custom and is decided by the community in a formal meeting of the village elders. But, in the case of both, the members of a community decide about the nature and degree of punishment for an offence, often depending on who the offender is, they do not themselves make a conscious distinction between a custom and a customary law. The punishment meted out may be soft or harsh depending on the age, gender, clan, etc. of the violator and not necessarily which customary law has been violated. It may also depend on whether a violation is a first or is repeated several times. Being often biased in favor of men, a man may be pardoned, but a woman may not be, even if their offence, such as infidelity, is similar.

Subba added in his paper that when one looks at the fast-changing tribal societies of the region, one tends to suspect that gradually the statutory laws will alone survive, but when one looks at the tendencies of the Christian tribal youths of the region to return to some of their select traditions, there is a possibility of their customary laws lasting longer than one would expect, especially the ones that are linked with their identity. He puts forward his argument that that the dominant discourse is in favor of statutory laws is clear when reference is often made about customary laws being discriminatory against women.

Amarjeet Singh's article deals with the land tenure system in Manipur during the colonial time and its far-reaching implications during the postcolonial period. It is indeed an extremely relevant topic in the contemporary context. Singh argues that the introduction of several administrative policies, the most remarkable ones were the administrative separation of the hill areas and the central valley, and the introduction of a land tenure system in the central valley had a deep impact on the state and the society in Manipur. Delegating the administration of the hill areas to the colonial officials not only undermined the authority of the Manipuri kings, but in due course of time became the main causes of hills-valley ethic divide which is more pronounced at present.

Singh elaborates that the present-day Indian state of Manipur was once a kingdom during the pre-colonial period which later became a native state in British India. It joined India from 1949 onward. Twenty years later, it became a state. Its topography consists of the hill region covering roughly 90 percent (20,089 sq.km.) of the total area, and the remaining area constitutes the central valley covering roughly 10 percent (2,238 sq.km.) only. Thus, the hills occupy about ninth-tenth of the total land. For want of better terms, the British used the words "tribes" to denote the Nagas and the Kukis, respectively, the "hills" to denote the hill areas, and the "valley" to denote the central valley of the state.

Singh briefly traces the ethno-economic roots of the unstable socio-political order in Manipur. Among the communities inhabiting the state, the Meiteis and the Pangals, who are considered as non-tribal, predominantly live in the central valley while the tribes, constituting about 40.88percent of the total population, mostly live in the hill areas. The tribes comprising several subgroups are now clubbed as either Nagas or Kukis although there are some who preferred not to identify themselves with either of the group. Some are recognized as the scheduled tribes, while others are not. Thus, the tribes enjoy the benefits of reservations in jobs, education, legislative assembly, parliament, and other welfare programs. The tribes are predominantly Christian whereas the Meiteis follow different religions such as Sanamahism, Hinduism, and Christianity. Since the data on Sanamahism was not recorded in the official Census so far, they are officially recognized as the Hindus.

Singh's paper analyzed the colonial land tenure structure to situate the contemporary conflict between hill tribes and inhabitants of the valley and plains. Land ownership in the state has been the main source that created animosity among different communities. The non-scheduled tribes cannot acquire or buy land in the hill areas of Manipur, whereas anybody can acquire or buy land in the valley areas. The valley communities are in favor of adopting a uniform land law, on the contrary, the hill communities are against it. In several states, the land where the hill peoples inhabit is not allowed to be transferred to the non-tribal people. Such restrictions can be traced back to colonial rule. The colonial policy of administratively separating the valley and hills after the British conquest of Manipur in 1891 paved the way for "strong geographical divide" which in turn led to "ethnic competition" between the inhabitants of the valley and hills and also within the hill people. Ethnic groups have become politically active in the name of defending their ancestral land not merely because of the material value but due to the symbolic role, the land plays in constituting their identities, security, and belongingness.

Singh's paper put forward his observation that uniform land law should be introduced as a channel to resolve the ethnic conflicts. He elaborated on how the hill communities resisted against allowing non-scheduled tribes to buy and settle in the hill areas fearing that they will lose the ownership of land, job, and identity. They consider this reservation as constitutional safeguard. He asserts that for the valley communities, a uniform land policy is necessary since the valley region is smaller in area. Concern over the fast-shrinking of paddy land and wetland, particularly in the valley, the Manipur Conservation of Paddy Land and Wetland Act, 2014 was enacted, for promoting agriculture by restricting rampant construction on the paddy land. He emphasized that for the valley communities, a uniform land policy is necessary since the valley region is small in area.

Cecile Mawlong and Theyiesinuo Keditsu added fresh perspectives on the growing gender discrimination in the reframing and dispensation of customary law. Cecile Mawlong's article offers keen analysis on the growing patriarchal trend and subversion of Khasi-Jaintia matrilineal structure. Very few societies now retain matrilineal structure and Khasi-Jaintia matrilineal structure is one of the few surviving forms of social organization that continues to survive into contemporary times. Mawlong traces gradual infiltration of patriarchal ethos into this long-survived institution. She argues that until recently, it was generally assumed that because the Khasi-Jaintia communities follow a matrilineal form of social organization in which descent and inheritance are traced through the female line, women therefore occupy a dominant position in society. Mawlong points out that Khasi-Jaintia society is frequently, though incorrectly, described as "matriarchal" rather than "matrilineal" and captions such as "Indian tribe puts women in control" or "Meghalaya: The Land Where Women Call the Shots," suggests that the terms are often used synonymously with little awareness for the variation in meaning and implication. In reality, among the Khasi-Jaintia, the lines of authority and descent do not converge. Thus while descent and inheritance passes through the female line, they seldom exercise authority in their kin groups, as is the case in matriarchal societies, of which there are very few examples worldwide. Nevertheless, matriliny where descent and inheritance is determined in the female line has an important bearing on gender and power relations in Khasi-Jaintia society.

Mawlong in the essay asserts that the above "popular" perception that Khasi-Jaintia matriliny is biased in favor of women is also shared by a number of Khasi-Jaintia men who consider their women-folk an "empowered" category because of their right to lineage and property. This has found expression in the founding of a Khasi Men's Rights Movement called the Syngkhong Rympei Thymmai, aimed at highlighting the gender-biased nature of the matrilineal system which from their perspective reduces men to mere "breeding bulls" and they have been advocating for a while now, for a reversal of the system. On the other hand, this view has been increasingly challenged in academic and non-academic circles, on the grounds that while Khasi-Jaintia society is organized along matrilineal lines, it reveals patriarchal values.[3] This is based on the fact that women have traditionally been excluded from political participation and decision-making in traditional political institutions which were and continue to be, largely the "preserve" of men.

Mawlong explained in the essay that the significance of the matrilineal clan structure as an organizing principle in Khasi-Jaintia society is also expressed materially in their megalithic tradition which lays particular emphasis on monuments that underscore the solidarity of matrilineal ancestry and veneration of ancestors that lie at the core of Khasi-Jaintia beliefs and practices. While the Creator-God is frequently called upon in rituals, it is ancestral spirits that have a more immediate bearing on the lives of people. These ancestral spirits – *Ka Ïawbei* (root ancestress), *U Suidñ ia* (first maternal uncle), and *U Thawlang* (co-creator) are frequently entreated on account of their status as progenitors of the lineage/clan. However, much greater reverence is accorded to *Ka Ïawbei* from whom sprang the family/lineage/clan, and she is invariably invoked in rituals especially those associated with death which lie at the core of the Khasi-Jaintia belief system. These rituals involving the internment of bones in the clan ossuary –the *Mawbah* – accentuates the importance of kinship bonds, as only the bones of kin-members can be interred together. So in life and in death, the bonds of kinship are paramount superseding all others.

Mawlong argues that in recent years, there has been a growing trend in non-western societies that experienced colonialism, to re-examine aspects of traditional practice, especially gender relations, from an indigenous perspective. This is discernable in the significant increase in writings by African scholars, especially women scholars, questioning the notion that pre-colonial African societies were inherently patriarchal in nature. Mawlong asserts that these studies suggest that most African societies were once "matriarchal" but external forces such as Islam, Christianity, colonialism, and education were largely responsible for the emergence of patriarchal institutions. She points out that such conclusions were based on research comparing the societal nature and gender relation at terms in the societies under study from the pre-colonial to postcolonial times. Mawlong observes that such reviews are necessary on account of the fact that frequently such conclusions are drawn on flawed or insufficient data or understanding of a society being studied. She essentially points out that in the case of Khasi-Jaintia matriliny, women have no "real" power despite their matrilineal social organization, since they have little or no role in the public space. However, contrary to what colonial and post-colonial writings suggest, there is reason to believe that Khasi-Jaintia matriliny was at one time a much more gender equal system. She finally argues that it is recorded in many parts of the world that increasing complexity in social relations is associated with the rise in population and the gradual replacement of kin-ordered societies by increasingly centralized socio-political structures. The transformation contributes in great measure to the gradual transformation in social and gender relations. In her view, this factor also played a role in the gradual change in gender dynamics in Khasi-Jaintia society. Mawlong also mentioned about other formidable factors such as the interplay of colonialism, Christianity, and the rise of indigenous revivalist movements which contributed significantly in effecting a gradual shift from a complementary gender model toward a conflicting one.

Theyiesinuo Keditsu's paper examines the evolution of the institution of marriage in the context of the Angami Naga community. Keditu traces the gradual infiltration of patriarchy and subversion of women's rights through the influence of colonialism and Christianity. The author attributes the subversion as an offshoot of "modernity" that negates the on-road "development" in a given society. Keditsu traces this process in the context of Naga society by analyzing a complex process. The author argues that patriarchy is founded upon the disenfranchisement of women.

First-world feminism in particular has built most of its theories and politics upon this premise, understood in its modern western sense. Yet challenging the notion of a monolithic feminism by third-world and indigenous feminists has necessarily highlighted the various forms of patriarchy and the complex negotiations of power that occur between women and the strictures which bind them. These strictures vary from and are specific to a culture. In Naga culture, as in many other indigenous sister cultures of the Northeast, orature in the form of folktales has been a narrative domain in which women as well as men have shared equal space and power. Using the Angami folktale of *Sopfünuo* as a site of analysis, this paper examines the rights and power of women within the institution of marriage – that bastion of patriarchal power. The article traces the movement of marriage from a traditionally loose institutionality to its transformation, via colonialism and missionization, to its current legal and sacrosanct avatar – a transformation that has curtailed the power women enjoyed within traditional patriarchy and had insidious implications on the modern rights women can claim today. The integrity and development of indigenous societies as desired by the postcolonial Indian state call for the enfranchisement of women as equal actors in policy formulation and implementation. Yet the violent resistance to the Women's Reservation Bill in the state as well as the conspicuous exclusion of women from significant decision-making bodies and spaces calls for an investigation in, among others, the cultural realm. This chapter scrutinizes the ways in which modernity has brought with it a certain narrative and practice of patriarchy that may be counterproductive to its own project of "development."

Keditsu herself is held from Chiechama, a northern Angami Village and reside in Kohima, also Northern Angami. Her work primarily dwells upon collecting oral histories and narratives. These are sourced from the people of this area. She thus builds this paper on the foundations for three folktales, two that come from the Northern Angami villages of Rüsoma and Kohima and one that is common to all Angamis. In Naga culture, as in many other indigenous sister cultures of the North East, orature in the form of folktales has been a narrative domain in which women as well as men have shared equal space and power. Using these folktales as sites of analysis, this paper examines the rights and power of women within the institution of marriage – that bastion of patriarchal power. Because marriage is the eye of the needle through which ancestry, inheritance, and consequently patriarchal authority are threaded and secured.

Binayak Dutta's paper addresses the issues of anxiety, immigration, and community relations in late colonial and postcolonial Assam. The paper locates the dynamics and challenges of legislations over land settlement in late colonial and early postcolonial Assam in the context of immigration of east Bengali peasant migration and community antagonisms between customary rights and colonial legislations that emerged in its wake.

Dutta argues that before the colonial advent, Assam had no compendium of codified laws and had enormous size of uncultivated productive lands. Despite having a huge scope for revenue generation, the revenue realization is comparatively negligible because of the absence of willing and enterprising population. Fundamental changes were introduced with the onset of colonial rule. Lawmaking was a primary occupation of the colonial rulers as they colonial sought legitimacy to introduce taxes and collect revenue. They adopted the policies to encourage the immigration of speculators, revenue farmers, and, if necessary, population transfer from other provinces as it introduced human resources to land to generate revenue. It is with the motive of revenue maximization that the English East India Company and the British Crown actively encouraged immigration of people from other provinces of colonial India to Assam. The expansion of representative politics in Assam along with the other provinces of colonial India opened politics of contests over immigration which, by the third and fourth decade of the twentieth century, turned into a wave. Laws were framed by the provincial government to meet political situations arising out of immigration of people from eastern Bengal into Assam. In this backdrop, Dutta locates the dynamics of lawmaking on immigration and settlement and migration of people from East Bengali migrants into the Brahmaputra valley districts of colonial Assam in the first half of the twentieth century. He analyses that settlement of this migrant population was a problem not only for the articulate middle class in Assam, who engaged among themselves on the issue of migration, but also for the tribal communities who shared space with the Brahmanical society of the Assam plains for generations. The colonial philosophy of land utilization and surplus was clearly at variance with the traditional indigenous idea of land settlement and utilization. Dutta locates the discontinuity in the disputes that arose between the migrant settler cultivators from East Bengal and the tribal communities on whose land peasant settlements came to be encouraged by the colonial state and legislations that came in the wake of such disputes.

Dutta's paper traces the integral link of contemporary citizenship debate with the colonial policies toward immigration, legislative practices, and the sentiment that emerged among the Assamese middle class and the tribal population regarding immigration. He argues that the significance of the issue of immigration in the legislative history of Assam lay in the fact that, for the first time, it brought the land question and tribal rights within the domain of colonial politics in all its dimensions. The popular sentiments were surged on the issue and demands arose for the protection of indigenous rights from all sections of Assamese society. The debates and the Enquiry Committee depositions highlighted the fundamental unity between the tribal and non-tribal populations of Assam which was also echoed in the debates on various issues affecting the community rights in the Assam Assembly. The unique position of the anti-immigrant debate in Assam lies in its success at appropriating the question of lawmaking from exclusively official to the domain of the popular. He asserts that legal change was recognized as a legitimate and just method to meet an impending political crisis and the amendment of 1947 was a product of a sustained movement to relate anti-immigration policy to protection of tribal and indigenous interests. In this larger background, Dutta traces the historicity of the Amendment to the Land and Revenue Regulations of1886 must be linked to the line system introduced in Assam.

Kaushik Thakur Bhuyan addresses the issues of censorship and legislation by focusing on colonial Assam and Northeast India. Bhuyan's paper in fact dwells upon a hitherto unexplored domain on the social–cultural history of the region, especially with regard to the genesis and development of cinema spectatorship in the Northeast. He offers copious narrative on the beginning of cinema in Assam. Starting with Joytiprasad Agarwala's *Joymot i*(1935) and *Indramaloti* (1939), a host of films based on historical figures selected from Ahom Buranjis, focusing on the Ahom dynastic feuds, Ahom Mughal conflict (1616–1682), Maomoria rebellion 1769–1805), Revolt of 1857 to mention a few; Assamese cinema in the vernacular has since colonial times grown out of a strong sense of middle-class consciousness evolving out of cultural interaction with its closest metropolis of Bengal as well as colonial introduction of western education, missionary activity, and the least acknowledged aspect, i.e., cinematograph legislations and middle-class participation of the regional intelligentsia in visual spectatorship. The paper explores various strands as well as historical facts regarding the development of cinema in Assam and colonial censorship. For example, he explores when and how were cinema to graph legislations enforced in the province and second how did Assam respond to censorship contestations being debated in the rest of India.

Erik Maaker's paper focuses on the significant areas of law and legislation relating to the conservation of land, biodiversity, and natural heritage in the Garo Hills in Meghalaya. He narrates that for some years, Meghalaya Forest Department advocated the creation of UNESCO World Heritage site in Garo Hills, the Garo Hills Conservation Area (GHCA). Garo Hills, the westernmost one-third of the Indian state of Meghalaya, is a biodiversity hotspot. It harbors large numbers of unique plant and animal species, including many that have so far not been documented. In recent decades, due to logging, as well as changes in the usage of the land, the dense forest that once covered much of Garo Hills has thinned, reducing wildlife habitats and eroding the diversity of plant species. In addition, coal mining creates substantial environmental pollution. The Meghalaya Forest Department manages a number of relatively small forest reserves, nearly all of which were created in the 1880s, at the time that Garo Hills became included in the colonial state. In addition, in the 1980s, the Nokrek National Park and the Balpakram National Park were established as major conservation areas. As national parks, these are included in a national-wide (i.e., all-India) scheme, while its management is being done by the Meghalaya Forest Department. Quite a few of the forest reserves, as well as both national parks, are located along an east-west axis, running through the southern half of the Garo Hills. Having been created at different moments in time, these various conservation areas are mostly disconnected. The GHCA was – certainly initially – envisioned as a contiguous area, which would encompass existing conservation areas, while also creating corridors among them. This means that the Garo Hills Conservation Area, as initially proposed, would also relate to land managed and held by villages which Maaker defines as customary communal ownership (*a'king*). This could be included either in the core area or (more likely) in a surrounding buffer zone.

Maaker is personally associated with this project. He was approached in early 2017 by one of the main advocates of the GHCA initiative to become involved in the effort. He has been actively engaged in this project since then and based on ethnographic fieldwork conducted in Garo Hills over a period of about two decades and published quite extensively on changing cultural attitudes toward land also in relation to Northeast India more generally. In the process of gaining recognition as a UNESCO World Heritage site, the Garo Hills Conservation Area would be proposed as a site of "outstanding universal value." Maaker elaborates that in such a site, various kinds of heritage combine, involving, e.g., natural, geological, and cultural values. As mentioned in the extensive literature on heritage studies, the distinction between natural and cultural heritage implies a specific (western) ontological perspective, which often has little relevance for the communities whose heritage it is supposed to describe al heritage, to fit the framework of UNESCO, typically emphasizes "the magical-supernatural aspect of local belief," to render it compatible with the "secular-rational" conceptual framework it is expected to fit in with. Such a demand can easily result in overlooking aspects of heritage that are locally considered important, yet do not fit this framework.

Maaker observes that UNESCO's application procedure entails a long and arduous process including legal ones, which includes the drafting of a hefty and very detailed dossier, and it was with respect to this bureaucratic exercise that my involvement was sought. He expresses the concern over the thinning of the forest cover of Garo Hills which is detrimental to the biodiversity in the region. He explains that mining creates severe pollution, and, more generally, communal land management is subjected to multiple pressures and the contemporary developments pose a severe threat to people and environment in Garo Hills. Simultaneously, as he observes, efforts at the conservation of the natural environment easily go against the interests of people who are living on and with the land, whereas their support, commitment, and knowledge should be central to any efforts made. Creating conservation areas has frequently resulted in people being evicted, as in the "hard conservation" that characterizes many national parks worldwide. That the Garo Hills Conservation Area is being proposed within the UNESCO category "outstanding universal value" therefore creates an interesting opportunity, since this can potentially foreground the meaning which land has for people who live on it. The GHCA could then call for conservationist's efforts to align with farmer's connections to land. In this paper, following up on his own involvement with the effort, he explores different interpretations of what cultural heritage in relation to the proposed Garo Hills Conservation Area might entail.

Moreover, the proposed GHCA is located close to the India–Bangladesh border and, in that sense, politically at the margins of the Indian state. More significantly, the Garo community, categorized within India as "tribal," is culturally and numerically marginal within the country.

The GHCA initiative could thus result in acknowledgment as a UNESCO World Heritage for an area that is in the margins both in a political and in a cultural sense.

Finally, Nandini Bhattacharyya Panda's paper traced the complex passage of legal formation in Northeast India to locate the historical roots of contemporary complexities in the legal scenario. "Law" was a prime instrument for the British rulers during the Empire-building process in India. For the British, law or legal governance was the more powerful instrument, no less than military operations, which solemnized the symbol of British sovereignty in the Indian soil. The lawmaking exercise of the British rulers was however not uniform in different parts of the Empire. The trajectory was also complex and frequently arbitrary. Yet the edifice of colonial "law" left its formidable legacy and the postcolonial legal structure is essentially based on the colonial "law" in terms of ideology, spirit, structure, and content. The legal structure in India despite the positive values and dominantly democratic dispositions entails several missing links, grey aspects, and paradoxes. Bhattacharyya Panda argues that the historical roots of such problems are largely traceable in the passage and mode of colonial legal formation, especially the economic backwardness, ethnic alienation from the so-called mainstream perspective and the notion of "difference" about the region and the people. The paper is written on the basic premise that "law" played a vital role in producing the fundamental changes in the given region. This is why "law" constitutes a formidable site of dissonance and contestation that is inherently linked with the past and as something that further adds to the contemporary disorder.

In this paper, the passage of colonial legal formation primarily focuses on threefold aspects: (a)fundamental changes in the pre-colonial patterns of land rights which were basically introduced in the plain or Lower Assam; (b) encroachment in the hills and forests and the process of making of tribal customary law through violence and violations; and (c) the introduction of Assam Code, an ambivalent and arbitrary text had been produced as a legal mechanism broadly designed to administer Assam as a resource frontier.

The construction of "law" relating to land, land revenue, and property rights through the passage of colonial state formation had far-reaching consequences. The colonial rulers arrived in the Northeast as "trustee" of human security and existing socio-legal structures. The brief analysis in the paper unfolds the history of how the material practices relating to land, revenue, and "property" of the pre-colonial era had been drastically restructured leaving a new legal mechanism which was inherited by the postcolonial state. The existing hierarchical structure in the pre-colonial era in land use and revenue structures had been disrupted by the colonial forces. Land, revenue, and existing notions and rights about "property" had been redefined within the European ideologies of private property rights by subverting the structure of communal holding. This chapter primarily focuses on the Lower Assam. The area was largely inhabited by hereditary landowners within multitiered land allotment arrangements. It highlights the functional role or revision of colonial land "law" in creating the conditions for complete access to resources. Northeast is still considered as a resource frontier.

The encounter between the tribal subjects in the Northeast and the British Empire is also briefly discussed to trace and analyze the process of the making of "customary law." The legal formation in Northeast India had been accomplished primarily through culturalization of the ethnic space, especially of the "tribal" subjects. The colonial archive is a repository of the expression of their anxiety regarding how to deal with the "savage" and "warlike" tribal subjects in the Northeast. They adopted various means to extend authority and control over the land in which they inhabit and enjoy resources for time immemorial. The chapter analyzes how the process of intimidation of those people through arms and draw them under the paradigms of civilization so that they are able to understand the governing principles of the colonial masters, especially the "law" by which they can perceive, modify, and regulate their demands and rights over resources. In other words, Bhattacharyya Panda's paper reveals the passage of violence through which customary law had been produced that devised the mainstream/periphery paradigms. Customary law is still a site of contestation and violence.

Finally, the paper examines the introduction of the "Rules," "Regulations," and "Acts" as introduced by the colonial rulers in Assam. The promulgation of several Rules and Regulations and their frequent revisions indicate the quest and confusion of appropriate legal governance to bring the land and the people under hegemony and control. The paper traces the crisscross trajectory of the legal formation that makes it a confusing and complex site of study. The chapter essentially reflects on two significant trends: (a) instrumentality of "law" toward expropriating resources and extending hegemony over the people, and (b) the confusion, arbitrariness, and fluidity in the sphere of legal governance in the Northeast. The confusion, arbitrariness, and fluidity still persist in India's Northeast frontier.

The volume examines the partial accomplishments of the policies and measures of the postcolonial state in the Northeast (formerly Look East and now Act East Policy) through the window of law. In this volume, the papers provide a deeper understanding of the impediments toward: (a) to improvement of the trade, commerce, and overall economy of the region, and (b) opening of the commercial and diplomatic corridor toward South and Southeast Asia. The book as a whole points out that along with other factors, the "Northeast problem" significantly contingent upon a situating "Law" in an unambiguous domain and the introduction of legal transparency is call of the day. The Indian state has been trying to address the challenges in the Northeast through several experimentations by geopolitical structuring, economic policies, liberal gestures, friendly negotiations, and hostile encounters. The Look East policy – later on, the Act East policy – marks significant endeavor to foster overall progress in the region as well as to open India's commercial passage toward South and Southeast Asia via Northeast India. Concerns have been expressed however by the policymakers, scholars, and the stakeholders over the limited success of the policy (so far) to yield both economic and diplomatic dividends leading to nationwide debate and discussion to locate more effective modus operandi to optimize the goal. The book examines and points out how a successful implementation of the strategic and economic policies such as Look East and Act East Policy largely depends on rational legal governance in the region. The volume is an attempt to locate the anomalies in the legal domain that dominate the policy perspectives, ethnic imagination, and stable socio-political order.

Nandini Bhattacharyya-Panda
Kolkata, 2024

Notes

1 Datta, P. S. (ed.), *The North-East and the Indian State: Paradoxes in a Periphery*, Roy Buman, B. K., "Policy Issues for the North-East and Tribal Areas", Vikash Publishing House, New Delhi, 1995, pp.78-87.
2 Melvil Perira, Bitopi Dutta and Binita Kakoti, (ed.), *Legal Pluralism and Indian Democracy: Tribal Conflict Resolution Systems in Northeast India*, Routledge, India, 2017.
3 For instance, see A. K. Baruah & M. Sharma," Matriliny, Land Rights and Political Power in Khasi Society,"in *Indian Journal of Human Rights*, Vol.3, No-1&2, Jan–Dec 1999, pp. 210–228.

1 Colonial State and Law and Customs in Northeast India

Virginius Xaxa

Introduction

India became a republic with the adoption of its constitution on January 26, 1950. With this, we became citizens in place of subjects. Citizen is a status of equality, reflecting a radical shift from the earlier status of hierarchy and inequality. In addition to citizenship rights, the constitution of India even granted special rights to tribal communities in India as evident in the provision of representation via reservation in status institutions such as state employees, higher education institutions, and political institutions such as the parliament, state legislatures, and local self-government institutions. Over and above, they are provided with special systems of administration in the form of the fifth and sixth schedules of the Indian constitution. Article 244(1) refers to the fifth schedule which provides for the administration and control of scheduled areas and scheduled tribes other than the state of Assam. The sixth schedule is referred to in Article 244(2) and concerns the administration of the tribal areas in the state of Assam. It was implemented in the states of Meghalaya, Mizoram, and, later on, extended to the Tripura and Bodoland areas of Assam. It was implemented in the then erstwhile hill districts of Assam such as in Meghalaya and Mizoram and later in Tripura and the Bodoland areas of Assam following the movement for a separate state by tribal people living in those areas. The sixth schedule of the Indian constitution makes provisions for autonomous district council with legislative, executive, and judicial power specified in the schedule. The objective of the two schedules is to preserve tribal autonomy, their culture, and economic empowerment to ensure social, economic, and political justice for the preservation of peace and good government (Chakraborty 2011: 86). The constitution makes provision for the preservation and protection of the age-old custom and their role and place in the administration of tribal areas of Northeast India. The term tribal areas is a constitutional category. At the time the constitution was adopted, it comprised the United Khasi-Jaintia Hills District, the Garo Hills District, the Lushai Hills District, the Naga Hills District, Cachar Hills, and Mikir Hills. They were all parts of the province of Assam. In providing for such administration for tribal areas of Assam, the constitution makes space

DOI: 10.4324/9781003539797-2

for legal pluralism, i.e., the coexistence of statutory and customary laws side by side. The place of customary law is thus formally recognized. The state-enacted laws at the parliament and state legislatures are not applicable in these spheres. This is the case for all the states with sixth schedule provisions and the states of Nagaland and Mizoram that enjoy the special constitutional status in the form of 371A and 371G, respectively.

As to what made such a space possible in the constitution entails an inquiry into the past. Accordingly, the chapter delves into the nature and type of administration in tribal areas in colonial India, in particular the interface between statutory and customary laws and the implications such arrangement had on tribal communities in Northeast India. This chapter is organized into five sections. The first section is concerned with meanings and concepts of law and customs and their general features. The second provides a synoptic view of the history of the region and its transformation from the notion of mere geographical territory to an embryonic form of the politico-administrative structure resulting in a form of northeasterner consciousness. The third discusses the general approach of the colonial state toward the administration of tribal people and tribal areas. The fourth examines the interface between law and custom in the colonial period. The fifth and final section engages with the national discourse on such arrangement and argues positively as it has ensured the people in the region in securing their land, territory, and identity.

Meaning, Concepts, and Features of Custom and Law

Laws and customs (in the sense of customary law) share one thing in common. Both are forms of rule of conduct and behavior. Yet, the two are distinct and are recognized so in jurisprudence and social science literature. Law is generally associated with an established central authority that spells out the rule of conduct for the people under its juridical authority. Such established authority has generally been conceptualized as the state, viz., an institution with the monopoly of the legitimate use of physical force. The state could be thought about as modern or pre-modern and so with the law. Law is generally clearly delineated in all its details, including the nature and quantum of punishment, and thus tends to be precise. Customary law, in contrast, remains vague and unspecified and evolves in the course of interaction among members of the community – be it a band or clan, or tribes or village. It does not have the kind of systematic elaboration found in the case of law, morality, and religion. There is certain vagueness and ambiguity concerning infractions of the prescribed code of conduct as well as punishment. Keeping this distinction in mind, social anthropologists working in Africa have made a distinction between state and stateless societies. Malinowski considers custom as an aspect of a binding obligation. It emerges more out of reciprocity and reciprocal obligation. According to him, besides the law, there are several other types of norms and traditional commandments, such as morals, manner, rules of craftsmanship, and ceremonial and religious precepts. To him, neither the force of habit nor respect of tradition nor public opinion nor the fear of supernatural beings could entirely account for conformity. He emphasizes the role of binding obligations such as the state in terms of its proclamation or enactment (Malinowski as cited in Bottomore 2010). Under custom, conduct is regulated by a traditional norm that is simply accepted rather than sanctioned and enforced.

Though customs are associated with the traditional society and laws with the modern society, modern societies are not altogether absent of the place of customs. Customs do play a role in modern society but the major forms of social behavior are regulated by law. Customs have been studied from various angles. Routine minute details as done in ethnographic studies are one of them. The other is to draw rules implicit in these routine and detailed activities, analyze them, and discern the cultural patterns. Custom is also studied as a distinctive nature of the whole culture of the community/society. In this sense, customs may be treated as a subculture within the larger culture of the community (Scott 2014; Oxford Dictionary of Sociology). The concern in the chapter is not custom per se but its interface with the colonial state, in particular with the statutory law. Custom has been hence taken as the whole culture of the community although the focus has been only on some aspects.

The Emergence of Northeast India into Regional Identity

The shaping of what is today referred to as Northeast India has gone through a different historical process. It all began with the British rule. The treaty of Yandaboo following the defeat of the Burmese at the hands of the British is considered the opening passage of the British to Northeast India. Yet, if one were to disaggregate the region, the entry of the British to the region may be traced even earlier. Parts of the region of what is Northeast today were already under the Mughals and with the Grant of Dewani in 1765, that is, the right to collect revenue from the territory under the control of the Mughals, these parts had already come under the British. With this, a vast area of Bengal, Bihar, and Orissa had become part of British India. Some regions of present-day Northeast India were already parts of Bengal then. The districts of Goalpara, Sylhet, and areas inhabited by some tribal groups in their vicinities had become parts of British India in 1765. And so has been the case with plain parts of territory under the Tripura kingdom. Much of these lands following the partition have gone to erstwhile East Pakistan, now Bangladesh. In 1793, these areas were brought under the Permanent Zamindari land and revenue Settlement. The other parts of Northeast India were brought under the British rule in different phases after the Treaty of Yandaboo in 1826. As per the treaty, the Burmese who had invaded and devastated Assam and Manipur were to leave the territory and rule to be restored by the earlier rulers. The Treaty of Yandaboo gave a foothold to the British in the region and, a few years later, they began to be brought under the British through annexation, war, and conquest. The earliest to come was the Brahmaputra valley, the lower parts of the valley in 1828 and the upper in 1838. In between, Cachar was annexed in 1832, Jaintia Hills in 1835, and the Khasi Hills in 1833. Other parts of the hills were annexed into the British territory somewhat later. The Naga Hills were gradually annexed into British India though the district had come to be constituted as early as 1866. The Lushai Hills were the last to fall under the British in 1890 following the protracted skirmishes between the hill and the valley people, especially the tea planters. Manipur following the Burmese war was a protectorate and became a princely state in 1891 (Rajiv Gandhi University 2016: 75–86).

Northeast India may not have gone many changes in its geography and territory from what was left as the British legacy; yet, in its political and administrative domains as well as economically and socially, it has undergone a phenomenal change. The North-East Frontier Agency is popularly referred to mainly as NEFA, Assam, Manipur, and Tripura. The NEFA today has been configured into a state. What was Assam has been reorganized into four states: Assam, Nagaland, Meghalaya, and Mizoram. In contrast, Manipur and Tripura as princely states outside of the direct control and administration of the British joined India as the union of states.

There have also been internal political and administrative subsystems within them, some with constitutional provisions and others under state laws. The evolution of such political and administrative arrangements has been the result of a long chain of articulation and movements at different planes and levels due to internal contradiction. These centrifugal tendencies raised doubt about the possibility and consciousness of a larger northeasterner regional identity. Yet, this has taken shape. In fact, no other part of India is thought of, described, and addressed as a distinct, economic, political, and social entity as Northeast India. The shaping of this identity came through the agenda of the post-independent Indian state overtime. The forces that led to this, however, had their roots in the region. Northeast India in the 1960s was in turmoil leading eventually to its reorganization in the form of carving out new states and union territories. Following this, the Northeast Council (NEC) was set up in 1972. All the chief ministers of the states of the region were its members. The aim was to secure balanced and coordinated development and facilitate coordination among the states. This was the beginning of Northeast's shaping into a distinct administrative entity. The NEC, since 2002, has moved away from being an Advisory Body to a Regional Planning Body for the region. The idea of the region got solidified with the setting up of the North East Development Financial Institution (NEDFI) in 1995 and a separate ministry for development of the region in 2001 in the form of the Ministry of Department for Development of Northeast Region (MODONER). The Look East Policy or more recent phrase the Act East Policy has given further credence to the idea of the Northeast as a region.

These developments have led to some degree of homogenization of Northeast India. Today, it is looked at more from the lens of the region.

This is so both in the Northeast and in the rest of India but more in the case of the latter. In this process of grand regional identity, the people and the diversity that marks the region have been overshadowed. It was precisely from this lens that the region was earlier looked upon. The people in the region are enormously diverse. They speak different languages; have a distinct culture, customs, tradition, and land tenure system; practice different religions; and inhabit territory ecologically diverse. The Indian constitution acknowledges this diversity and makes various kinds of special provisions for their protection and ensures their identity as distinct people.

Genealogy of Non-regulated Tract in India

To understand law and customs in colonial India, it is important to understand first and foremost the administrative system in place in different parts of India during the British rule. The system in place has been far from uniform. There were parts of India that the British directly administered. Some parts were under the native rulers/kings, popularly known as princely states. The British had residents in those states who oversteered the relation between the states and the British. The princely states ran as autonomous states though some forms of interference by the British with its interest at stake could not be ruled out. Both these systems were in place under the British in Northeast India. Whereas Manipur and the Hill Tripura represented the princely state, the rest were directly under British rule. Yet, the administration was far from uniform. The difference in administration revolved around geographical consideration. The introduction of such an administration in the Northeast was not new. They were already in practice in parts of India that were annexed into the British territory in the late 18th and early 19th centuries. Hence, a journey to a different system of administration under British India will not be out of place.

In fact, the British-introduced law varied from region to region in extent and enforcement. Whereas in certain parts it had been laws that predominated, in other places it was customs and traditions that held sway over the law. With the Government of India Act of 1858, the rule over India moved from the East India Company to the crown. The crown now ruled India through the Secretary of State for India, advised by a council whose members were appointed by the crown. Governor-General and Provincial Governors were all appointed by the crown.

The East India Company governed India through regulations and not laws, till the Charter Act of 1833. Regulation prevailed all over the territory they reigned. As mentioned earlier, regulation X 1822 introduced the concept of a non-regulated system. This system was put into practice for the administration of difficult areas. Under the provision, the executive could govern the area keeping in mind the principles and spirits of the regulation but also subject to amendments and modifications as may be ordered by the Governor-General in Council from time to time. Most of the areas so administered were referred to as an agency. Many of the princely states during the period were described as such. However, such practice was also extended to areas directly under the British administration but was located in difficult geographical terrain. Many of the areas so described were initially part of the regulation tract, viz., they were regulated by the general regulations applicable to British India (Misra 2012).

This caused havoc in societies inhabiting those areas. People living in such areas were different from those on the plains. They rose in open revolt against the British following the introduction of such alien administration. The Pahariyas of Rajmahal Hills, for example, revolted against the British as early as 1787. This forced the British to allow the system of administration traditionally in place in respect of the civil sphere and to some extent even the criminal sphere barring cases of what the British thought as heinous crimes. Such revolts kept on occurring in such areas in the early part of the British rule. Prominent among the revolts at this early phase were the Tamar Revolt (1789, 1794–1795), tribal revolt (1807–1808), and agrarian tribal revolts (1811, 1817, 1820) (Raghavaiah 1979; BosuMullick 1993). However, it was the Great Kol Insurrection of 1830–1831 that gave a big jolt to the British. Soon thereafter, the whole of what was then called the Chhotanagpur region spread over the present territory of Bengal. Orissa was brought under the non-regulated tract known as the South West Frontier agency. Similarly, the Santhal Parganas, which have been relatively close to the center of imperial power, were brought under the non-regulated tract following the Great Santhal Rebellion of 1855–1857. In the case of the Kolahan, (present-day Singhbhum district) following the Kol Revolt of 1832–1833, there was an introduction of what is known as the Wilkinson Rule in Kolahan or the Singhbhum district (BosuMullick 1993: 437–462). Under this, for the governance of the region, allowance was made for the old system of rule by Mankis and Mundas – the Mankis, who had under them 3–12 villages, were recognized as "police chiefs and revenue collectors" with powers to settle criminal and civil cases and Mundas were known as "police officers and revenue collectors" of the village under the control of the Mankis.

This was the beginning of the non-regulated tract. This meant that the general regulations will not be valid for tribal areas as the introduction of alien rule and administration has led to tension resulting in early struggles of tribes which were primarily to do with the issue of overthrowing the colonial rule and administration. Hence, it would not be altogether out of place to describe these early struggles as a kind of struggle for self-rule. Thus, the system of distinct administration in areas tribal people had inhabited had become a fairly well-established system of administration.

Then, the non-regulated tract came to be referred to by different names at different phases in British India. Yet, the essence underlying the principle remained. The early nomenclature used was the agency. Many tracts under the suzerainty of the British but not directly administered by the British were already being referred to as agencies. This system was also introduced in

British India in areas that had difficult geographical terrain and were not easily accessible. Tribal people inhabited much of such areas. The Government of India Act of 1870 introduced the concept of the backward tract, and areas tribes inhabited were generally considered a backward tract. The Government of India Act of 1874 introduced the concept of the scheduled district act. Tracts of British India known by such names as the agency or backward tract came under the scheduled district act.

Following the Montagu–Chelmsford report, the Government of India Act 1918/1919 was introduced. The act recommended that the backward tract be administered by the governors. They would decide if any of the acts of the Indian legislature should apply to such area or apply to such exemption or modification. The Government of India Act 1935 discarded the term backward tract introduced in the Government of India Act 1919. It classified the whole tract into excluded and partially excluded areas (Chaube 2012; Misra 2012).

Northeast India and Excluded and Partially Excluded Areas

It is important to note that all parts of Northeast India annexed after the treaty of Yandaboo were placed in different systems of administration as compared to regions that had come under British India before the treaty of Yandaboo. Except for Manipur and Tripura on the hill part of its territory, which did not form part of British India and were referred to as the princely states, all regions were part of the non-regulated system. This meant that the general laws and regulations governing British India were not applicable in the ceded British Northeast India. The Government of India Act of 1870 allowed Governor-General to legislate separately for the backward tract. This act also defined for the first time the areas along the Assam Frontier which were parts of neither British Indian nor any foreign state as Tribal Areas. Some areas in Assam Frontier also came under the Bengal Eastern Frontier Regulation of 1873. The regulation made it lawful for the government to prescribe and from time to time alter by notification, a line to be called Inner Line, and to prohibit any subject living outside the area from living or moving therein (Chaube 2012; Misra 2012). The present-day states of Mizoram, Nagaland, and Arunachal Pradesh came under this regulation. The system continues even today. Entry into these territories may be made by any foreigner after obtaining the Restricted Areas Permit while Indian citizens may visit these places only after obtaining Inner Line Permit.

The erstwhile non-regulated areas came under the purview of the Scheduled District Act, 1874. Assam, which was under the management of the Lieutenant Governor of Bengal, was put under a Chief Commissioner and the entire chief commissionership of the newly created province of Assam was declared to be a scheduled district. The term scheduled district was meant to refer to those remote or backward tracts or provinces of British India, where uncertainty prevailed regarding the local enforceability of the general Acts and Regulations. In such areas, the officers were supposed to be guided by the spirit of indispensable laws or were guided by such laws as had somehow or other been considered to be in force (ibid.).

Thus, within the system of administration falling under the scheduled district act, a distinction had already been drawn through the Government of India Act of 1870 and Bengal Eastern Frontier Regulation of 1873. Thus, the system of administration was far from uniform throughout the state. This had a different bearing on the interface between law and state in different parts of the region. Whereas in some parts, laws enacted by the British were more dominant and regulated the overall administration system, in other parts, such laws were not extended. Rather, the customary laws and practices and system of governance were more dominant. Yet, such arrangement underwent subtle change under the Government of India Act 1935. The act introduced the concept of excluded and partially excluded areas. Accordingly, the Northeast Frontier Tract, the Naga Hills, Lushai Hills, and North Cachar Hills came to be delineated as the excluded areas. The remaining hill districts, viz., the Khasi-Jaintia Hills, the Garo Hills, and the Karbi Anglong districts, were declared as partially excluded areas. The classification of the erstwhile non-regulated backward or scheduled districts into excluded and partially excluded seems to have its genesis in the Eastern Bengal Regulation Act of 1873. This difference in administration became sharper and sharper with the changing political and administrative setup in Assam.

Assam was part of the Bengal Presidency from 1826 to 1873. It was Chief Commissioner's province from 1874 to 1905, under Lt. Governor from 1906 to 1912, Assam Legislative Council from 1912 to 1920, Dyarchy from 1921 to 1937, and Assam Legislative Assembly from 1937 to 1947. With changes in administrative structure, some space for representation was provided to the native. Under the Lt. Governor, the province had 15 members of the legislative council in which Assam had two seats. With the return of the Chief Commissioner's province, Assam Legislative Council had 25 members, of which 12 were elected and the rest nominated. The Government of India Act 1919 increased the Assam's Legislative Council Members to 53, of which 33 were elected by special constituencies. Yet, the official groups and nominated had more power, and hence the rule was referred to as Dyarchy. The act also introduced local self-governing institutions with popular mandate and control over local affairs. As a result, many provinces enacted laws to intrude on local self-government. Under the Government of India Act 1935, the Council was enhanced into an assembly of 108 members and with more powers and, a little later, granted provincial autonomy and elected governments (Guha 1977; Chaube 2012). The act also divided tribal areas and backward tracts into wholly and partially excluded areas and excluded them from the purview of reform. While the former came under the purview of the Governor-General in Council, the latter was under the joint purview of the Governor and Governor-General in Council. The Simon Commission of 1930 reported the area under such administrative provisions to be 120,000 sq. miles with a population of about 11 million (Bijoy 2012: 9).

Law and Custom interface in Colonial Northeast

The overriding concern of the British for introducing the policy of non-interference in the affairs of the communities located in difficult inaccessible areas was the maintenance of law and order. Communities in such areas did enjoy a certain degree of autonomy of governance regulated by tradition and customs. At the same time, the presence of the British was not merely symbolic. To demonstrate its rule and authority, the British introduced house tax in place of land revenue as they refrained from introducing land and revenue settlements as they did elsewhere in India, including the Brahmaputra valley. The colonial state exercised its rule by introducing an administration that was alien to the communities. Such administration was marked by rules and regulations emanating from the system of knowledge, principles, and values antithetical to the system of knowledge, values, traditions, and customs of the communities. This did bring the administration into an interface with the practices of customs and traditions. How it is dealt with is the key concern in this segment of the chapter.

The colonial state ran its administration in Northeast India, especially in the hills in collaboration with the missionaries. Although distinct in the entity, the two shared the overall ethos of civilizing the tribes. After all, these two came from similar traditions and value systems and shared many things in common with their views and attitudes toward the tribal customs. Yet, they were far from identical. The colonial administrators were far more accommodating given the system of administration; the colonial state pursued in difficult geographical areas. This in turn related to the maintenance of law and order. The missionaries, on the other hand, were driven with a mission to mold the pagans into an entirely new value system and ways of life. Thus, though the British provided space for traditional self-governance through the administrative system of excluded and partially excluded areas, they did take or introduced certain measures which went against the traditional customs and traditions. On the whole, the British did not interfere with the land tenure system prevalent among the hill tribes. Rather than collecting revenue which would have entailed land and revenue settlement as has been the case elsewhere in India, including Brahmaputra valley, the British introduced tax. They also did not touch upon the core of their social and political organizations. In short, the colonial administration was strategic. According to Jiten Das as referred to in Ruchi Pant's article, the British rulers preferred to follow the policy of non-interference for this region in administrative matters. They did not alter the basic structure of the authorities, which dispensed justice, nor did they affect the general customs. They merely promulgated procedural rules for the administration of justice (Pant 2003).

Das is right in my opinion, as far as the basic structure is concerned. However, on the general customs, they did interfere. The nature of interference between the colonial state and its laws, regulations, and policies thus varied depending on the nature and type of custom. Customs, antithetical to the right to life such as killing a person either for human sacrifice as a part of protection from the impending catastrophe or ushering in prosperity for the community or head-hunting as was in practice among some of the communities of the region to earn honor and prestige in the community, were invariably acted upon. The policy was adopted to abolish the system (Chakravarti 1960; Lalsangpuii 2013–2014). The first evidence of witch-hunting in Assam was recorded in 1848 when a man (the general practice of witch-hunt has been a woman) from the Singpho community was accused as the witch. After this incident, Major F. Jenkins, the chief commissioner of Assam, banned witchcraft practices in the province (Basumatary 2021).

Even practices that affected basic human freedom and dignity were tampered with. The abolition of slavery in the region illustrates the point (Chakravarti 1960; Lalsangpuii 2013–2014). However, on this, the colonial administrators and others who worked among tribes have a somewhat different understanding. And hence whereas some tolerated and did not act against it, others were averse to such practices and articulated steps for its abolition. The system of slavery was one such instance among them. To illustrate, Mizos had the system of practice known as "Bawi," a sort of system of slavery. It meant persons who had no individual right to freedom of action. Yet, there has been a different understanding of the system. Lieutenant Colonel Shakespeare, one of the earliest and most knowledgeable of the Lushai Hills superintendents, had seen little wrong in the system and felt that a *bawi* in the Chief's household was as well-off as a "free" man. And village elders say that they were just below the Chief in status and considered members of the Chief's family. On the other hand, Dr. Fraser, who was a missionary, argued that the presence of bonded labor in the Chief's household was a clear instance of "slavery within the British empire." As such, they were against the constitution and should be immediately abolished. Fraser regarded it as blatant undisguised slavery which should be destroyed (Lalsangpuii 2013–2014). The officials were very confused about whether to abolish it or not. All the same, it was abolished leading to the emancipation of slaves but also resulted in the expulsion of Fraser and his friend H.W.G. Cole from Mizoram (Lalsangpuii 2013–2014: 228–229). The abolition of slavery/bonded labor and practices of head-hunting has been a glaring example of their direct interference with the customs and traditions.

About the British Policy toward tribes, Nagas to be more specific, Chakravarti refers to the policy of non-interference and the policy of isolation. The latter had restrained outsiders from moving into the Naga areas. Although the above was the policy of the administration, there were enough instances of intervention. The deployment of local police assisted by the Assam Rifles, the introduction of the court beyond the village council, and the institution of dobashi were the impositions of the above (Chakravarti 1960). These have been more of an add-on and did not interfere with the power and status of the traditional institutions. This may have been partly there as on why, despite the change, there has been no resistance. It did not affect the traditional system and customs directly but it did have an indirect bearing. Many of the changes that the societies in the hills went through were the results of various forces introduced from outside. Administration, trade, and commerce, and the presence of outsiders from the plains as teachers, clerks, traders, and shopkeepers did have a bearing on the life. Similarly, in Mizoram, for example, in 1898, Col. J. Shakespeare, the then Superintendent of the Lushai Hills District, formulated the land settlement policy which envisaged that each chief would get a certain area within which his people or subject could move about and cultivate land as they like. In doing so, the area under each chief and his people were demarcated. The British officers left the land revenue system as they found it. The entire area that formed the domain of the chief was known as "Ram." The superintendents of the then Lushai Hills District recognized the right of the chiefs. The whole territory of the Lushai Hills District was divided into 16 circles with an officer-in-charge and one interpreter posted in each circle. The interpreter's duty was to facilitate smooth relations between a chief and the officer-in-charge of the circle. The circle officers were to respond to the superintendent of the district. The superintendent on behalf of the government was empowered to interfere in the demonstration of the chiefs only when they went beyond their respective limits (Lalsangpuii 2013–2014).

More than law, it is through the policy and programs that they undermine customs and traditions. In this, Christianity played a critical role. The institution of youth dormitory which was an important institution of socialization and cooperative activities was destroyed by the civilizing mission of Christianity much more than the colonial administration. Indeed, the colonial administration aided the Christian mission in undermining many of these institutions.

At the same time, traditional institutions such as the institution of Chieftainship or headman were utilized by them solely for the maintenance of law and order, collection of house tax, and other related activities. They were in a way integrated into the structure of local administration. Further, as and when they required labor, especially for a public purpose such as construction and maintenance of roads and bridges, they even used forced labor which they had abolished (Ziipao 2016: 60).

The above have been the customs and traditions which the colonial state directly or indirectly undermined. However, there are others, especially of lesser significance, as far as the functioning of the colonial administration is concerned; the colonial administrators were either indifferent or accommodating. These concerned certain social and religious customs and festivals such as bachelor's dormitory, polygamous practices, and divorce (Roluahpuia 2016: 32). However, these were antithetical to the values of Christianity, which the missionaries through their evangelization and education aimed at eradicating, and have been greatly successful in the mission. Yet, customs related to property, inheritance, and succession from which women were excluded remained by and large intact.

Policy and Its Implications

How to understand the implication of such an arrangement? The understanding would vary depending on the perspectives one takes. If one is to look at it from the perspective of the Indian state and the larger Indian population, one would invariably be drawn to a different understanding/ perspective as compared to if one is looking at the same issue from the perspective of the people in reference. From the point of view of the Indian state, the policy is generally explored from three or four angles. The lack of consciousness of belonging to India or identification as Indian is attributed to the policy of isolation of tribes from the other segments of the population. The colonial policy of the British restricted interaction and exchange between tribes and non-tribes and thereby posed obstacles to forging larger national solidarity and the Indian national consciousness. The lack of development either in infrastructure or economically, politically, and socially such as education and health is also attributed to the policy of isolation (Kapai 2020). This is fairly tenable. Yet, there was a development of political consciousness relatively more advanced to worry about their place and identity in being part of India. Such concern was also echoed in the Constituent Assembly debate during the discussion on the sixth schedule provision of the Indian constitution. Kuladhar Chaliha from Assam went to the extent of calling the sixth schedule provision as the recipe for tribal stance and balkanization of India (Pereira et al. 2018). To the British, the policy served well, as their strategy was to ensure that the empire did not face any challenge, especially from those living on frontiers and geographically inaccessible areas. As for the tribal people, the policy protected them from the influx of people from outside the region. This protected them not only demographically but also from exploitation by people from outside in the sense of alienation of land, forest, and other resources from tribes to non-tribes. This is precisely what happened in tribal areas of eastern and central India, including areas that were partially excluded. This was largely due to the opening of the partially excluded areas for trade and commerce through the extension of roads, railways, and other means of communication. The result was large-scale migration of people from the plains into tribal areas and appropriation of their land and other resources through deceit, forging of documents, credit indebtedness, intimidations, etc. The shrinking landholding and landlessness pushed them out of their own territory for work and livelihood elsewhere. Today, they have become a numerical minority in their own territory. It is precisely because of this safeguard that tribes, especially in the excluded and partially excluded areas of Northeast India, were able to safeguard their resources under their control as well as protect their language, culture, and identity. It is this that facilitated the provision of the special constitutional arrangement in post-independent India, which provides space for people to govern themselves on matters granted under the constitutional arrangement. This has enabled them to safeguard and protect their interests as well as to develop according to their own genius. It is this control over resources as well as their distinct language, which has been a stimulant to their social and cultural development. Has there not been such a policy of protection under the British, it is unlikely that the post-independent India would have extended such provision of self-governance to tribal people of Northeast India. This is evident in the fact that such constitutional provisions were not extended to areas, which were marked by the absence of such protective administrative arrangements in colonial India.

References

Basumatary, D. 2021. 'Witchcraft Practices in Assam: A Sociological Analysis'. Ph.D. Thesis, Tata Institute of Social Sciences, Guwahati.

Bijoy, C.R. 2012. *Policy Brief on Panchayat (Extension to Scheduled Areas) Act of 1996*. New Delhi: UNDP.

BosuMullick, S. 1993. 'The Jharkhand Movement: A Historical Analysis', in Mrinal Miri (ed.) *Continuity and Change in Tribal Society*. Shimla: Indian Institute of Advanced Study.

Bottomore, T.B. 2010.*Sociology: A Guide to Problems and Literature*. South Asia edition. New Delhi: Bharat Law House.

Chakraborty, P. 2011. *Fifth & Sixth Schedules to the Constitution of India*. Delhi: Capital Law House.

Chakravarti, K.C. 1960. 'The Naga Policy: Old and New'. Economic and Political Weekly, January.

Chaube, S.K. 2012. Hill Politics in Northeast India, 1973, reprint, New Delhi.

Guha, A. 1977. *Planter Raj to Swaraj. Freedom Struggle and Electoral Politics in Assam, 1836–1947*, New Delhi: ICHR. (Anwesha Edition, Guwahati 2016).

Kapai, Y. 2020. 'Spatial Organisation of Northeast India: Colonial Politics, Power Structure and Hills–Plains Relationship', *Indian Historical Review*, 47(1): 150–169.

Lalsangpuii, R. 2013–2014. 'Bawi and Sal in Mizo Society', *Vidyasagar University Journal of History*, 2: 223–233.

Misra, B. 2012. Keynote Address. National Seminar on Governance, Socio-Economic Disparity, and Unrest in the 'Scheduled Areas of India. Tata Institute of Social Sciences, Guwahati Campus, 22–24 November.

Pant, R. 2003. *Exploring the Role of Community and Customary Law in Natural Resources Management in the Legal Pluralist Societies of North East India*. Bagdogra: ATREE-Eastern Himalaya Programme.

Pereira, Melvil et al. (ed.) 2018. *Legal Pluralism and Indian Democracy, Tribal Conflict Resolution Systems in Northeast India*. London: Routledge.

Raghavaiah, V. 1979. 'Background of Tribal Struggles in India', in A.R. Desai (ed.) *Peasant Struggles in India*. New Delhi: Oxford University Press.

Rajiv Gandhi University. 2016. *History of Northeast India 1228–1947*. Noida: Vikas Publishing House.

Roluahpuia. 2016. 'The Mizo national Question: A Study of the Mizo National Front (MNF) Movement'. Ph.D. Thesis submitted at the Tata Institute of Social Sciences, Guwahati.

Scott, J. 2014. *Oxford Dictionary of Sociology*. Oxford: Oxford University Press.

Ziipao, R.R. 2016. 'Infrastructure Development in Manipur. A Study in Social Dynamics'. Ph.D. Thesis submitted at Tata Institute of Social Sciences, Mumbai.

2 The Colonial Legacy in Manipur

M. Amarjeet Singh

Introduction

The present-day Indian state of Manipur was a kingdom for a long time. Its authority was significantly eroded as a result of its loss in the hands of the British in 1891. It was eventually recognized as a native state in British India. The kingdom had a brief period of independence just before becoming a part of India in September 1949. Manipur was granted statehood 20 years later (Government of Manipur 2021).

About 90 percent (20,089 km^2) of its territory comprises the hill region, while the remaining 10 percent area (2,238 km^2) constitutes the valley region. Thus, the hill region is about nine times bigger than the valley region. Interestingly, the majority of the state's population lives in the valley region. Thus, it is much more densely populated compared to the hill region (Government of Manipur 2021).

Among major ethnic groups of the state, the Meiteis and the Meitei Pangals are considered as the non-tribal people. They live predominantly in the valley, while the tribes (the scheduled tribes), constituting about 40.88 percent of the total population, mostly live in the hills. The tribes are broadly divided into Naga and Kuki groups although there are some who do not want to identify either of the group (see Oinam 2003). The Nagas and Kukis want to reorganize Manipur's boundary to allow for the formation of their own states/homelands, but others are against it. Since the tribes are recognized as the scheduled tribes, they enjoy the benefits of reservations in jobs, education, legislative assembly, parliament, and other welfare programs of the central and state governments. They are predominantly Christian, the Meiteis follow Hinduism, Sanamahism, and Christianity, and the Meitei Pangals follow Islam. Since the valley region has relatively flat terrain, it has better development infrastructure than the hill region.

All the non-tribals including Meiteis and Pangals are debarred from acquiring land in the hill region, but the tribals can acquire land in the valley region. With this background, this chapter examines the role of colonial policies in influencing future ethnic politics in Manipur. The chapter argues that these policies instead of integrating the hill and valley dwellers divided the

DOI: 10.4324/9781003539797-3

two apart. For want of better terms, this chapter uses the term tribes to denote the Nagas and the Kukis, respectively, the hills to denote the hill region, and the valley to denote the valley region.

From Treaties to the Office of the Political Agent

As mentioned above, Manipur was a kingdom in which the Meitei kings ruled both the hills and valley prior to the advent of the British (Pemberton 1835). However, unlike in the valley proper, the administration of the hill areas was restrained due to difficult terrain. R. Brown, the then Political Agent (July 1873–July 1876), acknowledged that hill territories were part and parcel of the kingdom. In this context, Brown (1975, 1) stated,

> ... The territory which constitutes the native state of Manipur consists of a large extent of hill country and of the valley proper of Manipur. Its boundaries on the north are the Angami country and the hills overlooking the valley of Assam; on the south the boundary is undefined and abuts on the country inhabited by the various tribes of Lushai, Kukis and Sutis; on the west, the British province of Kachar; and on the east by the Kubo valley and part of Upper Burma ... The total area of the kingdom isbetween7 and 8,000 square miles...

From the 18th century onwards, the British succeeded in establishing contact with the Manipur kingdom which subsequently led to the signing of several treaties. One such treaty (with the East India Company) was concluded in 1762 and included among others granting permission to the English for an open trade into and through Manipur free of all duties, to be considering the enemies of the British as the enemies of Manipur, and refraining from accommodation with the Burmese rajah without the knowledge of the English or the English should not do so without the knowledge of Manipur rajah (Sharma and Sharma 2021; Sanajaoba 1993).

The Treaty of Yandaboo of 1826 between the East India Company and the King of Ava recognized Ghumbheer/Gambhir Singh as the Rajah of Manipur by the King of Ava. Subsequently, in 1833, Gambhir Singh concluded a crucial treaty with the English in which the latter agreed to give up all claims on the hill ranges situated between the eastern and western bends of the Barak with the conditions that the Rajah should not obstruct trade, should undertake repair works of the road connecting eastern bend of Jeere/Jiri and valley of Manipur, and should assist the British government in the event of war with the Burmese (Sanajaoba 1993, 20; Sharma and Sharma 2021, 8).

In 1834, the Kabaw (Kubo) valley was transferred to the Burmese by the British on the condition to award a monetary compensation to the Manipuri king (Mackenzie 2011, 151–152). The British intended to grant a monthly stipend of five hundred sicca rupees to the king with effect from January 9, 1834, the date at which the transfer of valley took place. The people felt that they were unjustly deprived of their rightful possession and claim to the valley. Had Gambhir Singh been personally present, he would not have allowed the transfer of the valley. He died of heart failure on hearing the news on the same day (Rajkumar 2016, 44). These developments clearly showed that Manipur had already become a subordinate and protected native state, although the colonial interest was "more strategic and less commercial" (Rajkumar 2016, 38). Such treaties had benefited the English more than the Manipuris. Gradually, the kingdom became militarily and politically dependent on them.

In 1835, the office of the Political Agent was opened in Imphal, the capital of Manipur, under the supervision of the Chief Commissioner of Assam. Although it was meant to act as a medium of communication between Manipur and British, it became an important and powerful agency to further consolidate the English interest. Moreover, the rivalry among the Manipuri princes gave an added advantage to the Political Agent to interfere in the internal politics (Laldena 2012).

Intense factionalism took place in the royal families after the death of Sir Chandrakriti Singh in 1886. This provided an opportunity to the Political Agent to interfere in the succession to the throne. In 1890, the British even stood up to one of the most powerful princes, Bir Tikendrajit, for opposing a prince sponsored by the British for the throne. As he was seen as a potential threat to the British, it was decided to send him into exile. The task was not easy. While trying to execute the plan, a bloody confrontation broke out at the official bungalow of the Political Agent on March 24, 1891, leading to the death of four high-ranking British officials, including J. W. Quinton, the Chief Commissioner of Assam (Rajkumar 2016). Angered with this development, additional security forces were dispatched to Manipur, and the Anglo-Manipur War broke out. The people regarded this as a war of independence (Singh 1985). On April 27, the Manipuri army was defeated by the British army. "The Govt. of India under the British declared war against Manipur. The great Khongjom war was fought between Manipuri army and the invading British army. Manipur fell into the hands of British after fierce fighting" (Government of India, 2003, 6).

Post-war Development

After the war, Manipur was not directly annexed into the British territories and hence given a native state rule status "under such conditions as the Governor-General in Council may consider desirable, and in the person of such ruler as the Governor-General in Council may select" (Sharma and Sharma 2021, 63). Following that, the administration of Manipur was briefly (April 27 to September 13, 1891) entrusted to Major Maxwell, the Political Agent, under Brigadier General H. Collett, the General Officer Commanding (Singh 1985, 54).

Thereafter, the Governor-General in Council selected Churachand Singh, then a minor, as the chief and granted him the title of rajah in September

1891. The Political Agent who also acted as the Superintendent was granted "full power to introduce any reform into the existing administration" (Sharma and Sharma 2021, 128), although due regard should be given to the local customs and traditions. During the minor rajah, the civil and political administration of the state was vested in the Chief Commissioner of Assam, the Political Agent, and the Superintendent of State (Singh 1985, 57). The Political Agent became active and crucial, and the appointment of kings became the prerogative of the British.

Gradual reform in different aspects of administration such as judicial administration (such as the establishment of Cheirap and Panchayat Courts and the courts of the Political Agent and the Assistant Political Agent), finance (introduction of annual budget prepared by the Political Agent), and revenue was introduced. Due attention was accorded to revenue administration to levy taxes. Payment of house tax at the rate of two rupees per house for the valley and three rupees for the hills was introduced. The reason for imposition of the house tax was simply to raise tax in cash in line with the British Indian system. The *lallup* (the compulsory feudal service) was abolished and substituted by payment of cash for all services rendered to the state (Singh 1985; Sharma and Sharma 2021).

Churachand Singh assumed the full duties of the king in 1907 under the Manipur State Administrative Rules, 1907. The rules were prepared by the Judicial Department of Eastern Bengal and Assam, in which a Durbar comprising of the ex-officio president, the vice president, and six ordinary and additional members was to be constituted. The members were to be jointly appointed by the king and the Political Agent. Churachand Singh became the president, while W. A. Cosgrave became the vice president of the Durbar. Interestingly, the vice president was to be from amongst the members of the Assam Provincial Service Cadre. The Durbar had both administrative and judicial jurisdiction in matters involving Manipuris. But it had no jurisdiction in matters involving the hill tribes and the British Indian subjects (Singh 1985; Thokchom 2022). The vice president, not the president, was tasked with handling hill affairs, finance, and revenue of the state including preparation of the state budget. While the administration of the entire state was the responsibility of the Durbar of which the Raja was the president, the hill tribes were excluded from its jurisdiction (Parratt 2005a).

By 1916, the Raja ceased to act as the president of the Durbar, while the post of vice president was abolished. The president was entrusted with the responsibility of administering the hill tribes on behalf of the Raja. In addition, the president was to consult the Raja on all important matters concerning the hill tribes. "On the other hand, the British control over the Raja and his administration was all the more tightened by subjugating the Raja's actions to the approval of the Political Agent in Manipur, who in turn, was supervised by the Government of Assam" (Singh 1985, 97).

Four hill sub-divisions were created in 1919, namely the North-East sub-division with Ukhrul as the headquarters, the North-West sub-division with headquarters at Tamenglong, the South-West sub-division with headquarters at Churachandpur, and the Sadar sub-division with Imphal as the headquarters. Except for the Sadar sub-division, the administration was entrusted to the European sub-divisional officers. No role was assigned to the natives. Areas such as Mao and Maram in the north and Mombi area in the south-east and various tribes bordering the valley were administered directly from Imphal under the president (see Administrative Report of the Manipur State 1919–1920, Chapters 1 and 2). In addition, 13 armed outposts were set up in the hills. Thus, a separate budget for the hills was prepared. In due course of time, the hill sub-divisions and armed outposts were restructured.

The Durbar proposed in 1928 to hand over the administration of the hill areas to the Maharaja and that too without needing the approval of the Political Agent. The proposal was submitted to the Political Agent for onward submission to the Indian States Committee. But it was reportedly ignored by the Political Agent. The Political Agent even stated that it would be unsafe to entrust the administration of the hills to the Maharaja and the Durbar. Practically speaking, no significant changes took place in the power and function of the Maharaja and Durbar (Singh 1985).

Under the revised "Rules for the Management of the State of Manipur" (enforced on September 4, 1935), the king was assisted by the Durbar in which a non-native officer appointed by the Government of Assam acted as its president. The ordinary and additional members of the Durbar were also appointed. The non-native president was said to be responsible to the king for the administration of finance and revenue departments, and on behalf of the king, he exercised general supervision over other departments. But, in reality, the non-native president played an important role in the administration. There was a separate budget relating to the hill tribes and the other part relating to the state. The budget for both parts was drafted by the president. The hill tribes were governed by the president on behalf of the king and in accordance with rules approved by the Government of Assam. This was not good for the state because it created hill–valley divide. The Durbar tried all cases beyond the jurisdiction of the Chejrap court except those in which the hill tribes were concerned and those that arose within the British reserve (Sharma and Sharma 2021, 136).

One of the justifications for keeping the administration of hills separate from that of the valley was the likelihood of the exploitation of the hill tribes by the king, but there were other reasons because the British were not able to control the hills due to difficult terrain and the deployment of a few officials. In fact, the Christian missionaries were encouraged in the hills (Parrat 2005b). Thus, the "king's administrative power was confined to a small area in the valley" (Sanjeev 2020, 9). Thus, the policy of separating the hills and the valley by adapting separate administrative mechanism paves the way for ethnic division and polarization (Sanjeev 2020). Sir Andrew G. Clow, the then Governor of Assam (May 1942–May 1947), wrote on October 29, 1945, in Shillong his proposed plan for the future of north-east India:

> Manipur presents a more difficult problem. It is a state of 8,620 square miles in area... includes a small British reserve. Apart from this reserve, the state falls into two areas, the Imphal plain, this is a comparatively small part of the area but has about two-thirds of the people, and the hills. ... The plains are administered by the Maharaja with a darbar, but various powers are vested in the agent to the Crown Representative and his representative the Political Agent. In the hills and, indeed, over hill men generally the Maharaja's authority is merely titular and the darbar (apart from its President, an officer of the Indian Civil Service) has no authority at all. The administrative and judicial system is subordinate to the Governor as A.C.R.; but as in other hill areas, a considerable amount of authority is exercised by the peoples themselves.
>
> (Clow 1945, quoted in Syiemlieh 2014, 213–214)

Prior to the advent of the British, the king used to rule both the hills and valley of the kingdom. However, the king did not meddle with the village administration of the hills. The king received loyalty through the hill village chiefs. The chiefs were appointed in accordance with local customs. Initially, for hill administration, the king appointed Lam Subedars who were assisted by several Lambus. But the role of the king in hill administration was gradually taken over by officers appointed by the British government.

Unequal Landholding System

Both the hills and the valley used to have traditional landholding system in the past. Private ownership of land was unknown in the past. When a new landholding system was introduced in the valley, the old notion that the land belonged to the king was replaced by the notion that the land belonged to the state. The land patta was issued to the landholders with the right to transfer, sell, or inherit land. In 1894, in order to facilitate better land revenue collection, the valley region was divided into four sub-divisions, namely Ahallup Pana, Naharmp, Khabam, and Laipham Pana. For the purpose of collection of house tax, the valley was divided into three divisions (Singh 1985). Lakpa or tahsildars were appointed in each pana for the collection of revenue. They were given 10 percent from their collection at the first go and at the end of the year collected another 5 percent (Sanjeev 2020). Thus, the survey of the land in the valley was introduced.

The new landholding system was not introduced in the hills. The survey of the land was not introduced in the hills. If the issue was governance, the new landholding system could have been easily applied in the urban areas of the hills. This policy aggravated the geographical division, having a negative impact on the future politics of the state.

Like in Manipur, during the colonial rule, a number of laws to govern the administration of hill areas of Assam were introduced. The Bengal Eastern Frontier Regulations of 1873 prohibited the entry of all British subjects in the area within the Inner Line without a permit issued by the competent authority. Again, a considerable part of Assam was declared "backward" areas under the Government of India Act 1919. Further, from 1937, under the Government of India Act 1935, certain tribal areas of Assam were termed as "excluded" and "partially excluded" areas placing them outside the purview of the provincial administration and bringing them directly under the Governor of Assam. As a result, the tribals of the hill districts were encouraged to distance themselves from the plains men and developed a special kind of identity that had remained crucial for subsequent political developments. The British indirectly ruled over the hill districts that were left to the management of the traditional authorities who would be easily manipulated. It was a simple paternalistic British rule in the hills unlike the plain districts.

As a result,

> there are two types of land systems in the state. In the hill region, the landholding system is based on common property rights where the chief of each village has control over annual distribution of use rights on jhum land. Terraced cultivation has however private property characteristics. Except in some small pockets, the hill region is yet to be cadastral surveyed. In the valley region, private property rights have been fully established.
>
> (Government of Manipur 2019, 22)

Post-colonial Policies

The first legislative assembly in Manipur was constituted in 1948 under the Manipur State Constitution Act, 1947, which also marked the political transition from the rule of the king to that of a democratic government. However, the said assembly was dissolved as Manipur became a part of India, as a Part C state which was administered directly by the central government. As Manipur became a union territory, in August 1957, a territorial council consisting of 30 elected members and two nominated members was constituted. The territorial council was rechristened as the Territorial Legislative Assembly in 1963. In 1972, Manipur became a state with a 60-member legislative assembly. Since Manipur was not granted statehood until 1972, the hill–valley divide had grown more pronounced.

When Manipur was a union territory, the Manipur Land Revenue and Land Reforms Act, 1960, was enacted by the Parliament to consolidate and amend the law relating to land revenue in the erstwhile union territory of Manipur. Further, it prohibits the transfer of land belonging to the scheduled tribes to the non-tribes. This act has further crystallized the hill–valley divide because of the spatial distribution of ethnic groups in the state and also because the hill areas are predominantly inhabited by the tribes. The act is not extended to the hill areas, but the special provision that restricts the transfer of land from a member of the scheduled tribes to others further complicated the situation. The non-scheduled tribes cannot acquire or buy land in the hill areas, whereas anybody can acquire or buy land in the valley areas. As a result, the majority of Manipur's people cannot own land in the hills.

Thus, the question of land is a source of conflict in Manipur. It is not merely about geographical space which can be seen in terms of terrain, resources, and human inhabitants but the mechanism of authority and rights (Knight 1982; Penrose 2002). Ethnic groups are politically divided in the name of defending land not merely because of the material value but due to the symbolic role the land plays in constituting their identities, security, and belongingness (Walter 2006, 288). Since there is no uniform land law, the ownership of land created problem that created animosity among ethnic groups. These are root causes of exclusive identity politics of the ethnic groups. The spatial distribution of ethnic groups can affect both the capability and the legitimacy of how they mobilize for political action.

Territorial claims and self-determination claims are more difficult to invoke when the ethnic groups are widely dispersed and intermixed with each other. In such situations, group mobilization around issues such as civil or group rights and economic access is likely to be more prevalent (Reilly and Reynolds 1999, 15).

The valley communities are in favor of adopting a uniform land law; on the contrary, the hill communities are against it as they allege that non-tribals will take over the land. In several states, the land where the hill people inhabit is not allowed to be transferred to the non-tribal people. Such restrictions can be traced back to the colonial rule. The colonial policy of administratively separating the valley and hill areas paved the way for "strong geographical divide" which in turn led to "ethnic competition" between the inhabitants of the valley and hills and also within the hill people (Kipgen 2022, 83). Thus the advantage of one group is seen as a disadvantage by others. The hill people felt that introduction of a uniform land law will result in their "dispossession by them or affluent outsiders" (Sharma 2016, 12).

Fearing backlash from the hill people, the state government is unable to enact a uniform land law. Thus what is considered advantaged by some groups is considered disadvantaged by other groups. The hill communities are against allowing non-scheduled tribes to buy and settle in the hill areas fearing that they will lose the ownership of land, job, and identity. They considered this as their constitutional safeguard. For the valley communities, a uniform land policy is necessary since the valley region is small in area. Concerned over the fast-shrinking of paddy land and wetland, particularly in the valley, the Manipur Conservation of Paddy Land and Wetland Act, 2014, was enacted for promoting agriculture by restricting rampant construction on the paddy land. For the valley communities, a uniform land policy is necessary since the valley region is small in area.

The divide is further consolidated as hill districts enjoy limited district-level autonomy under the Manipur (Hill Areas) District Councils Act, 1971 (now the Manipur (Hill Areas) District Councils (Third Amendment) Act, 2008). The said act was enacted by the Indian parliament. The hill districts in Manipur have autonomous district councils in operation. These councils, which have limited district-level autonomy, serve as an institution of local governance in order to fulfill the aspirations of the tribes. Such autonomy, like decentralization, seeks to ensure administrative self-government. Under such arrangement, there is certain amount of demarcation of powers between the state government and the autonomous district council in which certain administrative departments which are usually under the state government are entrusted to the autonomous district council. Nonetheless, the state government continues to control key departments, such as general administration, police, treasury, election, and judiciary in those areas falling under the jurisdiction of the autonomous district council. But, the popular perception is that the councils have not yet proven themselves to be a credible institution of self-governance and an agent of economic development despite their existence for many years.

In fact, it only accelerated the divide between the hills and valley. Such autonomy is supposed to be the institution of self-governance and hence expected to play an important role in development of those districts. But the role of autonomy in managing conflict and development has been minimal and unclear. If the autonomy can bring development of the comparatively poorer districts, it will have a significant impact on the development of the state. Due to inherent difficulties and flaws, the entire objective of autonomy is still not being fulfilled. The councils are still unable to establish themselves as a reliable self-governance institution. In fact, it only accelerated the divide between the hills and valley.

Conclusion

The belief that the arrival of Hinduism in Manipur influenced the ties between plain and hill residents is not totally correct. It is due to the colonial policy of separating the lowlands and the highlands as different administrative units. Policies with far-reaching ramifications were introduced and tested in the name of administrative convenience. There was no attempt to blend the hills and valley. In conclusion, what had prompted the British to separate the Manipur hills from the valley? Being a small hilly state where ethnic groups are geographically concentrated, the colonial policies had created two Manipur. After independence, the divide has further compounded, and no concrete attempts have been made to bridge the divide. The policy of divide and rule adopted during the colonial rule has made the present situation politically explosive. The geographical distributions of major ethnic groups in the state make identity politics violent.

References

Brown, R. 1975. *Statistical Account of Manipur*. New Delhi: Sanskaran Prakashak

Clow, Andrew G. 1945. "The Future Government of the Assam Tribal Peoples." In *On the Edge of Empire: Four British Plans for North East India, 1941–1947*, edited by David R. Syiemlieh, 2014, 139–227. New Delhi: SAGE.

Government of India. 2003. *20 Years Perspective Plan Manipur*. New Delhi: Ministry of Tourism.

Government of Manipur. 2019. *Manipur Vision 2030- Leaving No-One Behind: Achieving Inclusive Growth and the Sustainable Development Goals*. Imphal: Planning Department.

Government of Manipur. 2021. *Economic Survey Manipur 2020–21*. Lamphelpat: Directorate of Economics & Statistics.

Kipgen, Ngamjahao. 2022. "Ethnicity, Food Security and Deprivation: The Marginalised Hill People and Distributive [in]justice in Manipur." In *Comprehending Equity: Contextualising India's North-East*, edited by Kedilezo Kikhi and D.R. Gautam, 80–97. Oxon: Routledge.

Knight, David. 1982. "Identity and Territory: Geographical Perspectives on Nationalism and Regionalism," *Annals of the Association of American Geographers* 72(4), 514–553.

Laldena. 2012. *History of Modern Manipur1762–1949*. Imphal: Reliable Book Centre.

Mackenzie, Alexander. 2011. *The North East Frontier of India*. New Delhi: Mittal Publications.

Oinam, Bhagat. 2003. "Patterns of Ethnic Conflict in the North-East: A Study on Manipur," *Economic and Political Weekly* 38(21), 2031–2037.

Parratt, John. 2005a. *Wounded Land: Politics and identity in Modern Manipur*. New Delhi: Mittal Publications.

Parratt, Saroj Nalini Arambam. 2005b. *The Court Chronicles of the Kings of Manipur: Cheithar on Kumpapa*, Vol. 1. New York: Routledge.

Pemberton, R.B. 1835. *The Eastern Frontier of India*. New Delhi: Mittal Publications.

Penrose, Jan. 2002. "Nations, States and Homelands; Territory and Territoriality in Nationalistic Thought," *Nation and Nationalism* 8(3), 277–297.

Rajkumar, Falguni. 2016. "Tikendrajit: Manipur's Struggle for Identity, Bir Tikendrajit andLittle Known Fighters Against the Raj-Figures from Manipur." In *"Koireng": Bir Tikendrajitand Little Known Fighters Against the Raj-figures from Manipur*, edited by Sanjoy Hazarika and M. Amarjeet Singh, 31–54. New Delhi: Global Books.

Reilly, Ben and Reynolds, Andrew. 1999. *Electoral System and Conflict in Divided Societies*. Washington, DC: National Academy Press.

Sanajaoba, Naorem. 1993. *Manipur Treaties and Documents (1110–1971)*. New Delhi: Mitttal Publications.

Sanjeev, Thingnam. 2020. "Surveying and Producing the Frontier in Nineteenth Century Manipur: Challenges and Practices," *Asian Ethnicity* 21(1), 122–136.

Sharma, Sushil Kumar. 2016. *Ethnic Conflict and Harmonization: A Study of Manipur*. New Delhi: Vivekananda International Foundation.

Sharma, Sushil Kumar and Sharma, Usha. 2021. *Documents of North East India: An Exhaustive Survey, Volume6: Manipur*. New Delhi: Mittal Publications.

Singh, Khwairakpam Ibochou. 1985. "British Administration in Manipur 1891–1947." PhD diss., Gauhati University.

Thokchom, Veewon. 2022. "Princely State of Manipur: Durbar, the Raj and Resistances c. 1900–1950." MPhil diss., Mizoram University.

Walter, Barbora F. 2006. "Conclusion." In *Territoriality and Conflict in an Era of Globalization*, edited by Miles Kahler and Barbora F. Walter, 25–61. New York: Cambridge University Press.

3 From Lines to Belts

Immigration, Anxiety, and Community Relations in Late Colonial and Post-colonial Assam

Binayak Dutta

Introduction

Immigration of Bengalis into Assam was not just a product of colonial administrative necessity but of economic exigency. While the colonial administrators like Jenkins were awake to the existence of extensive wastelands in Assam which were fallow and unexploited, they submitted a scheme for "colonization of Assam waste lands to the Government" as early as 1833.[1] When these proposals were being deliberated through private correspondence between 1830s and 1890s, even the Assamese middle class was supportive of the immigration of people from outside Assam. Anandanram Dekhial Phukan in a memorandum to AJM Mills urged that the people from some badly provided parts of Bengal could be invited to immigrate to improve the demographic structure of Assam. Similar position was also taken by Assamese elite like Gunabhiram Baruah and Babu Gunjanan Barua, Secretary of the Assam Association, who "submitted a memorandum to the Government, stating among other things, that, "as there is70.15% of land lying waste, the Government should give encouragement to their settlement by offering them on favourable terms...."[2] Cultural antagonism between the Assamese and Bengali gentry class notwithstanding, the Assamese elite were relentless in advocating a close communication between Assam and Bengal. The Assamese Literary Society represented by Jagannath Barooah and Manik Chandra Barooah submitted a memorial to the viceroy Lord Northbook in May 1872 urging for the introduction of a railway line connecting Assam and Bengal[3] (Guha: 19).

Though probably not realized by the memorialists, the completion of the Assam–Bengal railway gave a boost to Bengali immigration into Assam. While land settlement by immigrations grew leaps and bounds from 4,40,000 acres in 1881 to 7,97,800 acres in 1931, in actual terms the Bengali speakers in 1931 rose to 1,70,409 in Kamrup, 4,79,433 in Goalpara, 95,535 in Darrang, 1,93,349 in Nowgong, and 73,351 in Sibsagar (Nag: 98). Thus, despite middle-class antagonism developing over sites of language, culture, and government employment, the Assamese elite had no problem over

DOI: 10.4324/9781003539797-4

immigration of agriculturists from Bengal to Assam who were perceived as instruments of prosperity in Assam. Elites as Jagannath Bujar Baruah were unequivocal in their support for immigrants and saw no conflict between their interests and those of the immigrants. Jagannath Bujar Baruah in his deposition before the Assam Banking Enquiry Committee pointed out as late as 1929 that

> Immigration had led to all round prosperity in the Barpeta area. Many Assamese farmers turned to land speculators. They sold off their lands to immigrants at a good price; they then cleared new plots (pam) on wastelands and sold them again. The immigrants were financed by their own headman (matbar) as well as by Marwari and Assamese (Barpetia) moneylenders. Even the Hati (indigenous cooperative banks) funds of Barpeta were involved in this financing, to a small extent.
>
> (Guha: 167)

There was no doubt that the inflow of immigrants from Bengal had transformed the colonial economy of Assam, where land was abundant and labor was short. Landless immigrants from Bengal eager for living space flooded the waterlogged, jungle-infested riverine belts into productive agricultural plots by reclaiming "these malarial areas" (Guha: 166). While, initially, the Bengali peasants were reluctant to migrate to Assam, their reticence gradually gave way to steady migration.[4] Their manifold increase in migration began to attract Assamese attention as these immigrants began to encroach areas predominated by the Assamese cultivators and held by the indigenous landlords.

The inflow of immigrant cultivators from Bengal to Assam had a deep impact on Assamese agrarian society. While, on the one hand, it turned many Assamese landowners into neo-zamindars and land speculators, it also gradually ensured the spread of linguistic and cultural antagonism, which till the first decade of the twentieth century was limited to the middle-class elites of the two communities, into the agrarian sector. The colonial officials and the Assamese elite who had so long encouraged the inflow of immigrants from Bengal, being "stout and fanatical Mahommedans" of East Bengal and agreed that these peasants were "most eligible for immigration as they were hard working and prolific cultivators," were now eager to restrict their expansion. The Line System was an idea that was devised by colonial officers, first discussed in 1916 and introduced in 1920. The colonial administration devised it as a means to restrict the expansion of the Bengali immigrants into Assamese-inhabited areas. The system was first applied to the Nowgong and Barpeta subdivisions of Kamrup district. By 1920, the colonial state suddenly became aware about the dangers of unrestricted immigration. Probably, the untold rise in population of the Bengali immigrants in Assam served as an eye-opener.[5]

Bengali Population

District	1911	1921
Goalpara	77,000	1,51,000
Kamrup	4,000	44,000
Darrang	7,000	20,000
Nowgong	4,000	58,000
Sibsagar	14,000	14,000
Lakhimpur	14,000	14,000

Persons of Mymensinghi Origin

District	1911	1921
Goalpara	34,000	78,000
Kamrup	1,000	30,000
Darrang	1,000	12,000
Nowgong	1,000	52,000
Sibsagar	NIL	NIL
Lakhimpur	NIL	NIL

Love Turned Sour

The first official alarm was sounded in 1921 by Mr. Lloyd, who in his Census Report of 1921 for Assam, observed:

> In 1911, few cultivators from Eastern Bengal had gone goalpara..... In the last decade (1911–1921) the movement had extended far up the Valley, and the colonists now for man appreciable element in population of all the four lower and central districts ... In Goalpara nearly 20% of the population is made up of these settlers. The next favourite district is Nowgong where they form about 14% of the whole population. In Kamrup, wastelands are being taken up rapidly, especially in the Barpeta subdivision. In Darrang exploration and settlement by the colonists are in an earlier stage. They have not yet penetrated far from the banks of the Brahmaputra....... Almost every train and steamer brings parties of these settlers, and it seems likely that their march will extend further up the Brahmaputra Valley and away from the river before long.

If the colonial officials were raising consternation, the Assamese middle class was also alarmed by this huge influx. The number of Muslim population in the Brahmaputra Valley rose from 3,65,540 in 1911 to 5,94,981 in 1921, which channelized Assamese opinion against the immigrants. If the early immigrants from Sylhet and Dacca were disliked by the rising Western-educated Assamese middle class, this flood of immigrant agriculturalists from Mymensingh aggravated the antagonism. The Asamiya Samrakshini Sabha in its articulation of anti-immigrant position pleaded for restriction on the influx of people into the Brahmaputra Valley from Bengal and called for the assimilation of the immigrants with local language and culture (A. C. Bhuyan, S. De: 1999: 311, Pol. Hist. of Assam Vol. II). The Assam Association in its meeting at Nowgong in December 1925 also raised similar concerns and urged the government to immediately stop immigration from Bengal (Ibid). Concerns of the Assamese middle class were also articulated in the Legislative Council with Mahadev Sharma raising the issue through a discussion pointing out that

> The public of the Brahmaputra Valley are quite opposed to further immigration at present. Do not the governments think it worthwhile to protect the vital interests of the bona fide inhabitants?

Rapid occupation of land by the immigrants in the Brahmaputra Valley forced the native inhabitants to wake up to the scarcity of the resource on which an overwhelming section of population in the valley was dependent. Mahadev Sharma thus pointed out:

> The peculiar conditions of Assam have forced us to take recourse to such step. A piece of land is only source of wealth for the average people. They have no idea or ideal of industrialism. If however no provision is made for preserving lands for future developments our future generations will be jeopardized for want of new avenues....
>
> (Nag: 127)

Though articulated in the language of economic necessity, the Assamese middle-class perception of the immigrants and their opposition to them was built around threat to language, culture, civilization, and life of the Assamese as a result of immigrant habits and practices, as Mahadev Sharma pointed out:

> The immigrants brought with them a cultured following of thieves, burglers and forgers of currency notes. They are introducing with great rapidity crimes of the nature and violence hitherto unknown in this valley...
>
> (S. Nag: 128)

Violations of women and the killing of kine shocked the Assamese Hindus who built up crystalized opposition to the immigrants, who were perceived as people with alien culture and habits that went against the cultural ethos of the Brahmaputra valley. As frictions increased, the colonial officials themselves began to advise the immigrants to undergo a cultural transformation to assuage the Assamese middle-class anxiety over threats to their culture and language. Therefore, when a deputation of Bengali immigrants called upon the Governor of Assam Sir Laurie Hammand on February 7, 1929, the governor not only explained to the deputation the policy of the Assam Government in the matter but also advised them to settle down and become Assamese and have Assamese taught in their schools (Harendra Nath Barua: 1992: 58). The angst of the Assamese middle class over the immigration question was far from being resolved. A series of meetings were organized between 1925 and 1928, where orders were passed and proposals made to restrict the settlement of immigrants in the Brahmaputra Valley in deference to local sentiments.

Rai Bahadur, P.G. Mukherjee, Deputy Commissioner of Goalpara, in his opinion on the immigrant question, to the Assam Valley Divisional Commissioner in July 1926, pointed out that, "Public opinion seems generally .... In favour of legislation prohibiting transfer of periodic pata lands to Bengal Immigrants" (Line System Report Vol. III), and the Assamese middle class was gradually gearing up toward appreciating the efficacy of the Line System in protecting the Assamese community from immigrant "invasion." Naba Kumar Dutta, speaking in the Assam Legislative Council admitted that, "But for the line system it would not have been long before the Assamese became extinct ...... we cannot afford to allow our race to be wiped out" (Nag: 129). By mid-1920s, powerful and influential civil society groups began to sound alarm at the relentless immigration of agriculturists from Bengal into Assam. Benudhar Rajkhowa in his presidential address to the Annual Conference of the Assam Sahitya Sabha at Dhubri in 1926 called upon all nationalities in the sub-continent to limit themselves within their own territories, as he said, "Let all Nationalities of India follow their own path....let there be no attempts to merge one with the other" (Nag: 131). Similar attempts to emphasize Assamese autonomy vis-à-vis Bengal and India could also be seen in Tarun Ram Phukan who in his presidential address to the Assam Sahitya Sabha in 1927 lamented,

> we Asomiyas are a distinct nationality among Indians. Though our language is Sanskrit based, it is a distinct language... Alas... our neighbor is trying to swallow us taking advantage of our helplessness...
>
> (Nag: 131)

In a similar tone and tenor, Raghunath Choudhury, speaking at the Tezpur session of the Sabha in 1935, pointed out that

> Mere writing in the newspaper and lectures against the Bengalee attempts of 'cultural conquest of Assam' is not enough...
>
> (Nag: 132)

While the popular sentiments about immigration and immigrants were full of apprehensions, the atmosphere was further made combustible with the publication of the Census Report of 1931. This report became proverbial in Assam for its graphic narration of seamless immigration from Bengal to Assam. The Assamese leaders of Brahmaputra Valley also began to develop acute anxiety over immigration with reactions varying from alarm to paranoia. If Lloyd in his report of 1921 had presented a grim picture, the Report of Mullan in 1931 highlighted the invasive nature of immigrants, as he wrote,

> These are startling figures and illustrate the wonderful rapidity with which the lower districts are becoming colonies of Mymensingh ...
> (Census 1931, Line system Report Vol. VII).

The Census Report of 1931 clearly brought out in statistical terms the ever-growing Mymensinghi Bengali population in the Brahmaputra Valley Districts. Except for Sibsagar which showed a decline in Bengali population in 1931 in comparison with the figures of 1921, all the other districts including Kamrup showed a phenomenal inflow of immigration, as shown.

District	*Year 1921*	*Year 1931*
Goalpara	151 (78 MS)	170 (80 MS)
Kamrup	44 (30 MS)	134 (91 MS)
Darrang	20 (12 MS)	41 (30 MS)
Nowgong	58 (52 MS)	120 (108 MS)
Lakhimpur	14 (0 MS)	19 (2 MS)

(*Source:* Line System Report Vol. III, Census, 1931.)

Mullan's graphic description of immigrant movement from Bengal to Assam as an "invading corps" and his predictions that "it is sad but by no means improbable that in another thirty years Sibsagar district will be the only part of Assam in which the Assamese will find himself at home" sent the Assamese middle-class leadership into a war mode. The aggressive attitude of the immigrants often led them to encroach into areas predominated by the Assamese (Census 1931, Report of P.G. Mukherji from Nowgong Line System Report 1938, Vol. III). The Assamese elite felt that the task in hand, for them, therefore was to engage in aggressive cultural proselytization in the six districts of the Brahmaputra Valley. Speaking at the Assam Sahitya Sabha Session at North Lakhimpur in 1933, Gunabhiram Barua spelled out the forthcoming course of action.

"The district of Goalpara is our own. But some groups of people of the district do not speak in Assamese language. They speak in Bengali. This is very unfortunate. The first task of the Sahitya Sabha now is to completely Assamize the six districts...and to keep a watchful eye on Goalpara – Dhubri." Prolectionism movement began to gain strength with the emergence of new civil society bodies which began to engage in propaganda in the

Brahmaputra Valley on a large scale, ensured the participation of Ryot sabhas such as the North Mangaldai Ryot Sabha and the Na-Duar Ryot Sabha which pressed for the continuance of the Line System. The Assamese Press through organs such as the Asamiya and the Dainik Batori came out against the immigrants and the anti-line propaganda. If the Census Reports prepared the Assamese middle-class mentality, its impact seen in the deposition of the Assamese middle-class leaders before the Line System, the election results of 1937 to the Assam Legislative Assembly began to drive home the impact of immigrants on the provincial politics of Assam and further sharpened the rhetoric of protectionism among the Assamese in the name of protection of securing cultural spaces. In contrast to the Muslim League fortunes in other provinces of colonial India, the victory of the Muslim League candidates in 24 out of 34 seats reserved for the Muslim candidates in Assam gave a boost to the anxiety of parties and leaderswho opposed the League. The Asomiya Samrakshini Sabha, established in 1926, represented by Nilmoni Phukan and Ambikagiri Roy Choudhury submitted a memorandum to Jawaharlal Nehru when he toured Assam in November 1937. This memorandum, among others, argued that,

> For years together we have been standing face to face with extinction as people. Mass immigration of the Bengali speaking people from Bengal have been freely allowed in the face of strong opposition by the Assamese the Bengalees are developing a devastating attitude of linguistic imperialism over Assamese nationality for the linguistic conquest of Assam Valley.
>
> (Nag: 133: 134)

The situation was also summed up by Nehru who, in his notes on the travel to Assam in 1937, published in "Unity of India," pointed out that, "Some comments in the last Census Report have produced a powerful impression on the minds of the Assamese and they fear a suppression and almost an extinction of their culture, language and individuality..." (Nehru: 1942: 194–195)

Articulating Anxiety

From the second decade of the twentieth century onward, politics over immigration drew colonial Assam into a true Dickensian paradox. It was the most eventful of times and the worst of it too. If the annulment of the Partition of Bengal in 1911 revived Assam's autonomy, it also exposed Assam to the reality of a large-scale migration of people from East Bengal, more so from Mymensingh. This led to a serious debate among the officialdom on migration. The Census was a small reflection of the same. After the publication of the Census of 1911, colonial officials were repeatedly confronted with various demands for controlling this population transfer. One suggested solution was amending the Land and Revenue Regulations. But concrete efforts toward checking this problem could only be evolved at the dawn of independent India. The government came up with a legislation which amended the Land and Revenue Regulation and added the Tenth Chapter to it in the form of the Assam Land and Revenue Regulation (Amendment) Act of 1947 which attempted to meet the political crisis that emerged with the immigration of cultivators from across the Border of Assam from Mymensingh. Though the migration of people from Bengal was not limited to only one of the districts, the overwhelming number of migrants from Mymensingh in the second and third decades of the twentieth century turned popular and official attention to them. By the second decade of the twentieth century, the shadow of Bengal loomed over Assam, though the dimension and character of this interprovincial interface were different from the Bengali influence of the earlier century. The Census of 1921 brought to light statistical information about the unchecked population transfer from Bengal to Assam, especially from the district of Mymensingh, which alarmed the local population. The Census Report for 1931 articulated the alarming position. It observed that

> [p]robably the most important event in the province during the last twenty-five years – an event moreover, which seems likely to alter permanently the whole future of Assam and to destroy more surely than did the Burmese invaders of 1820 the whole structure of Assamese culture and civilization – has been the invasion of a vast horde of land hungry Bengali immigrant, mostly Muslims, from the districts of East Bengal and in particular from Mymensingh…[6]

The Report of 1931 was the culmination of a process that was started in the Census Report of the earlier decade. Though immigration was an inalienable part of the colonial policy on arable expansion and revenue maximization, it was only in the twentieth century that population trickle from Bengal turned into a tide. The Report of 1921 pointed out that

> In 1911, few cultivators from Eastern Bengal had gone beyond Goalpara, those censused in the other districts of the Assam Valley numbering only a few thousands and being mostly clerks, traders and professional men. In the last decade (1911–1921) the movement has extended far up the valley and the colonists now form an appreciable element in the population of all the four lower and central districts…[7]

The alarmist tone of the report had its impact on the politics of the day, and the Report of 1931 generated excitement. Mullan, the Census Superintendent, created a stir by his observation that

> …by 1921, the first army corps of the invaders had conquered Goalpara. The second army corps which followed them in the years 1921–1931

> has consolidated their position in that district and has also completed their conquest of Nowgong. The Barpeta subdivision of Kamrup has also fallen to their attack and Darrang is being invaded. Sibsagar has so far escaped completely but the few thousand Mymensinghi as in North Lakhimpur are an outpost which may, during the next decade, prove to be a valuable basis of major operations.[8]

There could be no doubt that Mullan set that one for a prolonged debate on land management and settlement policy in Assam by the publication of the Census Report of 1931.

The interprovincial migration of people from Bengal to Assam militated the minds of colonial officials and public-spirited Assamese middle-class leaders. The issue came to be first articulated as early as 1916, when the then Director of Land Record first put forward a proposal to create positions of Special Colonization Officers to regulate the settlement of immigrants. The matter died down as it was not favored by the Commissioner. It was revived by Sir William Reid in 1920, when he tried to formalize the practice of drawing lines in the villages across which the immigrants would not be allowed to settle, a practice which had already started in Nowgong and Barpeta by 1920. By 1923–1924, the practice had taken deep roots in Nowgong. Concern over immigration led to division of the land into various categories intended to restrict immigration. When the Government of India Act 1919 expanded participation of Indians in the government, concern over immigration echoed in middle-class leadership. When the Swarajists entered the Legislative Council, Shri Rohini Kanta Hati Baruah of the Swarajist Party proposed to move a solution recommending restriction on immigration.[9] In 1925, he again moved a resolution seeking preferential treatment to the Assamese settlers during the settlement of land. By the middle of the third decade of the twentieth century, the tide of popular opinion was slowly but steadily turning in favor of protectionism in favor of "children of the soil." In a report submitted on July 8, 1926, the Deputy Commissioner Goalpara was of the opinion that "Public opinion seems generally but not unanimously to be in favour of legislation prohibiting transfer of periodic patta lands to Bengal immigrants."[10] The proposals in favor of protecting the rights of the indigenous cultivator figured again and again in the Council. The provisions of the Assam Land and Revenue Regulations 1886 also figured in debates on the settlement question in the Council.[11] In 1926, the issue of immigration was again discussed in the colonial officialdom, and it was proposed that a conference of officials and "non-officials" would be convened at Shillong to discuss the subject.[12] With the object in view, a draft bill was prepared proposing an amendment to the Land Revenue Regulations whereby it was provided that transfer of land between the Assamese and the immigrants would be prohibited.[13] But the move for introduction of such an amendment was abandoned for want of public opinion in its favor.[14] But the assessment of the colonial officials returned a report in favor of the Line System but gave ominous indications of a conflict between the settlers and the tribals who had been the first settlers of certain areas. In 1934, a report from Nowgong indicated that serious difficulties were experienced by the Lalungs who were the original settlers of certain villages, when the colonial state decided to settle migrant settlers from the Surma valley of Assam in the southeastern areas of the district.[15]

The notification of the Government of India Act, 1935, changed the dynamics of Indian politics. Assam was equally affected. While it significantly widened the scope of representative politics in colonial India, it also transformed the idea of people's participation in politics and governance by introducing provisions for popular government in the provinces elected by widened, qualified electors on the basis of territorial constituencies. In the context of Assam, possession of the landed property was one such qualification which distinguished the electors from the on-electing subjects of the province. Part IX of the Schedule of the Act, which deals with Assam, clearly pointed out that

> No person shall be qualified to be included in the electoral roll for a territorial constituency unless he has a place of residence in the constituency, and a person shall be deemed to have a place of residence in a constituency if he ordinarily lives in the constituency or has his family dwelling place in the constituency and occasionally occupies it…[16]
>
> (Government of India Act: 1935)

The Act of 1935 and the politics that came in its wake drew both popular and government attention to immigration. The religious affiliation of the immigrants was not lost on the political parties who entered the electoral arena in the elections of 1936. The Muslim League which began its political fortunes in Assam in 1928 at the height of the Simon Commission Agitations began to use these immigrants as a vote bank and began to steadfastly espouse the cause of the immigrants.[17] The success of the Muslim League in Assam was spectacular. In view of the fact that it drew a blank in those provinces which later came to constitute Pakistan, League victory in 24 of the 34 seats reserved for the Muslims in Assam was immensely significant and helped it to claim some influence in colonial political space. This success also colored Muslim League politics in Assam after the elections were over and the Assembly was convened.

Muslim League Members of the Assembly, convened after the elections of 1937, began to condemn Mullan's classifications of the immigrant as land hungry "vultures" and "ants."[18] But such assertions by colonial officials also brought focus on the threat faced by the tribals from unchecked immigration from Bengal, which had been one of the main focus of Mullan's Report of 1931. It also began a new phase of tribal politics in Assam with a contest over the retention of the Line System. The system was viewed by the articulate elite leadership as a means of safeguarding tribal interests.[19] The Line

System Enquiry Committee under the chairmanship of a planter member, F.W. Hockenhull, was set up in January 1938 which, inter alia, highlighted that the tribals were the worst "victims of unregulated encroachment of vacant land by the aggressive immigrants from Mymensingh resulting in disappearance of many tribal villages. The tribal villagers moved further into sub-montane zone."[20] It was also the opinion of the revenue member in the colonial government, Mr Scott[21] that "there was much to be said for protecting the indigenous people if any good means could be devised of doing so."[22]

Toward Tribal Blocks

Though the colonial administration had almost become oblivious and counterproductive to tribal life and land management patterns through their forest policy and encouragement to settled cultivation in tribal areas, protection of tribal rights and interests became an interesting trope to resist the migration and settlement of immigrants from across the Bengal border. It is therefore interesting to note that tribal leaders from Assam were suddenly articulating the unique position of the tribal communities in Assam in their writings by the third decade of the twentieth century. Nichols Roy, one of the early leaders from the Khasi tribe, in one of his notes on the Khasi Hills in an encyclopedia in 1924, clearly pointed out that

> To a foreigner who goes up and down the Khasi Hills a great deal of land will seem like waste land not owned by anyone; but those who know the condition of the country will tell him that all the land belongs to some community.[23]

This position was not limited to the Khasi tribe alone but was more or less a universal condition among the tribes of Assam, which came to be threatened by the immigration and settlement policy of colonial provincial administration in Assam, more so by the Saadulla government, which caused great anxiety among the tribal leaders in Assam. On perusal of the Line System Enquiry Committee, it was evident that articulate tribal public opinion was in favor of devising special protection of the tribes and their landholding patterns, which was intrinsic to their life, livelihood, and identity. In his deposition before the Line System Committee, Dehiram Bora candidly observed before the Line System Enquiry Committee in his capacity as the Mouzadar of the Sekhar Mouza, Mongaldoi,

> If special protection is not given to the tribal sects they will sooner or later be extinct. Therefore no immigrant should be allowed to settle near them.[24]

The Deputy Commissioner Kamrup, Mr. C.B.C. Paine, believed that restriction such as the Line System had to be retained and argued that

> as it stands especially in areas inhabited by the Kacharis, Rabhas and other tribes that are unable to look after themselves. The protection of such people is an obvious duty of the Government.[25]

This demand for legislating and preserving exclusive tribal spheres of habitation was echoed not only in Kamrup but also across other districts. The Line System was, in a way, perceived as a useful intermediary between the tribes and the immigrants. The officiating Deputy Commissioner of Darrang pointed out that

> The Mymensingh Immigrants are aggressive by nature and to protect the indigenous people the presence of the line system is necessary for years to come. In Mangaldai Subdivision where Kacharis, Rabhas and other aboriginal people predominate the Line System will be very useful.[26]

While the conflict between the immigrants and tribal communities was on the rise across the Brahmaputra valley, the Deputy Commissioners such as the one at Nowgong reported instances of clashes between the immigrants and the tribal people over forcible dispossession of tribal land and cattle trespass.[27]

The coming of the Bordoloi Cabinet in Assam in 1946 brought into the government sensitivity over the alienation of indigenous communities from their land in the face of reckless immigration across the provincial borders with Bengal. The Bordoloi government accepted the report of the Line System Enquiry Committee but could do little else as it had to resign in view of the Congress agitation against a unilateral declaration by the Viceroy making India a part of the Allies in the Second World War. The Saadulla Cabinet which came back to power did much to enhance the interests of the immigrants but little for the protection of tribal interests and protection of tribal culture which was built around community ownership of land.[28] It was clear that the policy of the government was to facilitate private holding and ownership of tribal community and wastelands in Assam. The new government headed by Sir Muhammad Saadulla called a conference in May 1940 which was attended by almost all parties in the dispute on immigration, officials and non-officials alike, and which admitted for the first time the necessity of special protection for the tribal classes.[29] But its core focus was to evolve schemes for legitimizing the expansion of immigrants into new areas of habitation. This new scheme came to be called "Development Schemes."[30] In a Press Note dated August 3, 1940, the government claimed to have evolved a consensual compromise between indigene and immigrant interests on the basis of the dual principles of "justice" and "live and let live."[31] But despite perfunctory references to the balancing indigenous and immigrant interests, the practice of the Saadulla government was tilted toward protection of immigrant interest. The tribal people were greatly uncomfortable with the presence of the immigrants in their close proximity. The lifestyle, habits, and behavior with regard to land, cattle, and women made them, in tribal perception, undesirable neighbors and often at war with each other.[32] Therefore, there were demands made to amend the Land and Revenue Regulations, 1886, to secure the interests of the indigenous, especially the tribals.[33] But despite popular local sentiments which were against it, the Saadulla government introduced a scheme called the "Land Development Scheme"[34] according to which "all waste lands were to be divided into blocks and allotted to different communities including immigrants on the payment of a premium of Rs 5/- per Bigha. This policy further aggravated the situation since many immigrants were given settlements even in areas predominantly by tribals."[35] The political instability brought about by the Congress agitations against the War effort led to the fall of the Saadulla cabinet and the resumption of the administration of Assam by the Governor, Sir Robert Reid, under Section 93 of the Government of India Act, 1935, on December 25, 1941. One of the important steps taken by him was scrapping of the Land Development Scheme. But with the return of Sir Saadulla to power in August 1942, the fortunes of the immigrants were revived through the "grow more food" campaign. The Government of Assam came out with a resolution on August 24, 1943, which clearly pointed out that

> The cultivated area in Assam has been increasing steadily for some time; and the present urgent need of growing more food, coupled with the desirability of increasing the revenues of the Province and of providing for an increased number of landless persons having led government to review the present policy of land settlement....

But the interests of the tribals were blatantly ignored. Tribal interests were articulated only in 1945, when the Coalition Ministry came out with a land settlement policy. This policy superseded all previous policies and resolutions and stated inter alia that it was the proposal of the government to ensure

> protection of tribal classes in areas predominantly occupied by them against aggressive elements which are apt to endanger the normal economic and social basis of village life...[36]

This resolution on land settlement introduced the possibility of forming tribal belts and blocks in Assam. The government proposed to compile a report about cultivable waste lands in Assam and the percentage of tribal people living in those areas. It was decided that areas where the tribal population exceeded fifty per cent would be indicated on maps, and on the completion of the enquiry, Tribal Belts would be notified with boundaries of such belts being fixed along easily recognizable geographical features or the boundaries of the mauzas.[37] It was further proposed that "[P]rovisions will also be made for creation of Tribal Blocks side by side with the blocks of other communities in the Planned Settlement Areas where Tribal people have their villages and homes."[38] But with the resignation of the Saadulla cabinet and the dissolution of the assembly in 1945, these proposals were put on hold. The return of the Bordoloi Ministry in Assam after the elections of 1946 led to the revival of initiatives to secure the interests of the tribal communities in the Assam valley. Shri Hem Borah was appointed as the Special Officer to prepare a guide map for identifying those villages in which the tribal population was above 50 percent. The government therefore came up with a legislation which amended the Land and Revenue Regulation and added another chapter to it based on his report.[39] This amendment came in the form of the Assam Land and Revenue Regulation (Amendment) Act of 1947. The amendment led to the constitution of compact areas in regions predominantly inhabited by the tribes. In accordance with Section 160 of the Assam Land and Revenue Regulation Amendment Act 1947, Belts were large areas, and "Blocks had smaller areas considering with boundaries of the Mauzas." Therefore, as many as 35 Belts and Blocks were created in Assam till 1964. The same section enjoined the Government of Assam to notify those classes of people who were considered entitled to protection. Accordingly, the Government of Assam came out with a notification No. RD. 2/47/43 dated April 20, 1949, which declared that the Plains Tribals, Hill Tribals, Tea Garden Tribals, Santhals, Nepali Cultivator Graziers, and Scheduled Castes were the protected classes under Section 160(2) of the Amendment Act of 1947. However, the rules that were formulated in the wake of the regulations for the first time in 1894 and were printed in Part II of the Assam Land Revenue Manual, Volume I[40], held the ground facilitating the operation of the regulations.

Conclusion

The significance of the issue of immigration in the legislative history of Assam lay in the fact that, for the first time, it brought the land question and tribal rights within the domain of colonial politics in all its dimensions. The popular sentiments were surged on the issue, and demands arose for the protection of indigenous rights from all sections of Assamese society. The debates and the Enquiry Committee depositions highlighted the fundamental unity between the tribal and nontribal populations of Assam which was also echoed in the debates on various issues affecting the community rights, in the Assam Assembly. The unique position of the anti-immigrant debate in Assam lay in its success at appropriating the question of law-making from exclusively official to the domain of the popular. Legal change was recognized as a legitimate and just method to meet an impending political crisis, and the amendment of 1947 was a product of a sustained movement to relate anti-immigration policy to protection of tribal and indigenous interests. It is in this background that the historicity of the Amendment to the Land and Revenue Regulations of 1886 must be linked to the Line System introduced in Assam. Though deep connections exist between social histories and the history of laws and legislations, it is something that historians of this region are gradually waking up to. This article is only a partial attempt to bridge this historical hiatus.

Notes

1 Sajal Nag, *Roots of Ethnic Conflict: Nationality Question in Northeast India*, Manohar, New Delhi, 1990, p. 87.
2 Sajal Nag, *Roots of Ethnic Conflict: Nationality Question in Northeast India*, Manohar, New Delhi, 1990, p. 88.
3 Amalendu Guha, *Planter Rajto Swaraj*, ICHR, New Delhi, 1977, p. 19.
4 Binayak Dutta, 'The Stout Fanatical Mahomedan and Mulan's Burden: The History of Bengali Immigration in Colonial Assam (1871–1931)', *Man and Society*, Vol. XI, Winter 2014, 70–85.
5 J.N. Das, 'Genesis of Tribal Belts and Blocks of Assam', in B.N. Bordoloi (ed) *Alienation of Tribal Land and Indebtedness*, Tribal Research Institute, Assam, p. 29.
6 Census Report, 1931, pp. 49–50.
7 Census Report, 1931, p. 50.
8 Census Report, 1931, p. 51.
9 M. Kar, *Muslims in Assam Politics*, Omsons Publications, New Delhi, p. 34.
10 Line System Enquiry Report, Vol. III.
11 Speech of Khan Bahadur Sayidur Rahman in the Council as indicated in M. Kar, *Muslims in Assam Politics*, Omsons Publications, p. 39.
12 Report of the Line System Committee, Vol. I, p. 3.
13 Report of the Line System Committee, Vol. I, p. 3.
14 Report of the Line System Committee, Vol. I, p. 3.
15 Report of the Line System Committee, Vol. I, p. 4.
16 Government of India Act, 1935, p. 282.
17 For a detailed discussion on the impact of mobilization in the elections see B. Dutta, *Religion in Politics, Eastern India, 1905–1947*, Varanasi, 2009; also see A.C. Bhuyan & S. De, *Political History of Assam*, Vol. II Publication Board, Assam, Guwahati, 1978.
18 Census Report, 1931, p. 51.
19 For a detailed note on the issue see Suryasikha Pathak, Tribal Politics in Assam, *Economic and Political Weekly*, Vol. XLV, No.10.
20 B.N. Bordoloi, *Report on the Survey of Alienation of Tribal land in Assam*, Assam Institute of Research for Tribals and Scheduled Castes, Guwahati, 1999, p. 6. Also see Report of the Line System Enquiry Committee, 1938.
21 Reply of the Revenue Member Scott, in the Legislative Council on the 1st of October, 1936, online System, in Line System Enquiry Report, 1938, Shillong, 1938.
22 Reply of the Revenue Member Scott, in the Legislative Council on the 1st of October, 1936, online System, in Line System Enquiry Report, 1938, Shillong, 1938.
23 Rev Nichols Roy 'The Khasi Hills' in P. Lakshminarasiah (eds) *The Encyclopaedia of Bengal, Behar and Orissa, Indian Encyclopedias*. Compiling & Publishing Co., Madras, 1924–25, p. 118.
24 Report of the Line System Committee, Vol. III.
25 Report of the Line System Committee, Vol. III.
26 Report of the Line System Committee, Vol. III, p. 28.
27 Reference could be made to the case King versus Hapsing Kachari, Line System Enquiry Report, Vol. II, p. 19.
28 Entry on U Ram Khasi of Nodgjrong vs U Mon Lalu of Jowai by Rev Nichols Roy 'The Khasi Hills' in P. Lakshminarasiah (eds), *The Encyclopaedia of Bengal,*

Behar and Orissa, Indian Encyclopaedias. Compiling & Publishing Co., Madras, 1924–25, p. 118.
29 Resolution on Land Settlement dated 6th March, 1942, government of Assam, 1990.
30 Resolution on Land Settlement dated 6th March, 1942, government of Assam, 1990.
31 M. Kar, *Muslims in Assam Politics*, Omsons Publications, New Delhi, p. 55.
32 Line System Enquiry Report, Vol. II, p. 45.
33 Line System Enquiry Report, Vol. II, pp. 17, 20.
34 Announced on July 28,1941, see A.C. Bhuyan et al., *Political History of Assam*, Vol. III, p. 38.
35 B.N. Bordoloi, *Report on the Survey of Alienation of Tribal Land in Assam*, Assam Institute of Research for Tribals and Scheduled Castes, Guwahati, 1999, p. 7.
36 B.N. Bordoloi, *Report on the Survey of Alienation of Tribal Land in Assam*, Assam Institute of Research for Tribals and Scheduled Castes, Guwahati, 1999, p. 9.
37 B.N. Bordoloi, *Report on the Survey of Alienation of Tribal Land in Assam*, Assam Institute of Research for Tribals and Scheduled Castes, Guwahati, 1999, p. 9.
38 B.N. Bordoloi, *Report on the Survey of Alienation of Tribal Land in Assam*, Assam Institute of Research for Tribals and Scheduled Castes, Guwahati, 1999, pp. 9–10.
39 B.N. Bordoloi, *Report on the Survey of Alienation of Tribal Land in Assam*, Assam Institute of Research for Tribals and Scheduled Castes, Guwahati, 1999, p. 10.
40 K.N. Saikia, *The Assam Land and Revenue Regulation, 1886*, New Book Stall, Guwahati, 1965, p. 8.

4 Colonial Legal Formation in Northeast India

An Introspective Gaze in the Contemporary Context

Nandini Bhattacharyya Panda

Northeast India constitutes one of the most important portfolios of the Indian state since India became independent in 1947. Diverse in ethnicity and culture, rich in natural resources, and with human and geopolitical aspects, this region poses pressing challenges to the Indian state. Since independence, the Indian state pursued continuous dialogue at the policy level, political negotiations, academic discourses, and activism to understand and address the "Northeast problem." The entire region still remains within a twilight zone of hope and dystopia. Looking back at the colonial time, this chapter explores the historical root of contemporary complexities whirling over "law" that had begun in the colonial period.

The law-making exercise of the British rulers was, however, not uniform in different parts of the Empire. The trajectory was also complex and frequently arbitrary. Yet the edifice of colonial "law" left its formidable legacy and the post-colonial legal structure. "Law" in India is essentially based on the colonial legal structure in terms of ideology, spirit, structure, and content. The legal structure in India, despite its positive values and dominantly democratic dispositions, therefore entails several missing links, dark aspects, and paradoxes. The historical roots of such problems are largely traceable in the passage and mode of colonial legal formation. In this larger perspective, this chapter looks at the historical process of colonial legal formation in Northeast India to trace the roots of the current "Northeast problem," especially in the sphere of economic backwardness, ethnic alienation from the so-called mainstream perspective, and the notion of "difference" about the region. The chapter briefly focuses on the production of the Acts, Regulations and Code to trace the contested origin of customary law.

Customary law in the Northeast constitutes a formidable site of dissonance and contestation that is inherently linked with the colonial past and as something that further adds to the contemporary debates.

Northeast India as a geopolitical unit emerged in the colonial administrative and cultural discourses as "border" and "frontier" by situating the entire region in the spatial, civilizational, and ethnic fringes. This borderization and frontierization of the "Northeast" and the formation of the colonial state required formal legal structures in order to impose sovereign control over the

DOI: 10.4324/9781003539797-5

subject people. Legal hegemony was an essential prerequisite for various significant reasons. Extremely rich in natural and mineral resources, the British deployed every possible means to turn the entire region into their resource frontier. The cultural and ethnic composition was also complex and varied in the region. The colonial rulers encountered a large number of ethnic communities in the hills and forests whom they described as "tribes" and at the same time sizeable number of non-tribal population in the plains and valleys. Lawmaking was therefore a complex and challenging task for the rulers. This exercise did not follow a unilinear trajectory for the entire subject population. Unlike other parts of India, the British did not introduce any "Code," such as the Hindu and Muslim Code in Assam (which comprised entire Northeast of the present day). Instead, they formulated Acts and Regulations and created the edifice called "customary law" for the tribal population. In a very later stage of the colonial rule, a Code was compiled called the Assam Code which essentially endorsed and structured the Acts and Regulations.

There had been no orientalist ideologues such as Jones and Colebrooke *et al.* with at least preliminary training in the culture and language behind the formulation of "tribal law" in the Northeast or in other tribal belts. The lawmakers were mostly held from the military background with hardly any training in law. Bradley-Birt – one of the leading administrators and ideologues of the British Raj in the 19th and 20th centuries – delineated the passage of the formation of colonial tribal law in India as follows:

> The first pioneers of British rule were men of whom the Empire may well be proud. These records reveal them strong, quick to grapple with sudden and unforeseen events, fair and impartial in the administration of justice, and combining in themselves the multifarious of judge, soldier, lawgiver, and collector of the revenue. They were many-sided men who responded ably to the call to evolve order out of chaos, and to inspire a people who had hitherto known no restraint, save as such their own crude tribal customs and primitive institutions had taught them, with a respect for the first principles of law and justice.[1]

The law-givers in the Northeast region belonged to such genre of "many-sided men" in Bradley-Birt's definition. The British administrators encountered and had to deal with mixed ethnic groups in terms of culture, custom, socio-religious traits, and livelihood pattern. They responded to varied sets of circumstances with the avowed goal to uphold the pragmatic interests of the Empire. The making of "tribal law" in colonial India thus cannot be segregated from the cultural contour which essentially determined its legal framework. It is, however, striking that the "many-sided men" framed "law" even for the non-tribal population, and thus the legal structure in colonial Assam stood as an exception for being the "frontier" or periphery of the British Empire.

The colonial rulers in the Northeast "frontier" produced two sets of law: (a) Regulations and Acts and (b) customary law. It is evident from the colonial archive that these two sets of law operated in the overlapping domain to fulfill the essential and ultimate objectives: (a) expropriation of resources and (b) extending hegemony over each group of people to strengthen the expropriation mechanism. The analyses of the background and passage of the politics and production behind these two sets of laws in the Northeast would trace the link between the current politico-legal turmoil and the legal formation in the colonial past. The chapter will discuss how the law-making process was marked by prolonged violence, leading to ethno-cultural transformation. In this larger canvas, this chapter briefly focuses on the following significant aspects: (a) land and legal governance in Assam, (b) passage of the formation of tribal law, (c) religion and "law" in proxy, and (d) the Assam Code.

The Historical Background

The British colonizers started taking an active interest in Northeast India around the beginning of the 19th century. The English India Company (EIC) kept a watchful eye on the northeast since their arrival in Bengal in the 18th century first as trader and then as sovereign ruler in 1772. From the early years, the British rulers sustained manifold interests in the "Northeast frontier." In the first place, Northeast India comprised the lengthiest stretch of border with Burma (Myanmar), Nepal, Bhutan, Tibet, and China with further scope for expansion of the colonial territory and trade. Second, the land was the source of rich natural and mineral resources with oil, coal, timber, water, minerals, and other resources. The colonial rulers cherished twofold objectives to turn the Northeast into their (a) resource frontier and (b) corridor for territorial and commercial expansion.

The British rulers initially found the opportunity to be engaged with the political affairs in the Northeast in 1792 on the invitation of the King of Manipur. The king sought support and help of the British in the war with Burma. In response, the East India Company extended support as an external ally without being much ambitious for securing political control. Manipur was annexed by the British much later in 1861. In the early phase, the British cherished territorial and trading interests in Burma and assisted the King of Manipur against Burma to expand the commercial and trading interests. This chapter does not engage in narrating the prolonged history of the British conquest of Northeast India. In a nutshell, the British acquired control over the entire region through a series of military conquests through violent encounters at different stages. They finally established hegemony over Assam, the Naga Hills, the Lushai Hills, Garo Hills, Khasi and Jayantia Hills, the Mikir Hills, the Frontier Tracts, and North Cachar Hills by the middle of the 19th century.

As is already mentioned, colonial administrators had three lucrative concerns that drew them to the Northeast. In the first place, the entire region is situated alongside a vast stretch of the "frontier." The EIC cherished vested interest in defending the frontier and expanding further. Second, the entire region was endowed with rich natural resource such as land, water, energy, oil, natural gas, mineral, timber, plantation crops, horticultural products, and medicinal plants. The "frontier" was, however, inhabited by "numerous savage races" (as described by Alexander Mackenzie – a distinguished civil servant of the British Raj who wrote *The North East Frontier of India*[2] (earlier published as *History of the Relations of the Government with the Hill Tribes of the North-East Frontier of Bengal* in 1884)).

Following the conquests, the administration of the entire Northeast region became a difficult engagement for the British officials on account of the difficult nature of the terrain and the cultural diversity of the inhabitants. A major part of Northeast India was surrounded by hills and forests, while a part of the terrain was situated in the plains. The ethnic composition was equally diverse with not less than 200 communities inhabiting the region. Each community has its distinct socio-cultural traits, religion, tradition, and customs. Therefore, consolidation of the authority was a far more difficult task than conquest of the territory. As it is evident in the extant documents, "law" was the most crucial instrument in enforcing governance and control over the indigenous subjects.

In this larger background, this chapter analyses how land and land revenue have been the vantage point in the process of legal formation in Northeast India. The following section focuses on the engagement of the colonial administrators with (a) maximization of land revenue and (b) demolishing the power of existing landed aristocrats through the instrument of "law" who had the power and potential to challenge the colonial authority.

Land and Legal Governance in Assam

This section briefly discusses the ideology, motives, and driving concerns of the British rulers that determined the fundamental shifts from precolonial to colonial, which laid the foundation of the post-colonial structure of land ownership and taxation. The story of the plain (lower Assam) also reveals the colonial political economy of wasteland management and the emergence of plantation economy, especially tea plantation, that linked the entire region with global economy.

Control over land and the pragmatic exercises to revise the existing revenue structure in order to maximize the volume of revenue remained the major driving forces to frame the colonial land laws in lower Assam. The structure of colonial land laws and tax still remains the primary foundation of the pattern of land revenue and taxes in the post-colonial period albeit with periodic modifications and revisions. This section traces the fundamental transformation in the land revenue and tax structure by focusing on their encounter with Durrang Rajah in Assam. The encounter with the Rajah of Durrang essentially narrates the pattern of a fundamental restructuring of landownership and revenue arrangement in the plain.

The story in this chapter is built on the basis of the sources available in the colonial archive. The chapter does not claim to directly reflect the native voices. Yet, the archive is significant because it summarizes (a) colonial attitude toward hereditary landlords and native landowners, (b) investment in land revenue, (c) aggressive designs to expropriate rights over land, and (d) "law" as an instrument to accomplish the exploitation and expropriation of resources in favor of the colonial state.

The Durrang Rajah was a hereditary landowner who exercised control over a large estate. There had been six vassal chiefs under the Ahom King – Durrang, Dimarua, Rani, Barduar, Nauduar, and Beltola. Those vassal chiefs enjoyed complete autonomy in the internal administration of the territories, most importantly, revenue collection and administration of justice.[3] As it is evident from the extant documents, the Rajah had a sizeable portion of land and a large number of revenue payers under his control. At the same time, the Rajahs made endowment of land over time to different groups of his subjects under varied term with regard to payment of rent. The categories of endowment included *lakheraj*, *Nishksarraj*, *Brahmottar*, and *Debottar*. Different categories of land had been brought under divergent assessment patterns. The documents clearly indicate that colonial rulers perceived the existence of such large estates which had loyal subjects under their control as a threat to the newly established territorial foundation in Northeast India. Equally important for them was to acquire control over major portion of Rajah's land and its resources primarily through legal means.

The settlement of the land with the Rajah was made in 1837 by the Commissioner of Assam in direct communication with the government in Fort William.[4] The file contains lengthy correspondence on the right of the Rajah to alienate his own property. It stated that

> The Commissioner, it will be observed recommended that certain lands should be surveyed and settled for a term of 20 years at half rates with the Rajah and members of the family, and that at expiration of that period the land should be again surveyed to ascertain the increased quantity of land under cultivation, and that the rent should be again fixed for the like term at the half of the then prevailing rates, and so on in perpetuity.[5]

The above passage is significant to understand how the colonial rulers imposed the sovereign law, amounting to gross violation of the existing custom of land holding. The following passage, however, reveals how the British officials imported Western legal concepts that transformed the existing rights of the landholders and thereby the concept of property and land ownership:

> A second question arises namely how should the **alienations** from these lands be treated. It appears that these alienations have been considerable through public sales both for arrears of Revenue and in satisfaction of **decrees of Court**. The Collector of Durrang considers that the land **alienated** should now be settled at full rates, as the settlement at half

> rates was with the Rajahs of Durrang only. The Commissioner on the other hand considers that the half rental arrangement should extend to the lands which have been **alienated** as well as to those in the possession of the Rajah.[6]
>
> (emphasis mine)

The above passages show the colonial designs for withdrawing the existing customary rights of the hereditary Rajahs and landlords by framing new legal structures. The customary hereditary rights had been reduced to 20 years of occupancy rights against the payment of a fixed sum. Significantly, such radical transformations had been accomplished through the establishment of colonial institutions (that may also refer to Collector's/Magistrate's order as well as formal courts of judicature) and importation and application of the Western legal terminologies, such as "alienation" and "decrees of the Court."

Right to "alienation" is the elemental condition of private property rights that evolved in 17th-/18th-century England/Europe due to political philosophers such as John Locke, Thomas Hobbes, and David Hume, *et al.* John Locke proposed his theory of property in *The Second Treatise of Government.*[7] Locke's theory is rooted in his concept of "law of nature" that permits individuals to appropriate, and exercise rights over, "things" in the world, such as land and other immovable material resources. In other words, Locke propounded the theory of private property of which "alienation" is the essential quality. The intrinsic meaning of "alienation" is the right to "sale, gift, and transfer" of one's own property. Locke's theory provided rationale to *Laissez faire* theory of industrial capitalism and the welfare state of socialism.

I should mention briefly that the categories such as "alienation" were not part of the discursive genre on "property" in the Indian soil before the arrival of the British. In the classical *Dharmasatra* tradition, terms such as "property" and "alienation" may be approximately close to terms such as *Svatva* and *Svamitva*. But the Indian terms are by no means synonymous to the Western concepts. The Indian concepts evolved over millennia in a different civilizational background, while the Western concepts are also products of a particular time, political structure, economy, and socio-economic urges of a given class of people. Therefore, the intrinsic qualities of the Indian categories are foundationally different from the Western categories. The British sovereigns deployed those concepts to ensure control over resources and hegemony over the native subjects.

The British officials in Assam were anxious to secure a greater share in the revenue/rent which is evident in the correspondence with Durrang Rajah and other landed families. The officials were keen to establish the huge arrears of revenue of the Durrang Rajah and to sell a large portion of their property to realize revenue at higher rates.[8] Colonel Jenkins' anxiety was quoted below to indicate the dominant attitude of the imperial administrators:

> ...at the time of sale it was expressly declared that the lands were to be **transferred** to the purchasers with all the rights held in them by the Rajah viz: an assessment at half rates adjustable every twenty years. Had these provisions not been held out to purchasers it is clear that the lands would have been unsaleable or have been only for a trifle as other Khiraji lands liable to full assessment.[9]
>
> (emphasis mine)

Jenkins further added that the case of purchasers at sales for arrears of revenue would require "further explanation from the Commissioner should his Honour agree with the Board in opinion that full rates are to be imposed upon the **alienated** land". Jenkins anticipated that "some arrangements may have to be made with these purchasers but this does not affect the **principle now under discussion** which is accordingly submitted for the orders of the Lieutenant Governor."[10] (emphasis mine). The official further pleaded:

> ... this indulgence granted as it was on purely personal grounds to the Rajah and members of his family. Can not be pleaded now by third parties in bar of an assessment at the full rates of the District. Those who have purchased these lands at sales for decrees can of course urge nothing against such a cause. **The doctrine of "Caveat emptor"** applies to them in its very widest sense.[11]
>
> (emphasis mine)

It seems clear from the above passages that the British officials were ready to introduce certain **principles** relating to land laws, and those laws had to be transplanted from the Western categories and deployed through colonial courts of justice. Interestingly, **Caveat emptor** is a purely British legal term which means "the principle that the buyer alone is responsible for checking the quality and suitability of goods before a purchase is made." The application of this term had fundamental implication on the extant notions of "property" and existing practices relating to transaction of land. Contextually, the official tried to facilitate "alienation" or "transfer" of land and the liberty to impose rent according to their demand through the application of **Caveat emptor**. The buyer was not left with any choice but to accept the legal terms in order to legitimize their claim over acquired property. The modality of legitimization invariably meant increased rent. It is thus evident that the British officials tried to create a land market to acquire flexibility for increasing rent and maximizing the revenue. "Alienation" had been the prime instrument to create fluidity in the existing landholding pattern.

The British administrators throughout their rule adopted the strategy of labeling the precolonial regime as incompetent, worthless, and tyrant. A similar strategy had been adopted to expropriate Durrang Rajah's lands, which had been assigned to different groups of people on varied terms. A letter was sent to the Chief Secretary, stating that the Durrang Rajah "befel the whole district" into "extortion and misrule."[12] Captain Bugle wrote a statement justifying the claim of the British rulers over the resources of the land. It had been stated that the British did respect the rights of the landholders on the soil.[13] It was also pointed out that the British "did not conquer Assam from its inhabitants or native Govt. but from foreign invaders" (the Burmese) from whom the protection had been "solicited."[14] He continued:

> After driving out these foreigners, the natives residing with us from the first commencement of military operations we continued to occupy Assam, in my belief solely because it was impracticable for us to abandon the country injustice to ourselves and in mercy to a helpless people.[15]

Captain Bugle further stated:

> The imbecility and factions of the princes and nobles, and the divided debased and defenceless state of the people in general, made it imperatively incumbent upon us to retain military occupancy of the country for the peace and security of our frontier districts connected with it. And being obliged to provide for the protection of the country by our troops. We were necessarily compelled to take upon ourselves the management of its resources.[16]

The last line in the above passage is quite significant. Contextually, the statement referred to the Durrang Rajah. Nevertheless, condemnation of the precolonial regime provided the most convenient justification for the British toward establishing absolute hegemony over the land and its people. There was another very important reason which emanated from the official narratives. They traced the historical genealogy of the region. The discursive literature wanted to create a "fiction"[17] that the British entered into a vacuum and chaos. This argument had been drawn to justify the conquest and rule of the British in India. As has been pointed out by Nicholas Dirks, the early agents of the British Empire sought to prove that

> India had been unable to rule itself because its political system was commanded by grand but quarreling kings who would shamelessly exploit their subjects in order to accumulate unlimited wealth and prestige, and had neither attended to basic principles of justice nor concerned themselves with the formation of organized administration, and stable, centralized power.[18]

In this specific context, the imperial agents put forward a double-edged argument to justify "military occupancy" and expropriation of resources from the land. In the first place, they argued that they had to assume the role of the "protector" to ensure "peace" and "security" of the land and well-being of the people on account of the "imbecility" and "factions" of the precolonial rulers. This was an argument to establish their claim of a moral rule over the native subject. At the same time, the same regime had been claiming a "price" for deploying army to protect the land. And the price the officials claimed was quite high in the sense that they wanted the right to make and break the extant structure – including "law" – in order to establish absolute "claims" over resources.

The colonial rulers explored varied methods to withdraw the privileges of the existing Rajah and his family to hold the rights to endow rent-free lands. It had been clearly stated that

> If the individuals of the family are to be allowed to hold any lands they should hold the portion that may be assigned to them rent free, but I am greatly at a loss what portions to be recommended, for any measure applied to these *Lakheraj* lands will be expected to be extended not only to these *Lakheraj* lands will be expected not only to all *Lakheraj* lands but to all *Burmootoor* and *Durmattar* lands which are now equally assessed.[19]

It is evident that within seven years of occupation, the British Agent formulated their law to bring rent-free land under assessment. The officials also considered "money pension" in lieu of land, as it was stated: "granting money pensions in lieu of land to the individuals now in question."[20] The proposal, however, required a sizeable amount of money and thereby still remained under consideration in 1833 and also the officials apprehended resistance from the grant holders. It had been stated that

> I fear this would be very unacceptable to them and as a general policy very objectionable any sum the Govt would consent to give could only just support the family in the lapse of a very short time a degree above absolute poverty in barren indolence deprived of all influence and a useless burden upon finances.[21]

The officials observed that the population in Lower Assam essentially consisted of "rent payers and rent collectors," which left them uneasy due to "loss" in company's treasury as well as the power and influence enjoyed by this group over the rent payers. The colonial officials also expressed anxiety about "perpetual changes of Chowdries and the number of estates that have been sold in satisfaction of the arrears of their collection."[22] At the same time, they realized (presumably with comfort)

> All the Chowdries and Rajahs who undergo this operation [of sale on account of arrear] must if deprived of their rent free lands be soon reduced to the level of the Ryots, for the Govt. assessments would leave them insufficient incomes to maintain the struggle to support their former mode of life.[23]

The above passage provides an idea about the impact of the operation of colonial law of "alienation" (sale and transfer) on the existing social groups in the initial years of British rule in Assam. It led to thorough reshuffling of the power structure with the restructuring of ownership of land. As regards the *Lakheraj* lands, the officials pronounced that the

> Right to levy this assessment may be considered to belong to the Govt. as long its finances labour under difficulties, and **so might under pretences be continued forever, but the inhabitants understand that it was merely a war tax.**[24]
>
> (emphasis mine)

It is clear from the above passage that British agents deployed "law" with the hidden agenda of concealing their design to perpetuate their authority over the lands of dispossessed landlords under the garb of "war tax." The use of the word "pretence" is quite significant in the larger context. It indicates how law became the instrument to legitimize "pretence" to fulfill the imperial agenda.

The "pretence" of law had varied manifestations. The British agents decided on curtailing land holdings of Durrang Rajah and make a settlement favorable to the rulers. The British had decided unilaterally:

> The Durrang Rajah are not altogether devoid of rights nor the Govt. should recommend that instead of continuing light impact upon all the lands we should surrender one half of all now held by the family, the same to be held by them and their heirs, but not entailed under sunnuds rent free.[25]

The above passage suggests certain important aspects in the British policy toward the native subjects. In the first place, the arrangement between the British and Rajah was neither a contract nor a bilateral arrangement arrived at consensus. The lands were owned by the Rajah, and the assessment had been imposed by the British at their free will by deviating from the prevalent practices of the land. The decision to "allow" the Rajah certain portion of his holding subject to assessment of the rulers seems to be arbitrary. Such practices did not match with celebrated notions of "rule of law" and "equity" which the British claimed to have introduced on the Indian soil. What is more significant is that the British wanted the land acquired through "*Sunnud*" (land grant endowed by the previous rulers) to be brought under full assessment without scrutinizing the original deeds. They found that the arrangement (as proposed/introduced by the British) would "solve many difficulties" as it would "make the production, examination of original documents and taking the evidence unnecessary."[26] This decision glaringly violates the British legal tradition and as such the juridical tradition in India as well. Production, examination of original documents, and witness/evidence had been essential prerequisites to establish or dismiss one's claim over property. The British agents put forward "pragmatic" explanation to vindicate their act. They explained that "the anarchy that prevailed for many years in the country might be expected to cause a very tedious and unprofitable investigation."[27] The official file contains euphoric expression with the clearing of the obstacles to maximize the volume of revenue and consolidation of the power, which recorded:

> This measure would also enable us to consolidate the estates, now much divided and scattered greatly to public and private convenience, and it would be attended with an increase to our present revenue.[28]

It is even more significant that with this arrangement, as the officials exclaimed, "half of the waste would become the property of the **state**"[29] (emphasis mine). It had been stated further that "of the half lands **resumed** by the **state** and placed under full rate of assessment," the Collectors would be able to realize the arrears[30] (emphasis mine). Here we find that within a decade of occupation of Assam, the imperial agents had been using the word "state" to define and defend their authority as well as "resume" their control over soil. "State" is founded upon three branches of governance – executive, legislative, and juridical. After the military conquest, their claims of founding the "state" in Northeast India had been emphasized over and again even in the early years.

In sum, the colonial rulers followed the policy of fragmenting or dismantling the large zamindary estates in order to eliminate military and political challenges from the local magnates. The present author has already discussed the colonial attitudes against the large estates in many writings, especially in her previous book under the title: *Appropriation and Invention of Tradition: The East India Company and Hindu Law in Early Colonial Bengal*.[31]

The Ethnographic Hand Book of Tribal Law: Culture and Violence

This section briefly focuses on the passage from "custom" to "customary law." The fundamental differences in the definitions and usage of "custom" and "law" are already discussed in the introductory note. Custom is flexible while law is rigid and reified. "Customary law" was therefore a colonial edifice that was meant to convey to the tribal population about the "good will" of the sovereign. This was a gesture to proclaim that the rulers retained traditional "law" for the tribal population. In reality, the passage of transformation of custom to customary law was marked by intimidation and gross violence, leading to the dispossession and displacement of the ethnic communities from their ancestral habitat and their traditional practices. The history of the production of customary law is one of encroachment on the hills and forests and the culturization and peripheralization of the ethnic communities. It is reflected in the colonial discursive genre through lengthy narratives on cultural statements as well as mainland/frontier dichotomy. In the process, customary law has become the formidable cultural component and governing principle of the ethnic communities in the Northeast during the post-colonial period. It is the site of ethnic identity and rights which are administered through Autonomous District Councils in the Scheduled regions. Customary law is also a site of pervasive and frequent interethnic and intra-ethnic conflicts.

The British officials announced in the Northeast that they would not intervene in the "custom" of the tribal subjects. Instead, they would preserve the "customary law" of the tribal communities. This proclamation thus raises a critical question: could custom be made law without those having been made so? It leads to these questions: what was the passage of transformation from "custom" to "customary law"? The archive – the colonial archive – does not provide any direct answer. The colonial archive is in fact a repository of the expression of their anxiety regarding (a) how to deal with those "savage" and "warlike" tribal subjects in the Northeast, (b) how to extend authority and control over the land in which they inhabit and enjoy resources for time immemorial, and (c) how to intimidate those people through arms. In sum, the primary concern of the British rulers was to adopt appropriate policies in order to draw them under the paradigms of "civilization" so that they were able to understand the governing principles of the colonial masters, especially the "law" by which they can perceive, modify, and regulate their demands and rights over resources. The indigenous archive – as counterfactual – is hardly available to the researchers who would try to understand the history of anxiety and belonging of the tribal people. The folkloric traditions have some reflection of the native voices, although the cultural transformation of the proselytization and conversion acted as erasure of vital cultural components. The indigenous perceptions and reactions are therefore largely visible in the contemporary context. A researcher may perhaps derive the dominant trends from the violent encounters between the colonial sovereigns and the ethnic communities that ensued following the advent of the British. In sum, the passage of the introduction of colonial law in the hill Northeast was violent and complex. The process was prolonged and gruesome.

Among the contemporary administrator-writers, the chapter focuses on Alexander Mackenzie's book, which dominated the imagination in the contemporary period and currently inspires critical studies about the passage of colonization of the "Northeast frontier." He chronicled the British conquest of Northeast India in meticulous detail through his interpretative discourses. It was through his narrative that Northeast entered into the global map as a **strategic "frontier,"** a "wild tract," and a "savage" space. Mackenzie's narrative is closer to a discourse on ethno-history if the definition of ethno-history is dissolved from its rigid definition. Here it is commended to formulate a "frontier policy" to deal with "numerous savage and war like tribes whom the decaying authority of the Assam dynasty failed of late years to control, and whom the disturbed condition of the province has incited to encroachment."[32]

The word "encroachment" is contextually poignant as it symbolized two things: (a) the urge to restrict or deter the indigenous ethnic groups to claim their "primaeval rights" over land which they enjoyed before the British arrived[33] and (b) to delineate a "definite policy" on this frontier to dissolve the "indefinite nature of connexion subsisting between the Assam sovereigns and their savage neighbors."[34] By "indefinite nature of connexion," he meant rights and privileges endowed by the earlier rulers on the "savage neighbors" in land revenue matters.

Mackenzie, however, stated that the British have explored the "peculiar land system" of the "Native Governments" with an enlightened policy.[35] He further claimed that when the British "did arrive in any ease at a definite understanding as to the rights of any tribe, we were ready, as a rule, to treat them fairly and liberally."[36]

Mackenzie cited examples of the "success" of "fair and liberal" policy of the British toward the tribal subjects. Those examples may as well be cited as glaring examples of how the tribes had been forcibly drawn within the British legal system. As mentioned by Mackenzie, the British had demarcated the "frontier line" for each tribe in 1872–73.[37] The Deputy Commissioner of Durrang was in charge of watching the activities of "hill men" who used to come down in plains to trade and graze cattle. Sir G. Campbell recommended that this right should be given to them not "as a right" but "as a privilege" and as a "valuable means of securing their good behaviour."[38] The agreements signed between the tribal chiefs and the British sovereigns are, however, more obvious how the tribal communities had been forcibly subjected to colonial legal structure. A few examples are cited below.

An agreement had been signed between the Taghi Raja of Aka Purbat and the British, where the Chief was promised a pension of Rs. 20 against the following undertaking:

1 Myself, with my tribe, will confine our trade exclusively to the markets of Lahabaree, Baleepara, and Tezpur. We will not, heretofore, deal with the ryots in their private houses.
2 I will be careful that none of my tribe commit any act of oppression in the British territories.
3 We will apply to British Courts for redress in our grievances, and never take law in our hands.[39]

The third clause in that agreement is the most important to understand the modus operandi of coercing the tribal subjects under the British legal system that reflects the process of legal formation in Northeast India. Also, the clauses do not indicate that the British allowed their tribal subjects to retain their traditional "custom" as per their proclaimed policy. This was not just an agreement signed between the tribal chiefs and the British sovereigns. It was a "deed" of legal subjection of the autonomous tribes by the British Empire.

Mackenzie also recorded several instances of resistance from the tribal subjects. For example, in 1882, the forest guards reported that a large body of Aka and Duphla tribes came down and set up boundary marks, declaring that they would not allow anyone to cross the boundary and enter the British territory.[40] This is one of the myriad examples of how the indigenous tribes tried to offer resistance against the colonization process leading to loss of their land, traditional livelihood, custom, and cultural memory. Strikingly, Mackenzie cited from the Administrative Report of 1872–73 and the views of G. Campbell which stated: "Many Duphlas have settled as colonists in our territories and a few occasionally work on tea gardens."[41] Thus was the irony of history that the British colonizers in the Northeast had been describing the original inhabitants as "colonists" to whom the land originally belonged.

The archive makes it evident that the administration of law and justice for the tribal subjects had been a persistent source of concern for the British sovereigns in the Northeast. Mackenzie cited an extract from G. Campbell regarding the nature of law to be administered to those people:

> There may be, no doubt are, difficulties about the application of ordinary law in Assam and other districts peculiarly situated; but the Lieutenant-Governor considers that district officers should not raise and suggest difficulties. It is not for them to pick legal holes and find flaws, and to affect a pedantic legality. They should make the best of situation.[42]

The colonial archive clearly suggests that the British officers in the Northeast were by no means inclined to "pedantic legality." On the contrary, the production of customary law in Northeast India was essentially based on fluidity and arbitrariness, and that paved the passage for the production of customary law.

The next section briefly analyses the crucial role of the Missionaries in the process of subversion of custom and its gradual replacement by the sovereign "law."

Religion as "Law" in Proxy: Conversion and the Missionaries in Manipur

This section will briefly discuss how Missionaries played formidable agents in the process of transformation of the indigenous custom. The story of the Missionary enterprises in Northeast is complex that led to the cultural transformation of the land and the people. Missionaries were intimately connected with the passage of the formation of customary law. This section briefly analyses the passage on the basis of archival records from Manipur. The archival documents contain reports on rival Missionary activities in Manipur and their encounters with the tribal people. As is well known, Manipur was not directly administered by the British. The Political Agent in Manipur as the representative of the colonial state exercised the real authority while the king of Manipur was retained as titular head. Second, the Missionaries (all over Northeast) were not acknowledged as the direct "agents" of the state. But they were actively indulged in forging the link between the state and millions of tribal subjects. The following analysis is based on the letters written by the Governor of Assam to Mr. Watson, the Political Secretary, the Government of India. The letter narrates the rivalry between two Missionary institutions and its impact on the indigenous tribes. It also unfolds the *modus operandi* of the colonial state: (a) to forge a link with the tribal population via religion and English education and bring them under colonial authority and (b) to induct them to the ruler's creed in order to secure submission to the colonial state.

The king of Manipur expressed his disapproval to allow the Missionary activities in the plains of Manipur. The British authority allowed the American Baptist Mission represented by Reverend Pettigrew and Dr. Crozier – "with the permission of the Maharaja" – to start their activity in 1893 "strictly to the semi-civilized tribes on the Hills."[43] Interestingly, a rival mission also entered the scene with the similar objectives to "educate" (and convert) much to the displeasure of Reverend Pettigrew. Pettigrew voiced his protest on the restrictions imposed upon the mission to work in the entire hill. He claimed that Major Maxwell granted permission to them in 1894 on behalf of the Maharaja to introduce education among Tongkhuls.[44] Reverend Pettigrew further mentioned that the restriction had been imposed on:

In one isolated instance, an evangelist of the mission was fined for insisting an animist [of] Tongkhul village in defiance of the wishes of village elders and the villagers.[45]

Pettigrew further claimed in the letter of December 19, 1927, that the influence of American Baptist Mission existed over "unbroken chains of tribes from the Abors and Miris down to Chin Hills in Burma."[46] Reverend Pettigrew's petitions unfold the story of widespread Missionary activities in Northeast India and their efforts to bring the indigenous inhabitants closer to the rulers.

Another rival mission – The North-East Indian General Mission (formerly known as Thado-Kuki Pioneer Mission) – generated controversy over their mode of operation in the hills.[47] This mission had been consistently engaged in rivalry with American Baptist Mission over areas of operation. The representative of North-East Indian Mission complained against the "attitudes and policies of His Highness and the Darbar." The Rajah and his Darbar asserted that the "Manipuris are ardent Hindus" and strongly objected to "introducing Christianity to Manipur."[48]

The Missionary activities in Northeast India comprise a long story which is not a direct concern of this study. The documents refer to significant development through Missionary activities, which was directly linked with the passage of colonial state formation in the Hills. For example, the Governor of Assam wrote to the Secretary of State, the Government of India:

> To obviate friction between Animists who retain their aboriginal custom and Christians who perhaps may display resentment or be tempted to dispute the authority of a local Chief, the American Baptist Mission deliberately endeavours to arrange for a series of Christian villages, where the Christians live together apart from the Nagas and Kukis.[49]

The above passage is extremely significant to understand how the missions acted as direct agents of the state by creating a loyalist group through the device of "divide and rule" policy. Apparently, the rulers claimed that they segregated the "aboriginal" and "Christian" population in a village "to obviate friction." But the underlying motive behind this arrangement yielded different consequences, leading to internecine rivalry among the kins and villagers. Significantly, a petition was handed over to the Manipur State Durbar by a small group of Christian villagers from Mao village (who had been living apart over the past few years). They expressed their desire to live with "aboriginal" brethren in the same village.[50]

Reverend Pettigrew expressed his discomfort over the petition. He stated that

> The Heathen chief and elders of the village are wishing that these Christians remain with them, and that a pastor may come and visit them.[51]

Reverend Pettigrew, however, found the invisible hands of the king and the Darbar behind this petition. He expressed: "it sounds as if the Darbar has given the orders that no one is allowed to be a Christian." He made the following statement in defiance:

> The Missionaries of the American Baptist Mission would respectfully ask if the liberty of the individual and his convenience is considered the same thing in British territory.[52]

Reverend Pettigrew's statements in the above passage upheld the notion of "liberty" and "individual" which are exclusively Western concepts. More than that, he assumed the authority to defy the king and his Darbar being empowered by British "law" living in the "British territory," that is, Manipur.

Religion still remains the potent source of conflict and clash within and beyond the domain of the administration of customary law. Manipur is not the solitary example of the troubled interface of the ethnicity of religion. The trouble occurs in most of the states in the Northeast. In a retrospective gaze, one may trace the roots of current social, political, and religious conflict in Manipur in the colonial past.

The next section briefly reflects upon the Assam Code.

The Assam Code: Epistemology of Jurisprudence in the Politics of Omission

Assam Code was a cosmetic or thwarted gesture of the colonial rulers in Assam to introduce constitutional law. Assam Code, however, barely introduced any amount of transparency or clarification in the legal structure in the Northeast. On the contrary, the Code paved the way for contestation and conflict between the constitutional and customary law. In the contemporary time, contestation and conflict over "code" and "custom" are still formidable in the legal domain of Northeast India.

The Assam Code[53] contains "The Regulations and Local Acts in Force in the Province of Assam" in three volumes. The Code was designed to accommodate the "special law" for "different land and people." Captain Jenkins was keen to prepare a separate Code for Assam. The nomenclature Assam Code in itself is a kind of paradox because David Scott in consensus with the supreme authority in Fort William made it very clear from the very beginning that the Regulation intended for the people of Bengal could not be administered in the Northeast "Frontier," which was inhabited by "savage" and "rude tribes." Assam Code produced vehement debates and controversies during and especially after promulgation of the Code. Binayak Dutta cited H. K. Barpujari who asserted that the rules in *The Assam Code* "were respected more by violation than observance."[54]

Significantly, *The Assam Code* did not consciously provide an impression that it is designed as a completely separate Code/legal text, only meant for Assam. It is not clear whether it was a conscious strategic decision to uphold the "spirit and principles" of the "rule of law" implemented in Bengal. Otherwise, it reflected lack of expertise of the (military) officials in Assam to prepare a separate Code for the "de-regulated" region. The text began with Bengal Regulation 1 of 1793. In fact, it contains selective Regulations promulgated in Bengal. At the same time, *The Assam Code* contains the special Regulations for Assam. Assam Code therefore is a problematic legal guide, both for the law-givers and the stakeholders. The regulatory contents of the Assam Code are yet to be drawn under close scrutiny.

The Assam Code in three volumes contains elaborate administrative Regulations pertaining to Bengal. Simultaneously, the Code also contained Regulations relating to the administration of Assam. The document elaborately dealt with The Assam Labour and Emigration Act (1901) and its periodic amendments. Assam figured out most importantly in part 3: "Regulations made under the Government of India Act, 1870 (33 & 34 Vict., c. 3) and Government of India Act, 1915." This section dealt with the administration of Assam, for example: (1) Bengal Eastern Frontier Regulation, 1873, (2) The Assam Local Rates regulation, (3) The Assam Frontier Tracts Regulation 1880, (4) The Garo Hills Regulation, 1880, (5) The Sylhet and Cachar Rural Police Regulation, 1883, (6) The Assam Police Officers Regulation, 1883, (7) The Assam Frontier Tract regulation, 1884, (8) The Assam Land and land

Revenue Regulation, 1886, (9) The Assam land and Land Revenue Regulation 1889, (10) The Sylhet Jhum regulation, 1891, (11) The Assam Forest Regulation, 1891, (12) The Chin Hills Regulations, 1896, (13) The Assam Frontier Tracts Regulation (1880) Amendment Regulation, 1898, (14) The Assam Land and Revenue (Amendment) Regulation, 1905, (15) The Assam Forest (Amendment) Regulation, 1912, (16) The Assam Forest Amendment (Amendment) Regulation, 1922, and (17) The Bengal Eastern Frontier Regulation, 1925. Volume II of Assam Code contained two appendixes along with "Eastern Bengal and Assam Acts, 1907 to 1912".

It is quite significant that *The Assam Code* did not keep any provision for a proper judicial setup in Assam by appointing legal experts and Judges. The Commissioner had to function as the link between Assam and Fort William in Calcutta. He performed multiple and complex tasks being the administrative chief of a region; most importantly, he had to deal with the violent resistance and protracted armed encounters of the tribes.

The subordinate officials also felt the burden and difficulties of such an informal structure while they had to dispense all such duties in a remote and unfriendly region. For example, Colonel Jenkins wrote a petition to the Secretary to the Government of India regarding the creation of a new Zilla (district) called Jorehauth (Jorehat) and the release of funds to facilitate administration. He submitted that the funds would be managed by the Office of the Governor General's Agents in Northeast frontier. The Agency should be in direct communication with the President of Council. Jenkins, however, submitted his observation:

> The new divisions[55] be exempted from the ordinary control of the Sudder Courts and Board of Revenue as far as periodical and other returns but allowing Criminal and Civil Suits to take their usual course in subordination to the Sudder Dewanny and Nizamat Adawlat as now obtains in the Old Divisions of Assam under resolution of Government Judicial department of the 25th August 1834.[56]

The archive contains many such petitions which perhaps did not receive attention from the supreme authority. The archive recorded a letter of Colonel Hopkinson to implement "New Criminal Procedure Code in the Sudder Station of Gowhatty" and the first-class Magistrates should exercise their power "having held similar power under the former Code."[57] A few examples of the problems of the officials associated with the trials, especially in relation to civil cases, are discussed below.

Civil Cases

The archive recorded the narrative of an official who went for "tour in the Muffosil" in Goalparaby the "order of the Government in consequence of a large number of civil suits being on the file which could not be tried conveniently in camp."[58] It suggests that the colonial government did not pay as much attention as they did in the revenue matters, and it is evident from the narrative on trial of the cases from "camp." It is also evident from the list of cases recorded in the archive; almost each case concerned revenue matters. It had been further recorded in the archive:

> The official libraries of both the Judicial and Revenue sides have been re-arranged. In the course of this rearrangement several books and pamphlets which belong exclusively to the Revenue Department but which have hitherto been kept in the Judicial side have been transferred to the Revenue Library. Hence the large addition of 66 books this year.[59]

It may be derived from the above passage that the colonial state in the Northeast clubbed "revenue" and "judicial" matters together, especially in civil matters. In other parts of the Empire, for example, in Bengal, the English East India Company established Supreme Court as early as 1774, along with Sudder Diwanny Adalats in the Districts. The government maintained the structure of compartmentalized administrative, revenue, and judicial departments despite the imperial setup. The colonial government in the Northeast made no such attempts to introduce a formal judicial structure. It was further recorded that there had been "increase of 58 in the number of suits disposed of under Clause 4 Section 23, Act x of 1869."[60] As it had been stated, most of the suits related to "arrears of rent." The suits were contested between the zamindar and his tenants on account of the increase of rent on the tenants.[61] Such suits indirectly indicate the pressure of revenue on the zamindars which in turn passed on the burden over the tenants.

Assam Code and Land Revenue Administration: The Omission and Ground Reality

The omission to enact rules relating to land revenue points to the major lacuna in the Code. It is not clear whether the omission was deliberate to eke out space for arbitrary land revenue arrangements. Or it could be the product of the official confusion to prepare uniform legal structure given the uneven nature of the terrain and varied ethnic composition.

The colonial archive contains a very significant proclamation under the title: Rules for the Recovery of Land Revenue.[62] The proclamation was issued from the revenue department not judicial department. Yet it is significant for various reasons in relation to the legal governance in the Northeast. In the first place, the Assam Code did not contain any rules regarding settlement of land and power of the government to fix and raise the revenue and recover the land revenue from the defaulters. This document containing 25 clauses elaborately dealt with recovering "arrears of revenue" from defaulters. Second, the "Rules" had been repeatedly referred to as "Act" and the Clauses had been described as "Section." Third, Agnew, the officiating Commissioner and his team did not mention the formal official procedure by which the Clauses became "Rules" and "Act." Previous chapters analyzed how the rulers were keen to introduce permanent, heritable, and alienable rights on fixed rent while the ruler would reserve the right to raise it.[63]

The Lieutenant Governor of Bengal in consultation with the Board of revenue and local authorities wanted to introduce an effective land settlement. Earlier chapters have already analyzed the fluidity in the structure of land revenue settlement. The colonial rulers had been guided by the pragmatic considerations, such as (a) maximization of the amount of revenue, (b) reduction or displacement of the power and influence of the hereditary owners and their age-old loyalists who enjoyed rights over land over generations, and (c) transformation of forests, community holdings, wastelands, fallows, and lands used for other purposes such as trade, for example, in Sadiya – the *entrepot* trading center what now is called as border trade.

The most intriguing part of the record is twofold. In the first place, the "Rules" or "Act" proclaimed by Agnew elaborately dealt with the "defaulters" of the revenue and recovery of "debt" without referring to its status as legislative enactment. In view of this, the specific section analyzes those "Rules"/"Acts" to show how the colonial officials prepared their own trajectory to "recover" revenue within stipulated date. As it appears, the Clauses/"Acts" had been prepared in Assam under the "principle and spirit" of "Sunset Law"[64] as promulgated in Bengal Regulation 1 1793. At the same time, the arbitrary nature of those "Rules"/"Acts" in Assam becomes evident from the content and language of the document. The clauses are cited below.

The first clause proclaimed:

> Any instalment of assessment which is not paid (to the person entitled to receive the same) on or before the one which such assessment is payable according to the rules for the administration of land revenue in Assam and which date shall be specified in the *pattah*, shall be deemed as an arrear of revenue.[65]

Clause two instructed the Mouzadars (in charge of collection of revenue from the *ryots* and "other officers" to prepare an exhaustive list of "defaulter" *ryots* and submit the list to the sub-divisional officer. The Mouzadar should issue "separate warrants" to each *ryot* to pay the "whole amount" or due "instalments still due together with any expenses incurred by reason of the default and cost incurred in serving the notice, be paid within 10 days from the date of the notice being issued."[66] In case he failed to pay the due amount,

> He will be liable to arrest and imprisonment in the Civil Jail and that his property both moveable and immoveable will be liable to be attached and sold in satisfaction of the demand.[67]

The Clause is claimed to be the Act to "legalize" the policy of attachment of both "moveable and immoveable" property. Perhaps it was a strategy to implement the harsh measures under the pretence of "Act." *Ryots* were allowed only **ten days** to clear the dues and to save the attachment of their moveable and immoveable properties for sale. The sale was meant to recover the due "in satisfaction of the demand." This measure appears to be even more arbitrary because the value of the property had been assessed by the colonial officials. It is likely that there had been underhand dealings either between the purchaser and the Mouzadar or between the purchaser and the colonial officials or each party.

The British who claimed themselves as "law" abiding nation further added in Clause/Act four that

> It would be **lawful** for the defaulter on whom the notice has been served to appear in Court at any time previous to the expiration of 10 days and either by paying the amount of balance outstanding or by proving to the satisfaction of the Court that he is not liable on account of it, to save that his name be removed from the defaulter's list.[68]
>
> (emphasis mine)

The above passage shows that the colonial masters made "lawful" **concessions** to the *ryots* to allow the **privilege** to appear in the court either to clear the "arrear" **within 10 days** or **save** their property by submitting proof of their payment (emphasis mine). Clause/Act five further clarified the Rule:

> At the expiration of the 10 days specified in the notification if the defaulter's name is still in the list and he shall still neglect to pay the amount due, the District or Subdivisional officer shall issue a warrant directing the Nazir to arrest him and at the same time to attach all the moveable and immoveable property belonging to the defaulter.[69]

The reiteration of the "Rule" about attaching the "moveable and immoveable" properties is self-evident of the intention of the colonial rulers to create a land market toward maximization of revenue through sale in order to enrich the imperial treasury through the sale of "moveable" property. The archive did not record the individual gain of the officials out of the sale proceeds. Clause/Act six asserted that the defaulter should pay the due immediately. Otherwise, the property "shall be sold in public auction" within less than ten days and he would be imprisoned until the due was clear. Clause/Act seven declared that "personal property alone in the first instance be sold in the first instance." In case, the sale proceeds were "insufficient to liquidate the debt with cost," the rulers would attach "real property" of the defaulter and put it up for public auction and sale. The distinction between "personal property" and "real property" is not clear in the document. It is likely that "personal property" referred to moveables, while the real property meant immoveable or landed property.

Clause/Act eight was concerned about the purchasers and the terms are quite significant which are cited below:

> Purchasers shall be required to pay at the time of sale the full amount of purchase in cash, if this is not done the lot shall be resold at the risk of the first purchaser and the District or subdivisional officer shall recover the difference, if any from the first purchaser as arrear of assessment under **this Act.**[70]
>
> (emphasis mine)

It is interesting that the archive took the liberty to refer to such Clauses sometimes as "Rules" and occasionally as "Acts." *The Assam Code* promulgated Land Revenue Regulations for the first time in1886, whereas the "Rules" under discussion were recorded in 1870.

Clause/Act ten imposed stringent clauses on the defaulter regarding the transparency of his assets and holdings. It proclaimed:

> If it shall be proved that the defaulter or anyone acting on his behalf has either fraudulently or dishonestly made away with or concealed any portion of the defaulter's property and the amount realized from the sale of the portion allocated be not sufficient to liquidate the debt the defaulter may be imprisoned in the Civil Jail for a period of 2 months if the amount still due be less than 15 Rs. 4 months if more than 15 and less than 50 6 months in any other case.[71]

The Clauses/Acts above show that (a) defaulter would be jailed for non-payment and (b) the jail term would increase in case of "fraudulent and dishonest" act of concealing his actual assets and holdings. The defaulter was not given any grace period for procuring money toward paying off his "debt." The colonial authority did not keep any provision either toward payment of the dues in installments.

Clause/Act eleven proclaimed that "any person who has been imprisoned under the provisions of the last **preceding section** shall not again be liable to imprisonment for the same debt" ("section" refers to the Act, emphasis mine). The most significant part of "section" eleven was that "Any property he may subsequently acquire will be liable to attachment and sale."[72] Furthermore, "sections" twelve, thirteen, and fourteen proclaimed that the collecting officer would pay the jailor for the "subsistence" of the defaulter. The subsistence cost "shall not be less than 2 or more than 4 annas each day." But "any sums so paid shall be deemed 'Cost' and be recoverable from the defaulter."[73]

Such "Rules" and "Acts" upheld the "principle" and" spirit" of British "rule of law." For example, Clause/Act fifteen made the following provision:

> All complaints against Government Revenue officers relative to arrear of assessment, or on account of 'illegal' exaction of rent, or of any unauthorized cess or impost, or on account of the refusal of rent receipts for rent paid, or of disputed revenue accounts and all complaints of dispossession from the land, houses, premises, walls, watercourses and all disputed boundaries shall be liable under the Act.[74]

The above passage reveals the malpractices of the Mouzadars and other collectors of rent. It cannot be expected that the archive would openly state the collusion between the native rent collectors and colonial official for respective individual gains. The malpractices and collusion are, however, reflected in Clause/Act sixteen. The Clause/Act is quite lengthy regarding the offense and punishment for the Mouzadars or "other Government Revenue officials" who had been "found guilty for any of the following offenses specified in the preceding section." The guilty were those (a) who "omits to measure land as directed in the Rules for the Revenue administration of Assam," (b) who "knowingly delivers false or incorrect returns or accounts," and (c) who "in any way neglects his duty or wilfully disobeys any lawful order of his superiors." It had been proclaimed that such offenders

> Will be liable to a fine not exceeding 200 Rs or to suspension or dismissal at the discretion of the Deputy Commissioner or Assistant in Charge of subdivision, provided that if the latter suspend or dismiss a Mouzadar suspension or dismissal shall be subjected to approval of the Deputy Commissioner in the first place and in every case (whether the dismissal or suspension be by the Deputy Commissioner or Assistant Commissioner) shall be sanctioned by Commissioner to whom also all appointments shall be reported for confirmation.[75]

The above passage clearly indicates that the colonial administration devised the mechanism to restrain malpractices and collusion between native officials and British agents. Clause/Act seventeen further elaborated on this point, as cited below:

> Any person who maliciously or nexatiously [sic] makes a false complaint or resists any process issuing from any Revenue Court may be punished by fine not exceeding 100 Rs a portion of which at the discretion of the officer trying the case may be adjudged as compensation.[76]

Clause eighteen, however, added another clause evidently to protect the interest of other Mouzadars and other revenue officials. It clarified that the victims of oppression should lodge their complaints within three months of the "cause of action." The "cause of action" was listed as (a) illegal exaction of rent, (b) unauthorized cess or impost, (c) an account to further refusal of receipts for any dues paid, and (d) on account to stop extortion by confinement.

"Rules for the Recovery of Land Revenue in Assam" consist of a total of twenty-five Clauses/Acts. It is quite interesting that the initial Clauses did not mention the term Act. The term Act had been used from Clause eight onward. Clause nineteen unambiguously proclaimed the "Rules" to be considered as Act:

> All fines or awards on account of compensation or damages under this Act or under the Rules of Revenue administration of Assam may be recovered in the same way as an arrear of assessment under this Act.[77]

The subsequent Clauses/Acts elaborated on the judicial procedure for implementation. Clause/Act twenty elaborated on the authorized official to deal with such cases, as cited below:

> All cases under this Act shall be received and decided by the Deputy Commissioner or Assistant Commissioner in Charge of a Subdivision or may be referred by them for trial to any other Assistant Commissioner.[78]

Clauses/Acts from twenty-one to twenty-five[79] are the most significant enunciations to situate the "Rule"/"Act" under the existing structure of legal governance. It stated:

21 A sentence under this Act shall not be or affect any penalty or punishment to which the person so sentenced may be subject by Indian Penal Code or any other law for the time being.[80]
22 In all cases tried in the Revenue Deptt (Department) the officer deciding them may award expenses of suit at his discretion.
23 An appeal from all decisions and orders of the Assistant Commissioner shall be allowed to the Deputy Commissioner and from all decisions and orders of the Deputy Commissioner to the Commissioner provided such appeal be made in the former case within 15 days and in the latter case within 30 days from the date of the order appealed against.
24 The Commissioner may also if he see fit revise any order of a subordinate through the period of appeal may have passed.
25 Nothing contained in the Act shall be held to apply to suits between Lakherajdars and other private landowners and their tenants in Assam or to the recovery of any arrear of assessment due by a Govt (Government) tenant unless proceedings be instituted within 3 months of the date on which such arrears were due.[81]

The above Clauses clarified the legal foundation of the proclaimed "Rules" and "Act" which had been formulated without formal procedure and dispensed with arbitrary means. It was tailor-made to dispense "justice" toward the "savage" subjects of the Northeast Frontier. For example, Clause twenty-one clarified that under this "Act" no person could be "sentenced" by Indian

Penal Code or "any other law" (by adding the tailpiece) "for the time being." This tailpiece clearly explains that those were neither an "Act" nor even a "Rule" as endorsed by Indian Penal Code. It was primarily and essentially administrative directives to "recover"/expropriate land revenue. For example, Clause twenty-two talked about "discretionary" power of the serving officers. It was not mentioned in the document what kind of "discretionary" power had been allotted to the judicial magistrate and the extent of their power and jurisdiction. Also, it is questionable whether a subordinate officer could exercise "discretionary" power under any Act legislated by the supreme authority without any provision for the obligation to vindicate their action. Finally, certain categories of landholders, such as "Lakherajdar," "private landowner," and their "tenants," were virtually left beyond the orbit of the "Act." The entire discourse is intriguing. The archive does specify the category of landowners for whom the "Rule" or "Act" had been designed. The last clause mentioned a category of landowner called "private landowner." Such a conceptual category did not exist in precolonial Assam. The term had been imported from Western terminology in relation to colonial landholding structure, just as the introduction of the notion of "alienation."

The promulgation of 1891 Assam Code may raise the question as to what extent the "Code" ushered in any new policy measure or embodied the ideologies and measures that had already decided the legal destiny of Assam that occurred between 1826 and 1890. In sum, *the Assam Code* did not embody any coherent judicial directives that could ensure equity and justice for the subjects.

Next section will briefly analyze The Bengal Eastern Frontier Regulation, 1873. It poignantly addresses the question as to whether this Code created the legal edifice or whether it was a *post facto* endorsement of the legal or quasi-legal initiatives to produce and administer Assam as a frontier through different sets of "legal" principles.

"Inner Line" Regulation: Regulation of 1873 (Bengal Eastern Frontier Regulation, 1873) [August 27, 1873][82]

The Regulation of 1873, popularly defined as "Inner Line" Regulation is a landmark legal device in Northeast India. "Inner Line" Regulation had been introduced long before The Assam Land Revenue Regulation 1886. The Land and Revenue Regulation of 1886 is *post facto* "titles of law," for the policies and measures already introduced including the "Inner Line." "Inner Line" Regulation of 1873 was originally defined in the Code as "A Regulation for the peace and government of certain districts on the Eastern Frontier of Bengal." The "Inner Line Regulation" had been revised time and again during the colonial period as a strategic device to demarcate border and frontier of the British Empire. It was an equally important administrative tool to extend hegemony on the land and people. The Regulation has had an afterlife in the post-colonial period till date. It is difficult to evaluate the impact of the

Regulation of the material and cultural life of the people and the colonial policy of "exclusion" as well as a legal device to demarcate the British strategic border and frontier in this chapter. It is difficult to deal with the strategic, especially human and geocultural, complexities of this Regulation in this brief space. The chapter briefly focuses on the strategic, financial, and legal implications of the Regulation.

The "Inner Line" was initially applicable "to the districts of Kamrup, Darrang, Nowgong, Sibsagar, Lakhimpur, [GaroHills]. Kahsi and Jaintia Hills, Naga Hills and Cachar."[83] It had been declared in the Code that the Regulation had been approved by the Governor General in Council and then to be "published in the Gazette of India, and will be published in the Calcutta gazette, and will thereupon have the force of law, under the 33rd of Victoria, Chapter 3(1)."[84]

The Assam Code contained the basic tenets of the "law that would be effective in the places", mentioned above from 1st November 1873. "Inner Line" had been unambiguously defined as an "excluded area by Clause 2 of the Regulation", as cited below[85]:

> It shall be lawful for the local Government of Bengal,[86] with the previous sanction of the Governor General in Council, to prescribe and from time to time to alter by notification in the Calcutta Gazette,[87] a line to be called" The Inner Line," in each and any of the above-named districts.
>
> The Local Government [*4*] may, by notification in the Calcutta Gazette [*5*], prohibit all British subjects, or any class of British subjects, or any person residing in or passing through such districts from going beyond such line without a pass under the hand and seal of the chief executive officer of such district or of such officer as he may authorize to grant such pass; and the Local Government may from time to time cancel or vary such prohibitions [*6*].[88]

Clause 3 notified that any British subject, or any other person so prohibited, who after "the Inner Line" has been prescribed and notified in accordance with section 2 of this Regulation, goes beyond such line "without a pass, shall be liable, on conviction before a Magistrate"[*1*][89] (to imprisonment of either description which may extend to one year, or to a fine not exceeding one thousand rupees, or to both).[90] It was further notified that the Local Government may from "time to time prescribe by notification" in the Calcutta Gazette (revised as *Assam Gazette*) "a form of pass" (notified in *Manual of Assam Local Statutory Rules and Orders*, 1931, Vol. II) for each district "and map." Clause 5, however, explained the underlying objectives behind the promulgation of "Inner Line" Regulation. The following Clause clarified:

5.1 Any rubber, wax, ivory or other jungle-product [*4*][91] (or any book, diary, manuscript, map, picture, photograph, film, curio or article of religious or scientific interest) found in the possession of any person convicted of an offence under this Regulation may be confiscated to Government by an order to be passed at the time of conviction by the magistrate.

5.2 If the Magistrate has reason to believe that any article which if found in the possession of a person convicted under this Regulation would have been liable to confiscation under sub-section (1) has been acquired or wholly or partly written, made or taken by such person beyond "The Inner Line," the Magistrate after giving the person in whose possession the article is found an opportunity to show cause why an order under this sub-section should not be passed in respect of the article may, unless it is proved that the article was not acquired, written or made or taken as aforesaid order that such article be confiscated to Government.[92]

The above Clause is extremely significant in view of the arbitrary and omnipotent control of the colonial state over the people, land, and resources of the "excluded" zone. The above paragraphs made it quite evident that the vast expanse of the "Inner Line" region possessed considerable natural resources such as rubber, wax, ivory (of great value in national and international market), and other "jungle-products" (that might contain equally valuable commodities). The restrictions on the pass-holders to exit the region with any book, diary, manuscript, map, picture, photograph, film, curio articles, or articles of religious or scientific interest indicate the concern of the colonial administrators to keep the entire region under mysterious surveillance. In other words, "Inner Line" areas had been kept a closely guarded secret zone. One may speculate about the reasons behind this close-guarded policy. The strategic factor may be considered as only one of the various reasons, but there were more significant factors that the British sought to hide from the public eye. Clause 7 critically explains the major motive behind the restrictions, as it notified:

> It shall not be lawful for any British subject or other person, not being a Native of the district comprised in the preamble of this Regulation, to acquire any interest in land or the product of land beyond the said "Inner Line" without the sanction of the local Government or such officer as the Local Government shall appoint in this behalf.
>
> Any interest so acquired may be dealt with as the local Government or its said officer shall direct.
>
> The Local Government may also, by notification in the Calcutta Gazette [Assam Gazette] extend the prohibition contained in this section to any class of persons, Natives of the said districts, and may time to time in like manner cancel or vary such extension.[93]

The above passage provides essential clues toward understanding the real motive behind creating an invincible wall to closely guard the "Inner Line" regions. It was the avaricious investment of the colonial state in land and its resources. Violation of moral economy, moral law, and humanitarian policies had been kept beyond the public sight, and books, diaries, film, photography, manuscripts, and curio items reflect the hindsight of colonial policies. The Regulation also indicates it was an attempt to restrict unrestrained plunder of the British free traders and also native traders of the resources of the region. It is likely that the colonial administrations sought to reserve the rights to plunder the state. The introduction of "Inner Line" was not a peaceful historical passage. It is again a different story.

This chapter thus interrogates the essentialization of politico-economic policy focus in dealing with the knots historically and socio-anthropologically tied with the forces of "law." It examines the colonial legal formation in Northeast India had been accomplished primarily through culturization of the ethnic space as well as intimidation and violence against the native subjects which left irreversible scars on society, economy, and human relationships. The confusion and contestation over "Law" as happened during the colonial period still persists in Northeast India in different layers as a direct legacy of the colonial legal governance.

Notes

1 Bradley-Birt, F.B., *The Story of an Indian Upland*, Smith, Elder & Co., London, 1905, p. 15.
2 Mackenzie, Alexander, *The North East Frontier of Bengal*, Mittal Publications, New Delhi, 1999 (6th ed.).
3 Banerjee, A.C., *The Eastern Frontier of British India*, A. Mukherjee & Co. Pvt. Ltd, Calcutta, p. 13.
4 Assam Secretariat, Commissioner's Office, Revenue Department, 1859, Fileno.30.
5 Assam Secretariat, Commissioner's Office, Letter No. 19, January 1839.
6 Assam Secretariat, Commissioner's Office, Letter No. 19, January 1839.
7 Locke, John, *Two Treatises of Government*, First published by Awnsham Churchill, London, 1690.
8 Locke, John, *Two Treatises of Government*; Assam Secretariat Commissioner's Office, File No. 02, 1833; Assam Secretariat Commissioner's office, File No. 01, Revenue Department, 1846.
9 Assam Secretariat, Commissioner's Office, File No. 30, 1859.
10 Assam Secretariat, Commissioner's Office, File No. 30, 1859.
11 Assam Secretariat, Commissioner's Office, File No. 30, 1859.
12 Assam Secretariat, Commissioner's Office, Revenue Department, File No. 02, 1833.
13 Assam Commissioner's Office, Revenue Department, File No. 04, 1834.
14 Assam Commissioner's Office, Revenue Department, File No. 04, 1834.
15 Assam Commissioner's Office, Revenue Department, File No. 04, 1834.
16 Assam Commissioner's Office, Revenue Department, File No. 04, 1834.
17 This term has been used by Nicholas Dirks in *Castes of Mind*, p. 11.
18 This term has been used by Nicholas Dirks in *Castes of Mind*, p. 11.
19 Assam Secretariat, Commissioner's Office, File No. 01, 1833.
20 Assam Secretariat, Commissioner's Office, File No. 01, 1833.
21 Assam Secretariat, Commissioner's Office, File No. 01, 1833.
22 Assam Secretariat, Commissioner's Office, File No. 01, 1833.
23 Assam Secretariat, Commissioner's Office, File No. 01, 1833.
24 Assam Secretariat, Commissioner's Office, File No. 01, 1833.

25 Assam Secretariat, Commissioner's Office, File No. 01, 1833.
26 Assam Secretariat, Commissioner's Office, File No. 01, 1833.
27 Assam Secretariat, Commissioner's Office, File No. 01, 1833.
28 Assam Secretariat, Commissioner's Office, File No. 01, 1833.
29 Assam Secretariat, Commissioner's Office, File No. 01, 1833.
30 Assam Secretariat, Commissioner's Office, File No. 01, 1833.
31 Bhattacharyya-Panda, Nandini, *Appropriation and Invention of Tradition: The East India Company and Hindu Law in Early Colonial Bengal*, Oxford University Press, New Delhi, 2008.
32 Alexander Mackenzie, p. 7.
33 Alexander Mackenzie, p. 7.
34 Alexander Mackenzie, p. 8.
35 Alexander Mackenzie, p. 7.
36 Alexander Mackenzie, p. 7.
37 Alexander Mackenzie, p. 24.
38 Alexander Mackenzie, pp. 24–25.
39 Alexander Mackenzie, p. 24. Cited from Political Proceedings, 25th June 1857, Nos. 305–7; 19th May, 1859, Nos. 6–7; June 1860, Nos. 55–56.
40 Alexander Mackenzie, p. 25.
41 Alexander Mackenzie, p. 31.
42 Alexander Mackenzie, p. 31, cited from Political Proceedings, June 1871, No. 28, p. 30.
43 Foreign and Political Department, Political Branch, File No. 145, P/28, D.D. No. 169, 5 March, 1928, p. 2.
44 Foreign and Political Department, Political Branch, File No. 145, P/28, D.D. No. 169, 5 March, 1928, p. 2.
45 Foreign and Political Department, Political Branch, File No. 145, P/28, D.D. No. 169, 5 March, 1928, p. 2.
46 Foreign and Political Department, Political Branch, File No. 145, P/28, D.D. No. 169, 5 March, 1928, p. 2.
47 Foreign and Political Department, Political Branch, File No. 145, P/28, D.D. No. 169, 5 March, 1928, p. 1.
48 Foreign and Political Department, Political Branch, File No. 145, P/28, D.D. No. 169, 5 March, 1928, p. 3.
49 Foreign and Political Department, Political Branch, File No. 145, P/28, D.D. No. 169, 5 March, 1928, p. 3.
50 Foreign and Political Department, Political Branch, File No. 145, P/28, D.D. No. 169, 5 March, 1928, p. 9.
51 Foreign and Political Department, Political Branch, File No. 145, P/28, D.D. No. 169, 5 March, 1928, p. 9.
52 Foreign and Political Department, Political Branch, File No. 145, P/28, D.D. No. 169, 5 March, 1928, p. 9.
53 *THE ASSAM CODE*, in three volumes containing THE REGULATIONS AND LOCAL ACTS N FORCE IN THE PROVINCE OF ASSAM with Chronological Tables, Notes as to Scheduled Districts, and De-Regulationised Tracts and an Index, Printed at the Assam Government Press, Shillong, 1934.
54 Dutta, Binayak, "The Assam Code: Locating Law as the Instrumentality of Governance in Colonial Assam," Man and Society, *A Journal of North-East Studies, Indian Council of Social Science Research*, North Eastern Regional Centre, Shillong, Meghalaya, Vol. x, Winter 2013, p. 72.
55 The Assam Code.
56 Letter Issued to Government, Vol. 41, Part 2, 1863–64, Letter no. 112.
57 Letter Issued to Government, Vol. 41, Part 2, 1863–64, Letter no. 69.

58 Assam Commissioner, General and Judicial Department, Land Revenue of Goalpara, File no. 83, 1869.
59 Assam Commissioner, General and Judicial Department, Land Revenue of Goalpara, File no. 83, 1869.
60 Assam Commissioner, General and Judicial Department, Land Revenue of Goalpara, File no. 83, 1869.
61 Assam Commissioner, General and Judicial Department, Land Revenue of Goalpara, File no. 83, 1869.
62 Letter Issued to Government, Vol. 41, Year 1870.
63 The Assam Land Revenue Manual, Vol. 1, p. iv.
64 'Sunset Law' as promulgated in 1793 imposed the rule of payment of the revenue by the sunset of the stipulated date. In case of default, the Zamindari or estates were put up for auction for sale.
65 Letter Issued to Government, Vol. 41, Year 1870. Letter number not mentioned. It had been compiled as directive.
66 Letter Issued to Government, Vol. 41, Year 1870. Letter number not mentioned. It had been compiled as directive.
67 Letter Issued to Government, Vol. 41, Year 1870. Letter number not mentioned. It had been compiled as directive.
68 Letter Issued to Government, Vol. 41, Year 1870. Letter number not mentioned. It had been compiled as directive.
69 Letter Issued to Government, Vol. 41, Year 1870. Letter number not mentioned. It had been compiled as directive.
70 Letter Issued to Government, Vol. 41, Year 1870. Letter number not mentioned. It had been compiled as directive.
71 Letter Issued to Government, Vol. 41, Year 1870. Letter number not mentioned. It had been compiled as directive.
72 Letter Issued to Government, Vol. 41, Year 1870. Letter number not mentioned. It had been compiled as directive.
73 Letter Issued to Government, Vol. 41, Year 1870. Letter number not mentioned. It had been compiled as directive.
74 Letter Issued to Government, Vol. 41, Year 1870. Letter number not mentioned. It had been compiled as directive.
75 Letter Issued to Government, Vol. 41, Year 1870. Letter number not mentioned. It had been compiled as directive.
76 Letter Issued to Government, Vol. 41, Year 1870. Letter number not mentioned. It had been compiled as directive.
77 Letter Issued to Government, Vol. 41, Year 1870. Letter number not mentioned. It had been compiled as directive.
78 Letter Issued to Government, Vol. 41, Year 1870. Letter number not mentioned. It had been compiled as directive.
79 The writer of this document recorded Clause 25 as 23, presumably by mistake.
80 The writer of this document recorded Clause 25 as 23, presumably by mistake.
81 The writer of this document recorded Clause 25 as 23, presumably by mistake.
82 *The Assam Code*, Vol. 1, 246–249.
83 *The Assam Code*, Vol. 1, 246–249, p. 247.
84 *The Assam Code*, Vol. 1, 246–249, p. 247.
85 *The Assam Code*, Vol. 1, 246–249, p. 247.
86 The Chief Commissioner of Assam (Now, the local Government), *see* the Bengal, Bihar and Orissa and Assam Laws Act, 1912 (VII of 1912), s.3. Ands ch. D, Pt. III, *ante*. p. 247.
87 Now the Assam Gazette – *see* the Bengal, Bihar and Orissa and Assam Laws Act, 1912 (VII of 1912), s. 3. Andsch. D, Pt. III, *ante*. p. 247.

88 For notification prescribing and altering Inner Lines, and prohibiting persons from going beyond such lines without a pass, *see* the Manual of Assam Local Statutory Rules and Orders.

89 The words under square brackets were substituted for the words "to a fine not exceeding Rupees 100 for the first offence, and to a fine not exceeding three months, or to both, for each subsequent offence, by s. 2 of Regulation Vol f 1925.

90 The Assam Code, p. 248.

91 The words under square brackets were inserted by s. 3 of Regulation V of 1925.

92 The words under square brackets were inserted by s. 3 of Regulation V of 1925, p. 248.

93 The words under square brackets were inserted by s. 3 of Regulation V of 1925, p. 249.

5 Customary Law and Gender in Northeast India

Tanka B. Subba

Introduction

One of the dominant assumptions in the writings on the tribal societies of Northeast India is that they are gender equal. Some go to the extent of claiming that women among them enjoy a much higher status than the women in caste societies. However, it is also argued, quite frequently, that tribal customary laws perpetuate gender inequality in favor of men. This chapter will address the relationship between tribal customary laws and gender with suitable examples from India's Northeast.

During the colonial days, the "Excluded" and "Partially Excluded Areas" of the region were not directly administered, and they were allowed to be governed according to their own customary laws as long as they maintained peace and tranquility. But if they raided the plains villages or attacked the colonial survey teams or their plantations, punitive expeditions would be sent to them, which often burnt down their villages and granaries as no one would be found in the villages to punish. Even the domestic animals would have been set free. But when peace and tranquility prevailed, the hill tribes enjoyed considerable freedom from the colonial government in India.

It may also be recalled that the Law Research Institute (LRI), established in 1977 in Guwahati, has been documenting the customary laws and practices of the tribes of the region for almost four decades now. By the 1980s, 13 tribes were covered, and during 2003–2008, another 200 tribes were proposed to be covered with the help of one research team for each state of the region working under the overall supervision of the Chief Justice of Gauhati High Court (Sethi 2015). Although the mandate of the LRI was only documentation, it paved the way for codification of the customary laws that were actually flexible and underwent periodic revisions (Khutso 2018). Following their codification, they have assumed the force of law in the state of Mizoram, whereas in Nagaland, Naga customary laws are recognized under Article 371 (A) of the Constitution of India.

I argue here that, although the intention of the LRI might have been good, its project of documenting the customary laws has put the tribal communities of the region in a quandary because it made their customary laws rigid,

DOI: 10.4324/9781003539797-6

whereas customary laws are by nature flexible. In this context, I cannot agree more with Justice D.M. Sen who said:

> I am very much against codification. The moment you codify you make it final and firm and rigid. The societies, the tribal societies are developing much faster than any other societies and you yourself do not know what you are going to retain and what are you not. So codification means binding yourself.
>
> (Quoted in Wouters 2017: 23)

Flexibility, I argue, however, can be a double-edged sword, as it can also be misused. For instance, it is alleged that in Nagaland, customary laws are so interpreted by Naga men as to deprive Naga women of their political rights, in particular the 33 percent seat reservation in the urban local body elections in 2016 (Gangopadhyay 2017). Even the role of Nagaland state has come under a scanner in this regard in view of its ambivalent position with regard to the reservation for women. Instead of implementing the direction of the single judge bench of the Gauhati High Court, issued in October 2011, for holding the municipal elections, the state government managed to get a stay on this directive from a division bench of the same court. As if that was not enough, the state assembly passed a resolution on September 22, 2012, opposing reservation for women in civic bodies on grounds of customary laws. It was only in 2016 that it passed the Nagaland Municipal (Third Amendment) Bill, clearing the way for women's reservation in civic bodies (Khan 2017). And yet, the Naga men did not allow their women to contest elections to the urban civic bodies in 2016; those women who had already filed their nominations were asked to withdraw the same.

While state laws are rigid and cannot be amended without due legislative process and certainly not as frequently as societal changes would warrant, customary laws are, as stated above, by nature flexible. By giving them a legal status, some states of the region not only made their customary laws rigid but also made any breach of such laws punishable under statutory law. This led to the suffering of the common people, both financially and otherwise, on account of fighting endless litigation at the courts of law, unlike earlier, when some breaches of customary laws would be settled with a bottle of wine, and if the breach was more serious in the eyes of the village elders, with a pig or a cow perhaps. I am not claiming that every defaulter of customary laws got away by paying such fines in the past. On the contrary, at times, as the Naga ethnography shows, punishments led to ex-communication from the village, slavery, or even death.

But, as we all know, the court cases are often dragged for decades for various reasons. One such reason is that the hearings get postponed or remain inconclusive inclusive for many decades in some cases. No one, not the least a tribal person coming from a remote village and without any knowledge of law, is happy to attend the court hearings, for which the dates are often not honored by the courts themselves. Each time he comes to the district or state capital to attend the court hearing, he has to sell one of his valuables and bring the money as lawyer's fees. The lawyer assures him of early disposal of the case and a sure win, both of which remain assurances in most cases. Therefore, by legalizing customary laws, the state has made the common people vulnerable to legal machinations about which they are neither aware nor protected.

One other reason why I do not think that codification is a good idea is the issue of double templates. Even after customary laws are documented and codified, the society continues to adhere to their customary laws as before. Hence, one template of customary laws remains frozen while another template of the same keeps evolving in its natural setting, which over a period of time may move considerably away from the one that was codified. Such a situation leads to the creation of two templates, one which is constantly undergoing changes in response to societal changes and the other one that has been frozen. Yet the one that is codified and frozen may be picked up as the basis of legislation, making such legislation already obsolete.

Custom, Customary Law, and Statutory Law

A custom is a traditional practice followed by most members of a community living in a particular place at a particular time. It draws its strength from a reference to a social practice that has been followed "since time immemorial." It not only varies from tribe to tribe but also varies across time. It is a fact that many customs have vanished over the years and new customs have emerged. Some of the customs followed by the Naga tribes of the region clearly originated during the colonial era, as ably demonstrated by Wouters (2017).

It is, for instance, customary for a Khasi to offer *kwai* (betel leaf and areca nut with a dash of lime and sometimes a piece of ginger or even dry coconut) to guests and visitors. It is also customary for a Khasi man marrying the youngest daughter of the family called *khadduh* to go and live with her in his wife's mother's house. A customary practice being normative, any adherence to it will receive a general approval from the members of a community. But if the same is not followed, the only consequence that normally follows is a jeer, gossip, ridicule, and a kind of social disapproval. Such situations do arise at times because some members of any community may violate some customary practices once in a while. If some customs are not followed by a family for want of resources, the same may be condoned by the members of the community. The community members do not even expect the women in patrilineal societies, who have intermarried with people belonging to other communities, to follow their customary practices. In other words, a community evaluates each case of breach individually and contextually before considering even the mildest of actions against any person who has breached a custom.

But it is not always possible to have such a simple understanding of the word "custom." Violation of certain customs, such as those related to death, may be taken more seriously by the community than the violation of certain other customs, such as those related to birth or marriage. Hence, it depends on how important or not a custom is in the eyes of the members of a community at a given point of time and place. Certain customs which are vital for the membership of a community may be considered as important and may attract the severest punishment if they are, for instance, related to their rights and obligations or their very identity as members of a community. Such customs are generally called customary laws.

Otherwise, unlike customs, a breach of customary laws may attract some form of punishment, which has to be decided by the village councils or some such local bodies in a formally convened meeting. Such laws are important for the community because they help perpetuate certain community values and restrain deviant behaviors. Customary laws are, thus, slightly stringent types of customs whose violations will not go unpunished by the community, however mild the punishment might be.

In Khasi society, for instance, one customary law says that the youngest daughter in the family shall inherit the ancestral property and look after her parents, other dependent family members, including her unmarried uncles and aunts, and unmarried or separated/divorced brothers and sisters. If she belongs to their traditional religion called *Niamtre*, she will have an additional responsibility of performing the rituals when they die. But if she marries a non-Khasi man or indulges in an incestuous relationship with her maternal clan members, she will lose her privileges as the youngest daughter of the family.

There is, however, no clearly identifiable boundary between custom and customary law, except that the punishment for a breach of customary law is generally more stringent than it is for the breach of a custom and is decided by the community in a formal meeting of the village elders. But, in the case of both, the members of a community decide about the nature and degree of punishment for an offense, often depending on who the offender is; they do not themselves make a conscious distinction between a custom and a customary law. The punishment meted out may be soft or harsh depending on the age, gender, clan, etc., of the violator and not necessarily which customary law has been violated. It may also depend on whether a violation is a first or is repeated several times. Being often biased in favor of men, a man may be pardoned, but a woman may not be, even if their offense, such as infidelity, is similar.

The distinction between a custom and a customary law is therefore often arbitrary and pretty much the same as the difference between a folkway and a more, or between a value and a norm. Since the people themselves do not make a distinction between the two, it is likely that what is documented by the LRI of Guwahati as customary laws is, actually, and in many cases, customs.

The distinction between customary law and statutory law, on the other hand, is clear, that is, a customary law is interpreted and upheld by a community, whereas a statutory law is interpreted and upheld by the state.

More often than not, an FIR is to be registered in case of any violation of statutory law, and the accused is to be arrested and produced by the state police before a court of law, which will decide whether or not a bail is to be granted to the accused. If a bail is not granted, the accused has the liberty to approach a higher court. But, if convicted, the violator may eventually land up in jail for a period mentioned in the statutory law or as pronounced by the concerned judge presiding over a particular case.

Further, while some statutory laws have evolved through the codification of customary laws, most statutory laws in India were introduced by the colonial rulers. However, the tribes of the region seem to have accepted the statutory laws early in their history, in spite of not being administered directly like the plains people. For instance, in the early twentieth century, Major Play Fair reported that Garos were highly litigant. Other British administrators writing at the beginning of the twentieth century, like J. H. Hutton and J.P. Mills, not to exclude a relatively latecomer to the region like Christoph von Furer-Haimendorf, also write how the tribesmen in the areas under their administrative supervision came to them instead of going to their own chiefs or headmen for adjudication of their disputes as per their customary laws. There are writings on the tribes of the region that indicate that they had an early inclination for statutory laws and increasingly relied upon such laws, although they also continued to follow their own customary laws on many matters. The statutory laws were specially invoked for criminal offenses or for settling inter-village or inter-tribal disputes, which were once very common in the region, as each village or tribe had its own customary laws which were not binding on other villages or tribesmen.

Customary Law and Gender Inequality: Some Case Studies from Northeast India

A study conducted on gender implications of customary laws among five tribes of the region and funded by the National Commission for Women, New Delhi, has concluded that the tribes in the region interpret customary laws from a male perspective and justify individual ownership of land on the basis of the same (Fernandes et al. 2008). In fact, one scholar goes to the extent of branding all customary laws as biased against women (Kamei 2014), although, in some tribal societies of the region, including the Nagas, customary laws may also be biased in favor of the elderly persons of both genders. On the basis of the LRI reports on customary laws and practices among 13 tribes of the region, two important reasons stand out for marginalizing women's role in economy and thereby making them vulnerable to their customary laws. The two reasons are privatization of land and stoppage of shifting cultivation (Parwez 2012a). This is found to be particularly true of the Ao Naga tribe (Parwez 2012b).

One of the flashpoints of the customary laws denying gender equality was observed in Nagaland in 2016 when the election tour ban on local bodies was announced on the directive of the Supreme Court. The Naga (male) leaders invoked Article 371(A) of the Constitution which says:

> Notwithstanding anything in this Constitution, no Act of Parliament in respect of religious or social practices of the Nagas, Naga customary law and procedure, administration of civil and criminal justice involving decisions according to Naga customary law, ownership and transfer of land and its resources, shall apply to the State of Nagaland unless the Legislative Assembly of Nagaland by a resolution so decides.

And the Naga leaders claimed that according to their customary laws, there was no scope for the participation of women in their decision-making bodies, which was contested by the Naga women's organizations like the Naga Mothers' Association and the Joint Action Committee for Women's Reservation.

If customary laws are indeed the grounds for denying the Naga women the right to participate in the political arena, as believed by most women scholars writing on customary laws (Agarwal 1994, Zehol 2003, Ao 2010, etc.), it is difficult to explain how some of them contested assembly elections in the past, and one of them was even successfully elected in the parliamentary elections. While the Naga patriarchy may be one of the extreme types, it is methodologically difficult to draw one-to-one relationship between patriarchy and gender inequality among them. I think the answer instead lies in their long history of inter-village and inter-*khel* conflicts, mutual unintelligibility of their languages, headhunting, and insurgency, all of which marginalized the public role of women in their society. In my view, no other people in India have endured as much human rights violation as the Nagas have suffered ever since they came in contact with the colonial rulers about two centuries ago.

Traditionally speaking, the role of women has been limited to the domestic space in most societies, and Naga women are no exception in this regard. The public space has been monopolized by men from almost every community – tribal or not and in India or outside it – for centuries, and this is also true of the matrilineal Khasi and Garo tribes of the region. But gradually, and often grudgingly, more and more societies are opening up and giving such space to women. Even in Nagaland, it cannot be denied that it was men who passed the Nagaland Municipal (First Amendment) Act in 2006, providing 33 percent reservation for women, and it was again the men who passed the Third Amendment to this Act in 2016. It is difficult to believe that a Naga legislative assembly without a single woman member would have done it under some kind of external influence. Had there been some external influence, it would not have taken more than a decade to pass the First Amendment after the 74th Constitutional Amendment, providing women with 33% seat reservation in panchayat bodies and take another one decade to pass the Third Amendment.

To be fair to the Naga men, it is not only they who have shown a lackadaisical attitude toward issues related to women's empowerment in India.

Men from all states of India have shown such attitude. Otherwise, the Constitution Amendment (108th Amendment) Bill, 2008, which is also known as Women's Reservation Bill, would have seen the light of the day by now. Political parties of different orientations have come to power at the center but the Bill is remembered only when a party is in opposition, not when it is in power.

Conclusion

The codification of customary laws by the tribes of the region is an ongoing process. While there are a lot of publications on the impact of customary laws on gender inequality, such as Poumai Naga (Stephen 2021), Dimasa and Karbi (Parwez 2010–2011), Mizos (Gangte 2016), Kabui Naga (Kamei 2011), Nagaland (Khan 2017), and Northeast India as a whole (Buongpui 2013), I have not come across a single article or book on the impact of customary laws on men in tribal societies. I think it is time we research on the impact of customary laws on men as well, or why tribal societies want it so much to protect their customary laws. Is it merely to protect male dominance over their own women, or is the issue a little more complex than we assume it to be? To know the answer, a proper gender research is needed; what we have seen so far is mostly women's perspectives about women.

When one looks at the fast-changing tribal societies of the region, one tends to suspect that gradually the statutory laws will alone survive, but when one looks at the tendencies of the Christian tribal youths of the region to return to some of their select traditions, there is a possibility of their customary laws lasting longer than one would expect, especially the ones that are linked with their identity. That the dominant discourse is in favor of statutory laws is clear when reference is often made about customary laws being discriminatory against women. In a situation where there is hardly any male perspective in this regard, it is difficult to say if the customary laws are always favorable to men in tribal societies. It is also possible that men are more successful in breaking or circumventing the customary laws than the women generally are. Where women have been successful in resisting and maneuvering customary laws, such as the Kabui women (Kamei 2011), the women have even been successful in turning the customary laws to their benefit. To quote Kamei's interesting finding,

> Kabui Naga society is clearly marked by gender inequality. The Kabui customary laws especially the inheritance laws are biased against women. Kabui women however do not remain as passive subordinates. They just do not sit back but try to resist, or manoeuvre the customary laws according to their own advantage
>
> (2011: 66)

The 2016 directive of the apex court of India itself is the result of the long legal fight that the Naga women organizations put up against the Naga customary laws, which were interpreted in such a manner that the Naga women were excluded from contesting the urban local bodies election.

References

Agarwal, Bina. 1994. *A Field of One's Own: Gender and Land Rights in South Asia*. Cambridge: Cambridge University Press.

Ao, Temsula. 2010. Benevolent Subordination: Social Status of Naga Women. In Preeti Gill (ed.). *The Peripheral Centre: Voices from India's Northeast*. New Delhi: Zubaan, 100–107.

Buongpui, Ruth L. 2013. Gender Relations and the Web of Traditions in Northeast India. *The NEHU Journal*, 11(2), 73–81.

Fernandes, Walter, Melville Pareira, and Vizalenu Khatso. 2008. *Tribal Customary Laws in North East India: Gender and Class Implications*. Guwahati: North Eastern Social Research Centre.

Gangopadhyay, Jagriti. 2017. Debunking Myth of Naga Customary Laws. *Down to Earth*, 24 March.

Gangte, Mercie. 2016. Gender and Customary Law: A Case Study of Mizo Tribe in North East India. *Indian Anthropologist*, 46(1),17–30.

Kamei, Roselima. 2014. Customary Law and Women in North East India. *International Research Journal of Social Sciences*, 3(9), 59–62.

Kamei, Shellunglu. 2011. Customary Inheritance Practices and Women among the Kabui Naga of Manipur. *Indian Anthropologist*, 41(1), 55–69.

Khan, Saqib. 2017. Customary laws vs. Gender equality in Nagaland. RAIOT, February 4.

Khutso, Riku. 2018. Shifting Democratic Experiences of Nagas. In Jelle J.P. Wouters and Thoto Tunyi (eds). *Democracy in Nagaland: Tribes, Traditions and Tensions*. Kohima: Highlander Books, 143–158.

Parwez, M. 2010–2011. Customary Law and Women's Empowerment: Case of Dimasa and Karbi of Assam. *Proceedings of the Indian History Congress*, 71, 1196–1207.

Parwez, M. 2012a. Customary Laws and Practices in North East India: Records and Reports Preserved in Law Research Institute, Gauhati. *Indian Journal of Applied Research*, 2(3), 81–83.

Parwez, M. 2012b Women on the Margin: Customary Laws and Practices of Ao Tribe. *Proceedings of the Indian History Congress*, 73, 1366–1375.

Sethi, Nitin. 2015. Documenting the Northeast's tribal laws. *Down to Earth*, 7th June.

Stephen, Poukho. 2021. Customary Law and Women's Status in North East India with reference to Poumai NagaTribe. *International Journal of Humanities and Social Science Invention*, 10(7), 34–38.

Wouters, J. P. 2017. Land Tax, Reservation for Women and Customary Law in Nagaland. *Economic & Political Weekly*, L11 (9), 20–23.

Zehol, Lucy. 2003. Status of Tribal Women. In T. B. Subba and Sujit Som (eds). *Anthropology of Northeast India: A Textbook*. New Delhi: Orient Longman, 293–306.

6 Power Relations in Matrilineal Khasi-Jaintia Society

Revisiting Traditional Political Institutions from Precolonial to Contemporary Times

Cecile A. Mawlong

Khasi-Jaintia matriliny is a subject of considerable interest to scholars and lay people alike, given the fact that it is one of the few societies in the world where this form of social organization continues to survive into contemporary times. Until fairly recently, it was generally assumed that because the Khasi-Jaintia follow a matrilineal form of social organization in which descent and inheritance are traced through the female line, women therefore occupy a dominant position in society. In fact, Khasi-Jaintia society is frequently, though incorrectly, described as "matriarchal" rather than "matrilineal" and captions such as "Indian tribe puts women in control" or "Meghalaya: The Land Where Women Call the Shots" suggest that the terms are often used synonymously with little awareness of the variation in meaning and implications.[1] In reality, among the Khasi-Jaintia, the lines of authority and descent do not converge. Thus while descent and inheritance pass through the female line, they seldom exercise authority in their kin groups, as is the case in matriarchal societies, of which there are very few examples worldwide. Nevertheless, matriliny, where descent and inheritance are determined in the female line, has an important bearing on gender and power relations in Khasi-Jaintia society.

It is interesting to note that the above "popular" perception that Khasi-Jaintia matriliny is biased in favor of women is also shared by a number of Khasi-Jaintia men who consider their womenfolk an "empowered" category because of their right to lineage and property. This has found expression in the founding of a Khasi Men's Rights Movement called the Syngkhong Rympei Thymmai, aimed at highlighting the gender-biased nature of the matrilineal system which, from their perspective, reduces men to mere "breeding bulls" and they have been advocating for a while now, for a reversal of the system.[2] On the other hand, this view has been increasingly challenged in academic and non-academic circles, on the grounds that while Khasi-Jaintia society is organized along matrilineal lines, it reveals patriarchal values.[3] This is based on the fact that women have traditionally been excluded from political participation and decision making in traditional political institutions which were and continue to be largely the preserve of men.

DOI: 10.4324/9781003539797-7

The significance of the matrilineal clan structure as an organizing principle in Khasi-Jaintia society is also expressed materially in their megalithic tradition which lays particular emphasis on monuments that underscore the solidarity of matrilineal ancestry and veneration of ancestors that lie at the core of Khasi-Jaintia beliefs and practices. While the Creator-God is frequently called upon in rituals, it is ancestral spirits that have a more immediate bearing on the lives of people. These ancestral spirits – *Ka Ïawbei* (root ancestress), *U Suidñ ia* (first maternal uncle), and *U Thawlang* (co-creator) – are frequently entreated on account of their status as progenitors of the lineage/clan. However, much greater reverence is accorded to *Ka Ïawbei* from whom sprang the family/lineage/clan, and she is invariably invoked in rituals especially those associated with death which lie at the core of the Khasi-Jaintia belief system. These rituals involving the internment of bones in the clan ossuary – the *Mawbah* – accentuates the importance of kinship bonds, as only the bones of kin-members can be interred together. So, in life and in death, the bonds of kinship are paramount superseding all others.[4]

In recent years, there has been a growing trend in non-Western societies that experienced colonialism, to re-examine aspects of traditional practice, especially gender relations, from an indigenous perspective. This is discernible in the significant increase in writings by African scholars,[5] especially women scholars, questioning the notion that precolonial African societies were inherently patriarchal in nature. These studies suggest that most African societies were once "matriarchal" but external forces such as Islam, Christianity, colonialism, and education were largely responsible for the emergence of patriarchal institutions. These conclusions were based on research comparing the societal nature and gender relation patterns in the societies under study from the precolonial to post-colonial times. Such reviews are necessary on account of the fact that frequently such conclusions are drawn on flawed or insufficient data or understanding of a society being studied. In the case of Khasi-Jaintia matriliny, it has been argued that Khasi-Jaintia women have no "real" power despite their matrilineal social organization, since they have little or no role in the public space. However, contrary to what colonial and post-colonial writings suggest, there is reason to believe that Khasi-Jaintia matriliny was at one time a much more gender-equal system.[6] As recorded in many parts of the world, increasing complexity in social relations associated with a rise in population and the gradual replacement of kin-ordered societies by increasingly centralized socio-political structures contributed in great measure to the gradual transformation in social and gender relations. While this factor undoubtedly also played a role in the gradual change in gender dynamics in Khasi-Jaintia society, there are other influential factors that have received little or no attention such as the interplay of colonialism, Christianity, and the rise of indigenous revivalist movements that contributed significantly in effecting a gradual shift from a complementary gender model toward a conflicting one.

This chapter is therefore an attempt to explore the historical experience of matriliny through a re-examination of colonial sources, writings by indigenous scholars, and folk tradition, to make inferences about gender roles and power relations in precolonial "traditional" Khasi-Jaintia society as well as highlighting elements of continuity and change from post-colonial to contemporary times.

I The Khasi-Jaintia Matrilineal System

According to Khasi thought, roots to the matrilineal system lies in the biological fact that children are born of the mother and therefore lineage and descent should be traced from the mother who then becomes the ancestress of a descent group. The closeness of the mother–child bond is reflected in the Khasi saying that children are born of their mother's flesh and blood (*na ka doh ka snam ka kmie*) and given form and stature by the father (*u ba ai rynïeng*). Once elevated to the position of ancestress, she then has the responsibility of ensuring the unity, solidarity, and continuity of the descent group. Thus, while the Khasi-Jaintia acknowledge the concept of the creative god that is neither male or female in gender and addressed by various names as well as guised as male or female as the situation warrants, it is the progenitors of the clan – more specifically, *Ka Ïawbei* (the first ancestress of a clan) and her brother *U Suidñia* (the first maternal uncle of a clan) – that have a more immediate bearing on the lives and fortunes of clan members. As mentioned earlier, great reverence is accorded to *Ka Ïawbei* which may be inferred from the centrality of her character and role in folk narratives of clans. All calamities or misfortunes that befall members are traced either to *Ka DawÏing or Ka DawLum*, that is, "internal" or "external" causes, respectively. The former is more significant and is related to non-adherence to customary law and practices.[7]

On the basis of the matrilineal principle, the clan or *kur*, is an exogamous unit. Marriage between members of the same *kur* is taboo or *sang* and strictly prohibited. The basis of the *kur* is the belief that its members have all descended from a common female ancestress, *Ka Ïawbei Tynrai* or the root ancestress. However, since members of this group cannot actually trace their genealogical connection, the concept serves as a unifying myth, binding its members on the principle of kinship ties. The mother–child bond is therefore the basis of a wide network of relationships, which links one with one's kinsmen and community, for wherever one travels one will find someone with whom one has clanship ties. As the link between one generation and another is provided by the blood that is transmitted through the mother, a Khasi-Jaintia therefore traces his/her descent through the mother. The mother–child bond not only determines clan membership, but also determines rights to political institutions of *Syiem* or *Daloi* (chieftainship) and property, since succession and inheritance are transmitted in the matrilineal line. Further the clan is also a ritual concept implying exogamy which is strictly followed by the Khasi-Jaintia.[8]

The second inner tier in Khasi-Jaintia society is the *kpoh*, literally the "belly" or womb. Members of a *kpoh* trace their descent from *Kaïawbe iTymmen* or the old grandmother. Members of this group more often than not can demonstrate their genealogical connection with one another. It is, however, the extended family or *ïing* whose members trace their descent from *KaIawbei Khynraw* or the young ancestress of three or four generational depth that is the most important and basic unit of Khasi society.

The *ïing* institution represents a functional and corporate group, revolving round the core comprising the owner of ancestral property in the person of the youngest daughter or *Ka Khadduh* (the Khasi-Jaintia follow the principle of ultimo geniture) and the person holding the position of authority, namely, her brother.[9] It may be noted that although sisters other than the *Khadduh* do not have direct claim to inheritance (except in cases where ancestral property is large enough, then older sisters may also receive a share at the time of marriage over which they have full proprietary rights), they still have a potential claim to ancestral property in the event that the *Khadduh* dies before coming into inheritance. The natal family or *ïingseng* (Khasi) or *yungseng* (Jaintia) is the center of all family rituals, imparting sanctity to the house of origin, thereby making it difficult, if not impossible, for the *Khadduh* to dispose it off without the consent of siblings including brothers and maternal uncles. Thus the *Khadduh* or heiress is primarily the custodian of ancestral property, with enormous responsibilities both sacred and secular. It is these responsibilities that entitle her to the ancestral property or, at the very least, the lion's share of such property.

Among the Khasi, the residential pattern of marriage to a *Khadduh* is strictly uxorilocal, while marriage with a non-heiress is generally neolocal. In the case of the Jaintia until the very recent past, men invariably practiced the duo-local pattern of residence irrespective of marriage to an heiress or non-heiress. There is reason to believe that in earlier times the Khasi (*Khynriam*) also followed the duo-local pattern of residence.[10] Thus as some scholars have pointed out, in a matrilineal society there was always a latent conflict between the bonds of marriage and bonds of descent.[11] This problem was resolved by consistently emphasizing on the bonds of descent. The megalithic tradition of the Khasi-Jaintia underscores these ideas and concepts that are the bedrock of society, in a more concrete way. Thus a man after death cannot find a resting place in the bone repository of his wife's family. After cremation, his ashes and bones must be returned or transferred to his natal home to be interred in his kin group's *Mawbah*, which ensures that the bonds of matrilineal ancestry are maintained intact.[12] That is why when a marriage is dissolved between two persons for whatever reason and one of them decides to re-marry, the person seeking dissolution of ties must first perform a ceremony marked by the setting up of a stone monument called *Mawklim*, literally stones of adultery, to mark the formal severing of ties between two kin groups to which a couple belongs. How far this was actually practiced is difficult to verify, since remnants of the megalithic tradition is now practiced only in a few places in the Jaintia Hills.

In traditional Khasi-Jaintia society, family life is organized around the mother's house (*ïengseng/yungseng*) which is headed by the grandmother who lives with her unmarried daughters and her youngest daughter (even if she is married), and her youngest daughter's children. In addition, her unmarried, divorced, or widowed brothers and sons reside in her house. The youngest daughter never leaves home and eventually becomes the head of the household.[13] Older married daughters usually live in separate households adjacent to the mother's household. Furthermore, a woman never joins her husband's household, rather he joins hers. On the apparent "laxity" of marriage among the Khasi, H. Yule[14] observed, "The husband does not take his bride to his home, but enters her household, or visits it occasionally; he seems merely to be entertained to continue the family to which his wife belongs." He further states,

> In consequence of this loose system, we find that generally there is little or no attachments between a grown-up son and his father, as probably the latter has long left his first family, and perhaps others in the interval; whilst the affection between mother and son is very strong, and all the child's attachment rests with his mother's kin. A Khasia if asked after his father, will often tell you that he is dead, meaning only that all connection between them has ceased.[15]

This is still evident among the Jaintia where some men practicing the traditional faith continue to observe the duo-local residence pattern, living in their wife's and mother's households.[16] In this context, the observation of anthropologist Chie Nakane[17] that even when a married man resides with his wife's family, he spends much if not most of his time in his mother's or sister's household is significant as it underscores the greater importance given to kinship bonds over matrimonial ties, a fact that is often overlooked, deliberately underplayed, or ignored in the writings of local scholars as we will demonstrate. Nakane's comment reiterates the views of David Roy,[18] who asserts that the "matriarchal" (sic) system of the Khasis have made men and women extremely independent of each other.

Thus, while the status of Khasi-Jaintia women in traditional society was relatively high owing to the matri-local residence pattern that offered a support system and investment in the human capacity of their daughters, many important decisions in society remain the domain of men. This may be inferred from a widely known phrase such as "War and politics for men and children and property for women."[19] Yet when it comes to ancestral property, the heiress (*Ka Khatduh*) is frequently described as merely the "custodian" of inherited property while the maternal uncle as the authority figure plays a key role in the management and distribution of ancestral property and lineage/clan holdings. Furthermore, it emphasizes the exclusion of women from access to and participation in decision-making bodies and holding of offices in the tribal political structure. According to sociologist Tiplut

Nongbri,[20] "Women do not participate in politics, civil defence or justice and priesthood is a male profession." Along similar lines, a distinct sex-based division of labor in Khasi-Jaintia society is articulated by Hipshon Roy Kharshïing[21] who states that

> In their social system the Khasis are matrilineal and they recognize the matrilineal descent but it should not be confused with a matriachaite society. The woman is the mistress of the household and the custodian of wealth and property but not the proprietress. The man is the master in war and peace. The maternal uncle is the undisputed director of the ancestral wealth and property where the father is the provider, the master and guide of his family. There were a clear division of function between household and the world outside. The woman is the receiver and the custodian and therefore must not stray into the field of politics. She is not to take part in the affairs of the state, her domain is the home.

The fact that men zealously protected their rights in the political arena from where real power emanates is also highlighted in another well-known saying that equates a woman who voices her opinion on public affairs as a "hen that crows," thereby effectively rendering it as something unnatural. But the question is how far is Kharshïing's statement consistent with the nature of Khasi-Jaintia matriliny? If anything, it appears to be a distortion of the structure and character of gender relations in Khasi-Jaintia society, when considered against our earlier discussion on Khasi-Jaintia matriliny. Take for instance his statement that the maternal uncle is the "undisputed" director of ancestral wealth and property, or the father as the "provider," "master," and "guide" of his family. None of these terms seem to fit the traditional or precolonial matrilineal society described by Yule, Nakane, or Roy, but seems to be more in keeping with changed or more recent perceptions as a result of contact with patrilineal societies from the valleys and/or the impact of colonialism which brought with it new ideas of family life and roles for women and men. While there is no disputing the significant role played by the maternal uncle in the context of traditional Khasi-Jaintia society, the almost dictatorial portrayal of the maternal uncle regarding the management of ancestral wealth and property is to suggest that the ancestress who heads the *ïing* institution had no role to play. It is also difficult to explain how she as head of the household could be ignored in matters relating to ancestral wealth and property, even if she is merely the "custodian" of the same. As far as the role of the father described as master, guide, and provider of the family, it is a misrepresentation of Khasi-Jaintia matriliny since these are attributes that rest with the maternal uncle who is the authority figure in his sister's home. In fact, in the Khasi-Jaintia matrilineal structure, the role of the father or spouse is essentially a supportive one, as a begetter of children, and he has no authority over his spouse or children. Further, he is often described as "*U Khun Ki Briew*" meaning "someone else's child" or, simply put, an "outsider" since he belongs to a different clan. Moreover, the idea of a strict division of public–private spaces is also problematic given the fact that Khasi-Jaintia women were very independent, self-reliant, and industrious, performing a wide variety of subsistence activities, including "providing" for their families (given the tenuous nature of the wife–husband bond), which often took them away from the confines of the domestic domain.[22] It must also be noted that while the ideas expressed in Kharshïing's statement are shared by other Khasi-Jaintia men, over time they appear to have been internalized by women as well.[23] It is against this backdrop that we will briefly describe the traditional polity and draw inferences from there on gender and power relations in traditional political institutions from the precolonial to contemporary times.

II Polity Formation

According to Khasi-Jaintia tradition, they first came to occupy the Khasi-Jaintia Hills, as groups of clans occupying and colonizing particular areas of land. Families belonging to the same clan (*kur*) lived together in clusters. Thus, the political community was clan based. The eldest male, from among the members of the founding clan/clans, combined in his person both secular and sacerdotal powers.[24] In his role as the mediator or spiritual authority between the community and the unseen powers, he was called *ULyngdoh*or *Saidnia*, while as the head of clan administration he was called *Basan*. As founding clans were gradually joined by other clans and as clans grew in size, families or even whole branches moved away to start new settlements in other parts of the hills. Over a period of time, clans amalgamated giving rise to the development of territorial entities called *raids* or communes. In due course, these *raids* too merged, paving the way for the emergence of chieftainships called *himas* under the rule of *Syiems* or chiefs. However, in some cases, *himas* emerged as direct confederacies of clans without going through the intermediate stage of forming raids.[25] But founding clans as dominant clans that were numerically preponderant in their settlements, representing as it were the earliest "traditional elite," continued to retain control of administration through their respective clan representatives.

In traditional Khasi-Jaintia society, right and access to political participation in traditional institutions was based on kinship, with the matrilineal clan as the basic institution around which the socio-political structure is built. Therefore the centrality of women in Khasi-Jaintia society cannot be disputed, as the matrilineal principle not only determines clan membership, but also determines rights to office, for example, *Basan*, *Lyngdoh*, *Syiem*, *Daloi*, and *Myntri*. Therefore, given the importance of kinship as the organizing principle and the matrilineal clan as the bedrock of Khasi-Jaintia society, therefore all institutions including political ones are rooted and determined by the matrilineal clan organization.

Studies on Khasi-Jaintia polity by indigenous scholars[26] rarely fail to mention the so-called democratic nature of traditional political institutions.

As stated by J. J. M. Nichols-Roy, one of the architects of the Sixth Schedule of the Indian Constitution, "The Khasis, in both the Khasi and Jaintia Hills, have been used to democratic institutions from time immemorial. There is nothing new to them in the system of adult franchise as their headmen and *sirdars* have all along been elected on the basis of adult franchise.[27]" Evidently, Nichols-Roy's statement highlights the primacy of male functionaries whether as "headmen" or "*sirdars*" in the traditional polity and women were clearly an excluded category. In fact, this is not the only limitation to Khasi-Jaintia democracy since access to political office was also not open to all adult males as the right to be elected as functionaries to political offices from the grass-roots upward (*shnong*/village, *raid*/commune, and *hima*/chieftainship often equated with a native state) is restricted to members of select clans such as founding clans who enjoy a higher ritual status than others. Therefore, the nature and degree of political participation in the traditional polity was circumscribed as it were by "tradition."

Nevertheless, while acknowledging that Khasi-Jaintia women were not "traditionally" dominant in the political sphere of action, we question the idea that they had no role or influence whatsoever in traditional polity. This may be inferred from the fact that according to tradition, society, religion, and politics are all clan based. In other words, men's participation and access to political offices is determined by their membership of a clan. As pointed out by Fabian Lyngdoh,[28] "men are to all intents and purposes the mouthpieces of their clan." Therefore if a kinship group or clan dies out (*ïap duh*) because of the absence of a female line, the male members of that clan forfeit their right to political participation in the traditional political bodies, as they no longer represent the views of a clan from which their political identity emanates. He further draws attention to the fact that the earliest political organization was the clan council or *dorbarkur*, in which "all" clan members, that is, men and women, could participate. It appears that only when it came to participation in political institutions that involved several clans, that is, at the level of higher political entities such as the *raids* and *himas*, that women were debarred from participation. However, their voices and interests were nevertheless represented by their matrilineal male relatives, who were bound to abide by the decisions taken at the clan council in which we emphasize both women and men participated. This suggests that power relations between men and women in Khasi-Jaintia society in precolonial times was one of interdependence, and clearly women were integral to decision making at least at the level of the Clan Council. Therefore misogynistic sayings that equate women who voice their opinion on public affairs as "hens that crow" need to be analyzed carefully as it could well be a later development.

The likelihood that a conscious and deliberate process of gradually eroding female influence in politics by articulating a strict separation of public and private spaces and of distinct male/female roles in society cannot be ruled out. This may be inferred from statements expressed in several works[29] by leading male figures particularly of the indigenous faith in the post-colonial period, despite evidence to the contrary which reveals Khasi-Jaintia women as a productive force in the precolonial and colonial society and economy.[30] Take, for instance, the assertion by R. T. Rymbaithat,

> [In] our matrilineal society, contrary to the mistaken idea of outsiders that women rule, we find man doubly honoured. In his sister's home he is *U Kni ha ka iap ka im* (an uncle in life and death) for he protects and defends the home. In his wife's house he is *U Kpaubalahbaiai* (a father able and steadfast) for he is God's instrument to increase the tribe of his wife. Indeed the Khasi-Pnars deprecate over lording women.[31]

These statements, especially the last line, is an example of male chauvinism which hinges on gender-role stereotypes that obscures the more complex complementarity of roles in traditional Khasi-Jaintia society and economy which repudiates a strict separation of public and private spaces. Rather, it is an attempt to subjugate and keep women under male control.

It may be pointed out that gender relations in Khasi-Jaintia society as portrayed in vernacular literature produced by leading figures of the Seng Khasi are challenged by folk traditions and ritual practices documented in many parts of the Khasi-Jaintia Hills. Take, for example, folk traditions from Ri-Bhoi (located in the northern slopes of the Khasi-Jaintia Hills) recorded by Kharmawphlang,[32] which highlight the key roles played by *KaÏawbei* and *USuidñia* in family and clan narratives. In these tales, *U Thawlang* as co-creator or "father" figure is never mentioned as he has no role to play in ritual practices that are associated with the matrilineage since he belongs to another clan. In fact, in most narratives that highlight the matrilineal principles, the father figure is conspicuously absent. This is in sharp contrast to the manner in which *U Thawlang* is depicted in accounts and descriptions that are dominant particularly in the Khasi uplands, wherein the role of the maternal uncle (*U Kñi)* is frequently overshadowed by that of the father (*U Thawlang*).[33] Furthermore, as discussed elsewhere,[34] the participation of women in ritual practices and, in some cases, even officiating at religious ceremonies is also not unknown. It is also significant that a good number of Jaintia and Bhoi folktales trace the origin of practices, knowledge systems, and institutions to women.

There are also several legends and folk tales that refer to women rulers and chiefs such as *Ka Syiem Ïaw Saring, Ka Syiem Ïapngar, Ka Syiem Latympang, Ka Lar Syiem, and Ka Lieh* that are strongly suggestive of the likelihood that in former times, women were not excluded from holding public office at least in some parts of the Khasi-Jaintia Hills. This view is also reiterated by historian Hamlet Bareh[35] who in a discussion on laws regarding succession of *Syiems* maintains that while they vary from "state to state" (referring to *himas*), in the absence of heirs from the male line, women were eligible, in which case the eldest sister of the deceased would become *Syiem*, failing which the eldest daughter would rank next followed by the eldest granddaughter of the sister of the *Syiem*. This was apparently the practice in the *himas* of Nongkhlaw, Mylliem, Nongspung, Langrin, Myriaw, and Malai-Sohmat. He also asserts that traditions clearly indicate that in many *himas*, both male and female *Syiems* were elected. Further, both male and female *Syiems* used to nominate their successors who were recognized as legitimate heirs. The important point to note here is that, contrary to the idea that women "never ever" had access to political institutions in the traditional polity, it appears that when the situation warranted, women did hold decision-making authority. In fact, according to one tradition,[36] a community referred to as Thaiang spread over seven villages located in the Bhoi region of the Khasi-Jaintia Hills was founded by a woman warrior *Kaïang Lyngdoh* or the black priestess whose descendants till date officiate as priests and preside over religious ceremonies. However, their responsibilities and commitment are reported to have diminished considerably on account of their conversion to the Christian faith.[37] Unfortunately, such folk narratives that highlight women as being active in warfare and providing leadership in sacred and secular matters are hardly known. Indeed, women in the role of leaders, warriors, or decision makers in former times are hardly ever considered or highlighted in discussions on gender dynamics and power relations in traditional Khasi-Jaintia society.

It is in this context that views that allude conclusively to the "total" exclusion of women from leadership or ritualistic roles in traditional Khasi-Jaintia society must be examined more carefully. Similarly, there are many instances where there is ambiguity in the description of women's role in the performance of religious ceremonies. Take, for instance, the *Behdeinkhlam* festival, celebrated annually in the month of July in Jaintia Hills. This festival is one of the most important religious events in the Jaintia calendar performed after sowing is done. According to Rymbai,[38] a leading member of the Seng Khasi, "Women do not take part in the public celebrations of this festival. Their role is to offer prayers at home...." However, elsewhere[39] he describes the same festival at length, there is frequent mention of a "priestess" or *Ka Langdoh* described as the "head" of the community religion, whom male celebrants must consult with on the outcome of various sacrifices performed in the course of the three day festival, to seek divine protection from disease and plague, as well as blessings for peace and prosperity. Therefore how can the head of a community religion in the person of the "priestess" or *Ka Langdoh* be without a significant public role? Similarly the ritual role of the *Syiem Sad*, the eldest female relative of the chiefs of *Hima Khyrimat* whose residence rituals associated with the Khasi religious festival of *Pomblang/Ka Shad Nongkrem* are performed and wherein the *Syiem Sad* assists the *Sohblei* or priest, is hardly ever highlighted rather more often trivialized.[40] Our argument is that ritual roles of a priestess or for that matter any ritual role cannot be without influence and if we keep in mind that Khasi-Jaintia religion is family and clan based with women as the keepers of family and clan religion, then it also follows that women in the person of the ancestress or head of the *ïing* institution, the locus of socio-religious practices, and as custodians of family/clan/community religion must have played meaningful and effective roles at least in former times.

The appearance of centralized polities in the form of chieftainship followed by a gradual process toward state formation (in the case of Jaintia Hills) appears to have contributed to the weakening of the clan structure and kinship relations which, in turn, led to the gradual marginalization of women from political participation. This process seems to have accelerated in colonial and post-colonial times as a result of the impact of patriarchal colonialism and Christianity and critically, the establishment of the Seng Khasi which contributed in various ways toward the subjugation of women through a re-interpretation of folk tradition.[41] This may be inferred from frequent references to "hens that crow" that serve to underscore the uncharacteristic and absurd notion of women's involvement in politics, aimed at safeguarding men's rights by marginalizing and excluding women from the political process of where "real" power resides. That these ideas gained legitimacy is indicated by the portrayal of women in various kinds of literature of the twentieth century in an increasingly submissive and dependent role.[42]

In contemporary society, the clan has lost its true institutional character and has been largely replaced by the nuclear family as the basic unit of society. This change has had far-reaching impact in all spheres of social life. To begin with, the maternal uncle's role is by and large nominal with his position now replaced by the father as the head of the nuclear family, especially in urban Christian households. This is not surprising since Christianity is a patriarchal system that encouraged husbands and fathers to take a more active role in their children's upbringing as well as the running of their homes as opposed to traditional households. While these changes did improve the quality and stability of family life, it also fostered an increase in nuclear families as opposed to extended families. This in turn has led to changes in the structure of the household or *ïing* institution, with husbands/fathers becoming heads of households replacing the maternal uncle as authority figures.[43] Given these sweeping changes, the clan council has also become defunct with no substantive political role. The village council or *dorbarshnong* has replaced it at the grassroots level. Therefore, adult males who participate in these councils do so, not as representatives of their clan, but primarily in a personal capacity, representing their own interests and that of their nuclear families. Similarly the role of women in producing heirs necessary to maintain perpetual succession to the office of clan representatives is no longer necessary and, to that extent, has lost their truly traditional character and therefore should be open to all, irrespective of gender. However, surprisingly, women continue to be largely excluded from access to political offices in these tribal councils or *dorbars*, in the name of traditional practice, which is undemocratic and discriminatory. It may be noted that while a handful of women in a few localities in the state capital of Shillong hold executive positions, they are the exception rather than the rule. Furthermore, the top posts including that of headman continue to be the exclusive preserve of men.

III Traditional Political Institutions

Works[44] on traditional institutions of governance in Khasi-Jaintia Hills invariably highlight that they pivot around the institution of the *Dorbar* or tribal council associated with the three-tier levels of administration – the village council or *Dorbar Shnong* under the leadership of the headman or *Rangbahshnong*; the *Dorbar Raid* headed by the *Sirdar*, and the *Dorbar Hima* headed by the *Syiem, Daloi, Whahadadar*, or *Lyngdoh*, depending on the type or nature of the chieftainship under study. Such *durbars* are usually held in the open and its members sit in concentric circles.[45] The composition of the *Dorbar Hima* differs from one *hima* to another. However, in the case of the *Dorbar Shnong* as a grassroots institution, all adult males are members of the *dorbar*. The conduct of the proceedings of *durbars* at all levels of administration is strictly as per customary laws which must be adhered to. All decisions are taken by consensus either by the counting of heads or by the raising of hands. The Khasi-Jaintia consider the workings of the *durbars* as sacred and serious affairs in which ancestral spirits are also invoked necessitating that discipline is maintained throughout its proceedings. No disparaging remarks and scandalous or defamatory expressions are allowed.[46] There is no greater transgression than to treat the proceedings of the *dorbar* with contempt which is punishable by debarment from future attendance or even loss of citizenship and ostracization from society.

As pointed out in the preceding sections, Khasi-Jaintia society and polity is clan based, meaning that the basic and earliest political institution is the *Dorbar Kur* or Clan Council. Yet, hardly any work ever discusses the *Dorbar Kur* or Clan Council and its role headed by the senior-most maternal uncle or *Basan* (as he is also referred to), as the chief political representative of the clan. In the Clan Council, all male and female members can participate as it concerns the interests of all clan affiliates. Indeed as asserted by Fabian Lyngdoh,[47] "a clan council in which no female clan member is present, would be invalid." Lyngdoh[48] further asserts that while it is frequently stated that only male adults are permitted to partake in a Khasi *dorbar*, the actual position was that "only male adults who represent the clan, and on behalf of the womenfolk are entitled to participate in the *dorbar*." Therefore, according to tradition, men that attended the *durbars* had no right to express their personal opinions other than to support the arguments of their respective *Basans* which is in line with resolutions adopted at the Clan Council expressing the views and interests of all clan members.[49] The fact is the Clan Council as an institution and particularly as a political body is now defunct and has lost its true institutional character and has been replaced by the Village Council or *Dorbar Shnong* at the grassroots level. Therefore, how can traditional institutions of contemporary times maintain that they are genuinely representative of traditional practices? As highlighted earlier, adult males who attend the *Dorbar Shnong* do so in their own capacity and to represent their own interests and that of their nuclear families and not that of the clan. Consequently, if they have changed character and are no longer strictly traditional, then on what grounds can the continued exclusion of women from access to key positions including that of headperson, if they are capable, be justified by invoking tradition? Perhaps more pertinent to the present discussion is a vital point raised by Fabian Lyngdoh in a thought-provoking article[50] that links the Clan Council as a political body with land holding in a community. Therefore only men representing clans that were permanent resident landholders could participate in *dorbors* associated with the three tiers of administration discussed earlier. He further argues that "in rural areas, it is women who have more title to ownership of land and other forms of property than men." In fact, in most Khasi villages, fathers are referred to as "*Ki shongkha*" loosely translated to mean "incoming husbands" who generally hail from other villages since in a matrilineal system, it is the husbands that join their wives' home and village and not the other way around. Consequently, it is the women folk who are the permanent residents and in many cases landowners as well, which entitle them with greater rights to be involved in village administration. This is perhaps the reason why there is so much emphasis on describing Khasi-Jaintia women as "custodians" rather than owners of land, given that land is the source of power and influence and therefore "managed" by the brother of the "custodian" in the capacity of the *Kñi* or maternal uncle.

Our readings suggest that the establishment of the revivalist organization, the Seng Khasi in 1899, has played a critical role in the subordination of women. As moral "guardians" and "preservers" of Khasi-Jaintia culture and tradition, the vernacular literature spawned by the Seng Khasi expresses a strongly androcentric perspective articulated in their writings on religion, customary law, folktales, proverbs, etc. The late nineteenth and early twentieth centuries mark an important watershed in Khasi-Jaintia history marked by a growing trend toward the consolidation of folk tradition and the shaping of a composite "Khasi identity."[51] This factor played an important role in promoting the growth and spread of vernacular literature with the Seng Khasi spearheading the movement.[52] In the process, diverse folk traditions and ritual practices were gradually subordinated by dominant traditions underscoring homogeneity and increasing gender bias. As discussed elsewhere,[53] the authors were invariably men and therefore represent a "male perspective," which was in no small measure a counter to the challenge of colonialism and Christianity seen as responsible for the erosion of Khasi-Jaintia culture and traditional values. Undoubtedly the matrilineal system of Khasi-Jaintia society must have been viewed as peculiar and unnatural to the colonial masters and its impact on the psyche of the burgeoning Khasi-Jaintia male intelligentsia may have been a source of embarrassment, needing a corrective. Furthermore, the exposure of the founding members of the Seng Khasi (who were by and large educated in the southern foothills at Shella and Sylhet) to the language, culture, and patriarchal norms of the plains people could not have left them unaffected. Therefore, it is reasonable to surmise that the influence of patriarchal notions may have been a critical factor resulting in the conscious construction or re-shaping of folk tradition that may be inferred from the increasing importance given to the role of father/husband encapsulated in the term *U Thawlang*. Not surprisingly, *U Thawlang* gradually becomes the locus of authority, replacing the role of the maternal uncle or *U Kñi*, as the "protector" and "defender" of the family or *ïing* as discussed in earlier sections. Therefore, the portrayal of the father as "provider" and "master" of the family or *ïing* institution is, in our opinion, historical at least in the context of "traditional" Khasi-Jaintia society.[54] These arguments are based not only on a critique of the sources but also on the fact that the structure of matrilineal societies are not based on subordination, but rather on cooperation and complementarity of gender roles. The views of the Seng Khasi were very influential, becoming the dominant or determining narrative, and their impact continues to inform the understanding and experience of Khasi-Jaintia matriliny in contemporary times.

Thus in Khasi-Jaintia society, as in most societies worldwide, the universal dichotomization of masculine/aggressive versus female/passive that associates men's role in warfare to leadership roles in society is used to enforce and legitimize their domination in public life, since it is postulated that males, not females, usually engage in fighting, as warfare like hunting requires strength and quick bursts of energy and therefore is generally male dominated. It is also generally argued that combat situations are incompatible with childrearing or that women's fertility is more important to a population's reproduction and survival than their usefulness as warriors. Further, men's control of weapons, particularly iron, an important resource, may have further augmented their role in public life. These essentialist assertions are discernible in the writings of the Seng Khasi serving to enforce gender roles in society.

Today, while traditional institutions continue to co-exist alongside their modern counterparts, they have lost much of their independence, control, and, to some extent, status, to hybrid institutions such as the Autonomous District Councils (henceforth ADCs). Created under the provisions of the Sixth Schedule of the Indian Constitution, ADCs were conceived as instruments of institutional accommodation in post-colonial India, intended to preserve the distinct cultural and ethnic identity of indigenous communities in some areas of India's northeast. Meant as facilitators between the traditional or modern state apparatus and traditional institutions, ADCs are increasingly perceived as having largely failed to function as instruments of effective governance and democratization at the grassroots level. There are a number of studies[55] that have highlighted the tension that exists between the traditional institutions, non-traditional institutions, and the ADCs. Some of these problems include overlapping jurisdiction, power struggles, mutual trust, and competing interests.

For the purpose of this article, the relationship between the Khasi and Jaintia Autonomous District Councils (henceforth KHADC and JHADC) and the traditional institutions is of greater interest as it underscores the symbiotic relationship shared by the two and also reveals how the former is above all concerned with safeguarding the interests of the latter. Inaugurated in 1952, the United Khasi and Jaintia Autonomous District Council was bifurcated in 1964 into separate Khasi and Jaintia Autonomous District Councils.[56] Of the constitutional powers entrusted to the ADCs, their powers of appointment of chiefs and headmen, inheritance, marriage, and social customs are of particular interest, as they have an important bearing on gender and power relations in contemporary Khasi-Jaintia society. One of most important bills passed by the Khasi Hills Autonomous District Council is the Khasi Social Custom of lineage Act, 1997. This piece of legislation was an attempt to codify and preserve the community's traditional social and customary practices. However, members of the Syngkhong Rympei Thymmai opposed it, objecting in particular the provisions of the Lineage Bill that debars sons in the absence of daughters from inheriting family property, by providing for an age-old custom of adopting a daughter termed "*rap-ïing*" from within the family lineage or clan (*kpoh/kur*), as the custodian of ancestral property. Further, the bill also stressed on strict compliance with the system of descent of tracing one's name in accordance with the matrilineal principle. This too did not go down well with members of the Syngkhong Rympei Thymmai who are in favor of patriliny and the option for offspring to adopt their father's name. The influential Khasi Students Union also lent support to the position of the Syngkhong Rympei Thymmai by opposing the codifying of what they termed as an "outdated system" advocating for the "modernizing" of their kinship system and further proposed that only children who separately are Khasi should be regarded as Khasi.[57]

Subsequently, in 2018, under the chairmanship of (L) H. S. Shylla, the KHADC passed the controversial Khasi Lineage Amendment Bill which sought to strip a Khasi woman of her Scheduled Tribe status and other associated privileges, if she marries a non-Khasi man. Offspring of such a union would also be considered non-Khasi and ineligible to land and other rights. Justification for the bill was made on the claim that allowing Khasi women to marry men of their choice has led to the abuse and misuse of privileges afforded by their scheduled tribe status by unscrupulous non-tribal men. The bill was opposed by many women's organizations who described it as "unconstitutional" and have questioned why women are targeted as the exclusive cause of all ills and misfortunes that have befallen the community. Ironically, acts by men folk, specifically in their role as headmen, *Syiems*, or other official capacities, within the traditional political structure which have been detrimental to the well-being of community, have not attracted the same kind of condemnation and action from the ADCs given that one of their mandates is regulation of the affairs of the traditional institutions.[58] Women who have publicly criticized the bill have been branded "elitist" and "international," divorced from their own cultural moorings. Legal experts too have opined that the bill went against the fundamental rights of women to choose their life partner. The bill was, however, returned to the KHADC by the then governor and appears to have been shelved for the time being at any rate. More recently, the Chairperson of the KHADC has tabled the Khasi Inheritance of Property Bill 2021, aimed at "equitable distribution" of parental property among siblings in the Khasi community. According to a newspaper report,[59] the bill has now been referred to a select committee, to examine and submit "their considered views and suggestions." The Chief Executive Member of the KHADC, Totosstarwell Chyne, is quoted to have said, "I would not like to rush to pass the bill at this junctures in since it is a very important bill which relates to the customary practices of the Khasi people."[60] He further stated that the select committee would seek the views of all stakeholders and social organizations concerned with customary practices.[61] If implemented, this bill would modify the age-old practice of inheritance.

Another bill passed by the KHADC that has come under the scanner is the Village Administration Bill, 2014. The bill was the outcome of the Central Government's efforts to amend the Sixth Schedule with the objective of making the ADCs more efficient as instruments of democratic decentralization. The Draft Meghalaya Village Council Act 2011 was framed more or less in line with the Panchayati Raj institutions, but the district councils of Meghalaya opposed it as they felt that it contravenes the provisions of the Sixth Schedule meant to protect customary laws and tradition. So the KHADC countered by bringing out its own Village Administration Bill purportedly to usher in an efficient system of administration within the framework of the existing system of traditional governance and adjudication. However, both the original document and the amended one have come in for several criticisms from various quarters and one organization in particular has described the bill as a "shoddy piece of legislation that betrays the call of the people to democratize the *Dorbar Shnong* and the *Rangbah Shnong*" and that "it fails to respect and protect traditional village level autonomy and processes and to help them transform into legally consistent institutions to meet modern day demands for transparency, accountability, inclusiveness and participation."[62]

It may be noted that there's ambiguity in the language of the bill itself which uses gender-neutral terms in some places and biased ones at others. Take, for instance, the use of the term "Traditional Head" for the office of *Rangbah Shnong*or Village Headman or the provision that the *Dorbar Shnong*or Village Council will include "all" Khasi inhabitants of eighteen years and above and that the *Rangbah Shnong* should be a "person" above twenty-five years of age and a resident of the village for at least ten years. The terms used imply a breakaway from tradition by making the institution open to all, irrespective of gender. Yet in the same document, there are also references to *Rangbah Shnong* and "his" *dorbar* unfortunately suggesting otherwise. In any case, the bill has sparked off a lively debate for a re-examination of the traditional system of governance especially at the grassroots level, to effect changes for the empowerment of women by offering them equal opportunity to participate and to hold office in village councils making them truly democratic institutions.[63] In this sense, the Panchayati Raj system has done much more to empower women at the grassroots level by providing at least thirty-three percent (in some states even as high as fifty percent) reservation for women, offering them an opportunity and platform to air their views and hone in leadership skills in decision making. By contrast, traditional institutions in the Khasi-Jaintia Hills have done little, if anything, to democratize or make governance at the grassroots level more inclusive and participatory in nature.

Thus despite the fact that the Khasis are a matrilineal society seemingly oriented around women by way of marital residence pattern, their kinship system, and the fact that they have contributed significantly, if not more, to the society's economy in the past and present, they continue to be largely left out of the decision-making process as indicated by their miniscule numbers in key political institutions. There are but a handful of women legislators: a few members in the KHADC with only one woman heading it for a brief period in 2014 and a lone woman member in the JHADC despite the latter's existence since 1964. As discussed in the preceding sections, attempts are being made by the KHADC to bring about changes in the traditional system of inheritance by allowing both female and male children to inherit family property. But there appears to be much greater resistance from men folk, especially those holding offices in traditional institutions as well as the district councils, to accept or welcome changes in the traditional system of governance.[64] However, it is heartening to see that there are a rising number of both male and female voices[65] not only questioning the role and effectiveness of traditional institutions and the district councils but also asserting the pressing need to empower women by giving them access to traditional political institutions and decision making which has been denied to them through a discriminatory invocation of tradition. In fact according to a fairly recent newspaper report,[66] the women of Nohwet village located in Meghalaya's East Khasi Hills District approached the High Court of Meghalaya when they were denied the right to vote and elect their Headman and the High Court subsequently ruled in their favor. Unfortunately, the judgment which was hailed by women of the state as a positive step in the right direction has not prevented the continued denial of voting rights for women in other similar cases under the pretext of upholding customary law. The KHADC on its part has done little to resolve such issues in line with democratic principles as mandated by the Sixth Schedule of the Indian Constitution. Rather, it continues to safeguard traditional institutions and practice regardless of how regressive they may be, as it is linked to their continued survival. It is to be hoped that the voices calling for gender equality and greater accountability in governance gain momentum, encouraging traditional institutions and the district councils to introspect and adapt, to vindicate their relevance in contemporary society.

Notes

1 See for instance P.R. T. Gurdon, *The Khasis*, Low Price Publications, Delhi, 1990(rep), p. 76, where he talks of the prevalence of the matriachate amongst the Khasi. A similar view is expressed by D. Roy in "Principles of Khasi Culture" in *Folklore*, xlvii, 1936, pp. 381–382.

2 The *Syngkhong Rympei Thymmai* (Home-Hearth Restructured) is a Khasi Men's Rights Movement founded in Shillong on April 14, 1990. One of its leading founding men K. Pariat is in favor of reversing the matrilineal system which, in his opinion, treats Khasi men as mere "breeding bulls.".

3 For instance see A.K. Baruah & M. Sharma, "Matriliny, Land Rights and Political Power in Khasi Society," in *Indian Journal of Human Rights*, Vol. 3, No-1 & 2, Jan–Dec 1999, pp. 210–228.

4 See C.A. Mawlong, "Megaliths and Social Formation in Khasi-Jaintia Hills", in M. Momin and Cecile A. Mawlong (eds.) *Society and Economy in North-East India*, Vol. 1, Regency Publications, New Delhi, 2004, pp. 35–56; see also H.H. Mohrmen, "The Stories of the Iawbei," in *The Shillong Times*, May20, 2013.

5 Refer to Niara Sudarkasa, "The Status of Women in Indigenous African Societies" in *Feminist Studies*, Vol. 12, No. 1. Feminist Studies Inc., 1986, pp. 91–103; Sefinatu A. Dogo, "The Nigerian Patriarchy: When and How", in *Cultural and Religious Studies*, Vol. 2, No. 5, Sep–Oct 2014, pp. 263–275.

6 These issues are discussed in some detail in Cecile A. Mawlong, *Interrogating the Past: Reading Gender & the Megalithic Tradition in Khasi-Jaintia Society*, DVS Publishers, Guwahati and Delhi, 2022, 978-93-85839-46-7.

7 H.O. Mawrie, *The Khasi Milieu*, Concept Publishing Company, New Delhi, 1981, pp. 36–37.

8 See Chie Nakane, *Garo and Khasi: A Comparative Study in Matrilineal Systems*, Paris, 1967, p. 106.

9 See Chie Nakane, *Garo and Khasi: A Comparative Study in Matrilineal Systems*, Paris, 1967, p.120.

10 See Chie Nakane, *Garo and Khasi: A Comparative Study in Matrilineal Systems*, Paris, 1967, p.125.

11 See Lt. Yule, "Notes on the Kasia Hills and People", in *Journal of the Asiatic Society of Bengal*, No. 152, 1844, p. 624; see also Chie Nakane, *Garo and Khasi: A Comparative Study in Matrilineal Systems*, Paris, 1967, p. 125, where she summarizes the role of the Khasi man in his wife's house; N.C. Shadap-Sen, *The Origin and early History of the Khasi-Synteng People*, Firma KLM Private Limited, Calcutta, 1981, p. 190.

12 Refer to Cecile A Mawlong, *Interrogating the Past: Reading Gender & the Megalithic Tradition in Khasi-Jaintia Society*, DVS Publishers, Guwahati and Delhi, 2022, 978-93-85839-46-7, pp. 117–136.

13 See especially H. Lyngdoh, *Ka Pomblang Nongkrem Bad Ka Thang Syiem Sohra*, Ri Khasi Press, Shillong, 1990 (3rd ed.) pp. 11–20; see also Soumen Sen, *Khasi-Jaintia Folklore*, National Folklore Support Centre, Chennai, 2004, p. 78; P.N. Dutta, *Impact of the West on the Khasis and Jaintias*, Cosmo Publications, New Delhi, 1982, pp. 5–6; D. Roy, "Principles of Khasi Culture", pp. 375–393.

14 See Lt. Yule, "Notes on the Kasia Hills and People", in *Journal of the Asiatic Society of Bengal*, No. 152, 1844, p. 624.

15 See Lt. Yule, "Notes on the Kasia Hills and People", in *Journal of the Asiatic Society of Bengal*, No. 152, 1844, p. 625; see also P.R.T. Gurdon, *The Khasis* (1st edition 1907, London; Reprint, Delhi 1990), pp. 82–83; Chie Nakane, *Garo and Khasi: A Comparative Study in Matrilineal Systems*, p. 125 wherein she summarizes the role of the Khasi man, in his wife's home.

16 See H. H. Mohrmen's, illuminating article "Thiah Chloor or the Night Visit System in Jaintia Hills," in *The Shillong Times*, dated February 21, 2022, p. 6.

17 Chie Nakane, *Garo and Khasi: A Comparative Study in Matrilineal Systems*, p. 126.

18 See David Roy, "Principles of Khasi Culture", pp. 381–382.

19 Most Khasi are familiar with this phrase which encapsulates the nature of Khasi matriliny, wherein the lines of authority and inheritance do not converge.

20 T. Nongbri, *Development, Ethnicity and Gender* (New Delhi, 2003), p. 187.
21 See H. Kharshiing, "The Khasis" in H. Kharshiing (ed.), *Where Lies the Soul of Our Race*, Seng Khasi Series No. 2 (Shillong, 1982), pp. 3–4.
22 Refer to Cecile A. Mawlong, *Interrogating the Past: Reading Gender & the Megalithic Tradition in Khasi-Jaintia Society*, pp. 61–113.
23 Kharshiing's views that emphasizes the strict separation of the public from the private space and the home as women's domain are also echoed in the writings of R.T. Rymbai, "Ki Dorbar Shnong", in *Lyngkhuh Snem BaShiphew*: 1982–1992, Seng Khasi Mawlai, Shillong; p. 51; see esp. K. Singh, "Khasi-Jaintia Religion", in *Seminar on the History of Meghalaya, SCERT*, (Shillong, 1979), pp. 27–28, wherein he expresses strongly androcentric views that not only reiterates the above dichotomy of public and private spaces, but describes feminine qualities that reflect strongly patriarchal values in the following words; "God has created woman to procreate and to multiply"; "Virtue and purity are her essential attributes"; "No religious ceremonies are performed in marriage if a woman is no longer a virgin"; or "She is the one who must prepare and make ready all the articles necessary in the performance of all religious rites. But being a woman she cannot perform the rites herself." That women had internalized these ideas is indicated in the words of Sitimon Sawain who when addressing the Sein Raij, Shillong, on 26.6.66, stated that she was not used to public speaking, since in the Khasi-Pnar system, women did not speak in a *dorbar* or public platform. But she could not refuse the request made by leaders (men). She went on to justify the exclusion of women from public speaking on the grounds that they are supposed to be short-sighted or lack vision, etc., expressed in *Lyngkhuh Snem Ba Shiphew*: 1982–1992, Seng Khasi Mawlai, Shillong; p. 44. See also Dakamon Mawroh, *Representation of Women in Khasi Literature* (Shillong, 2008), esp. pp. 1–3, which brings out quite clearly how deeply patriarchal values had been internalized by Khasi women.
24 L.S. Gassah, "Traditional Khasi Polity," in *Lest We Forget*, Seven Huts Enterprise, Shillong, 1994, 81-86467-00-9, pp. 11–15. See also relevant chapters in Surajit Sinha (ed.), *Tribal Polities and State Systems in Pre-Colonial Eastern and North Eastern India*, K.P. Bagchi & Co., Calcutta, 1987.
25 Soumen Sen, *Social and State Formation in Khasi-Jaintia Hills*, B.R. Publishing House, Delhi, 1985, pp. 136–138.
26 See Hamlet Bareh, *The History and Culture of the Khasi People*, Calcutta, 1967, pp. 275–277; H.O. Mawrie, *The Khasi Milieu*, Concept Publishing Company, New Delhi, 1981, pp. 90–101; N.C. Shadap Sen, *The Origin and Early History of the Khasi-Synteng People*, Calcutta, 1981, p. 186; R.S. Lyngdoh, *Government and Politics in Meghalaya*, Sanchar Publishing House, New Delhi, 1996, p. 78; Helen Giri, *The Khasis Under British Rule* (1824–1947), Regency Publications, New Delhi, 1998, 81-86030-67-0, pp. 11–12.
27 Quoted in D. R. Syiemlieh, *British Administration in Meghalaya: Policy and Pattern*, Heritage Publishers, New Delhi, 1989, p. 215.
28 Fabian Lyngdoh, "When the Hen Crows" in *The Shillong Times*, September 3, 2014 and "Women and Dorbarin Khasi Society Today", in *The Shillong Times*, last updated on November 13, 2021.
29 Refer to *supra*, 23n.
30 For references, see *supra*, 21n, pp. 61–96.
31 See R.T. Rymbai, "Some Aspects of the Religion of the Khasi-Pnars", in *Khasi Heritage*, Seng Khasi Mawlai, Shillong, p. 113.
32 See D.L. Kharmawphlang, *Essays in Khasi Folkloristics*, RiKhasi Book Agency, Shillong, 2016, pp. 59–78.
33 *Supra*, 21n, pp. 104–106.

34 *Supra*, 21n, pp. 97–116.
35 Refer to Hamlet Bareh, *The History and Culture of the Khasi People*, pp. 251–254. Bareh, however, maintains that succession to the *Syiem's* office by a woman was rare in the past and that the practice is now abandoned.
36 D.L. Kharmawphlang, in *Essays in Khasi Folkloristics*, p.81; See also Fr. Sngi Lyngdoh, "Social Festivals in the Ancient Thaiang State", in K.R. Marak and R. Wankhar (eds.) *Festivals and Ceremonies in Meghalaya*, Historical and Antiquarian Studies, Dept. of Arts and Culture, Govt. of Meghalaya, Shillong, 1994, pp. 107–119.
37 D.L. Kharmawphlang, in *Essays in Khasi Folkloristics*, p.81.
38 See R.T. Rymbai, "The Festivals of a Khasi and Their Influence on His Life", in U Hipshon Roy (ed.) *Khasi Heritage*, RiKhasi Press, Shillong, 1979, pp. 140–141.
39 *Idem*, "Some Aspects of the Religion of the Khasi-Pnars", in U. Hipshon Roy (ed.) *Khasi Heritage*, RiKhasi Press, Shillong, 1979, p. 113.
40 See for instance Kynpham Singh's "Khasi-Jaintia Religion" in *Seminar on the History of Meghalaya, SCERT*, Shillong, 1979, pp. 27–28, wherein he underscores the subsidiary role women play in the performance of religious rites and ceremonies stating that, "She is the one who must prepare and make ready all the articles necessary in the performance of ALL (emphasis mine) religious rites. But being a woman she cannot perform the rites herself." Yet as we have tried to demonstrate in the text, female roles in religious rites are not insignificant and conceivably downplayed and undervalued.
41 Refer to relevant chapters in Cecile A. Mawlong, *Interrogating the Past: Reading Gender & the Megalithic Tradition in Khasi-Jaintia Society*, DVS Publishers, Guwahati, 2022, 978-93-85839-46-7.
42 Refer to *supra* 23n.
43 See Cecile A. Mawlong, *Interrogating the Past: Reading Gender & the Megalithic Tradition in Khasi-Jaintia Society*, pp. 45–60.
44 For details see Hamlet Bareh, *The History and Culture of the Khasi People*, pp. 273–277; L.S. Gassah, "Traditional Khasi Polity," in *Lest We Forget*, Seven Huts Enterprise, Shillong, 1994, 81-86467-00-9, pp.14–15; Soumen Sen, *Social and State Formation in Khasi-Jaintia Hills*, B.R. Publishing House, Delhi, 1985, pp. 132–152.
45 Hamlet Bareh, *The History and Culture of the Khasi People*, p. 274.
46 *Supra* 41n.
47 See *supra* 27n.
48 *supra* 27n; See also Fabian Lyngdoh's interesting article on important concepts that underlay traditional political institutions in Khasi Hills titled "Some interpretations on Ka Sad-Ka Sunon", in *The Shillong Times*, November 12, 2014.
49 *supra* 27n.
50 See *idem* "Women and Dorbarin Khasi Society Today", in *The Shillong Times*, last updated on November 13, 2021.
51 Refer to Cecile A. Mawlong, *Interrogating the Past: Reading Gender & the Megalithic Tradition in Khasi-Jaintia Society*, pp. 1–19.
52 Refer to Cecile A. Mawlong, *Interrogating the Past: Reading Gender & the Megalithic Tradition in Khasi-Jaintia Society*, pp. 10–16; see also Kynpham Singh, "Seng Khasi", in *Where Lies The Soul Of Our Race* (Seng Khasi Series No. 2, Shillong, 1982), p. 7.
53 Cecile A. Mawlong, *Interrogating the Past: Reading Gender & the Megalithic Tradition in Khasi-Jaintia Society*, pp. 97–116.
54 Cecile A. Mawlong, *Interrogating the Past: Reading Gender & the Megalithic Tradition in Khasi-Jaintia Society.*
55 See A.K. Nongkynrih, *Autonomous District Councils: The Case of Khasi Hills, Meghalaya*, Department of Sociology, NEHU, Shillong, 2020; see also, relevant

chapters in H. Srikanth and Rooplekha Borgohain (eds.)*Ethnicity and Political Economy in Northeast India*, DVS Publishers, Guwahati, 2016, 978-81-86307-91-5. There are also a number of write-ups and letters to the editor, *Shillong Times*, that highlight these issues. For instance, refer to H.H. Mohrmen's article "Future of the Traditional Institutions in Khasi Jaintia Hills," in *The Shillong Times*, January 19, 2015; Fabian Lyngdoh, "The Knotty Issue of the Rangbah Dong," in *The Shillong Times*, May 13, 2015; Albert Thyniang, "Critiquing the Institution of the Dorbar Shnong," in The Shillong Times, September 16, 2020; Toki Blah, "Meghalaya Grassroots Governing Institutions," September 29, 2020; M.M. Mohrmen, "MDA Govt Demolishing the Foundation of Matrilineal Social System," in *The Shillong Times*, January 11, 2021; Fabian Lyngdoh, "Understanding Paragraph 12A of the Sixth Schedule," in *The Shillong Times*, September 16, 2021; Toki Blah, "Meghalaya's Traditional Grassroot Institutions: Who Owns Them?" in *The Shillong Times*, November 22, 2021.

56 For details see A.K. Nongkynrih, *Autonomous District Councils: The Case of Khasi Hills*.

57 See N.K. Das, "Indigenous Feminism and Women Resistance: Customary Law, Codification Issue and Legal Pluralism in North East India" in *Journal of Cultural and Social Anthropology*, Vol. 1, Issue 2, 2019, 2642-8236, p. 23.

58 One only has to go through the editorial page of *The Shillong Times* dating back from 2014 to the present to get a sense of the increasing frustration felt by people at large. See for instance *supra* 54n and letters to the editor, *The Shillong Times*, by Dominic S. Sahkhar, "Laughing Stock of the Country," January 19, 2015; Timmy Lyngdoh, "Why Defend Corrupt Rangbah Shnong?", dated January 29, 2015; Toki Blah, "Is Ravaging the Forests a Khasi Tradition?", November 22, 2021.

59 Refer to *The Shillong Times* November 9 and 11, 2021.

60 Refer to *The Shillong Times*.

61 Refer to *The Shillong Times*.

62 See critique by Thma U RangliJuki (TUR) or Progressive People's Collective in https://raiot.in/village-administration-bill-its-amendments-and-ramifications/ August 28, 2015, accessed on 11/8/21.

63 Refer *infra* 65n.

64 See for instance the views of Ainam Manik Syiem acting Syiem of Mylliem in *The Shillong Times*, October 25, 2021.

65 See *The Shillong Times*, October 25, 2021, p. 4; Patricia Mukhim, "Women's Day: Has Anything Changed?" in *The Shillong Times*, March 7, 2014; Fabian Lyngdoh, "When the Hen Crows," in *The Shillong Times*, September 3, 2014; Karen Wahlang, "Silly Turf Wars" in *The Shillong Times*, May13, 2015; Fabian Lyngdoh, "Why Appeal to Tradition Not to Propagate Injustice? What About Justice?" in *The Shillong Times*, July 7, 2015; Albert Thyniang, "Critiquing the Institution of the Dorbar Shnong," in *The Shillong Times*, September 16, 2020; Toki Blah, "Meghalaya Grassroots Governing Institutions," in *The Shillong Times*, September 29, 2020; Benjamin Lyngdoh, "Khasi Dorbar Shnong Must Move with the Times," in *The Shillong Times*, November 9, 2021; Albert Thyniang, "Pulling the Tail of the Elephant," in *The Shillong Times*, November 10, 2021.

66 Refer to the report in *The Hindustan Times*, February 1, 2020.

7 Turning to Stone

Transformations in Angami-Naga Patriarchy

Theyiesinuo Keditsu

Patriarchy is founded upon the disenfranchisement of women. First-world feminism in particular has built most of its theories and politics upon this premise – understood in its modern western sense. Yet challenging the notion of a monolithic feminism by third-world and indigenous feminists has necessarily highlighted the various forms of patriarchy and the complex negotiations of power that occur between women and the strictures which bind them (Mohanty et al. 1991; Menon 2004; Suzack et al. 2010; Simpson 2014). These strictures vary from and are specific to a culture. In his keynote lecture, Prof. Xaxa talked about how categories such as "Northeast" run the danger of homogenizing the myriad peoples and cultures in this region.[1] I would like to take this further by joining a long line of scholars who contest the notion of Naga and Naga culture as some kind of single entity (Hutton 1965; Elwin 1969; Jacobs 1990; Sanyü 1996; Lotha 2007, 2013, 2016). We are over 66 tribes spread across this part of Southeast Asia of which only 16 inhabit the Indian state of Nagaland. All these 16 indigenous tribes of the state of Nagaland are patriarchal but the nature of each varies from tribe to tribe and even within a tribe varies from region and village. Temsula Ao (2013: 125) notes the "varying degrees [of patriarchy] among different tribes." For Walter Fernandes (2009: 177), the "somewhat high social status of Angami women [is] because they as well as most other tribes keep a clear separation between the family and social sphere.". Bhattacharya (1976: viii) observes that "the customary laws that evolved through the ages not only differed from tribe to tribe but also from village to village of the same tribe" (also Vizol 1976). I have thus very consciously specified that this chapter covers the scope of the patriarchal practices of the Angami Naga tribe and that too with much trepidation, because among Angami villages too, patriarchy ranges from intractable to looser forms (Hibo 2009, Kekhrieseno 2009; Peirera 2009; Kekhrieseno & Hibo 2014–2015; Kharütso 2015; Ao 2013; Goswami 2013).

Temsula Ao's (2013: 126) account, of how patriarchy came to be, corresponds with established folklore as well as personal accounts. "Life in those days was fraught with danger, to say the least. Not only did the people have to struggle with difficult terrain for sustenance, they also had to contend with

DOI: 10.4324/9781003539797-8

the wild animals of the forest who posed constant danger to life and limb. But above all, they had to protect themselves from the periodic raids from hostile neighbors.[2] In all these endeavors, the superior physical prowess of the mad had to play a crucial role in order to achieve desired results. For instance, the hard work of clearing the jungle of trees and thick undergrowth was done by men because women lacked the physical ability to do it. So was the case with securing protection from wild animals and enemy attacks. In short, it was the man who was the "protector" and hence it was easy for him to assume the superior status in the male–female dichotomy. What emerged from these practical situations facilitated the exclusion of women from the decision-making seat – of governance in society."

Hence the rationale for traditional patriarchy and its concomitant allocation of power traces its origins to folklore. In their seminal book, *Folk Law: Essays in the Theory and Practice of Lex Non Scripta (Vol I)*, Alison Dundes Renteln and Alan Dundes (1995: 2) propose folk or unwritten law (lex non scripta) as having "the same characteristics of folklore in general, that is for myths, folktales, legends, folksongs, proverbs, riddles...these characteristics include multiple existence and variation." Further, folk law, like folklore, is so old it is timeless and its origins are always "anonymous" (1995: 3). While Renteln and Dundes reject the term "customary" as a stand-in for folk law, their definition of folk law as "traditional law, law passed on orally from person to person, from generation to generation" (1995: 4) corresponds with the manner in which the phrase "customary law" is used by others, the closest to home is the late Naga statesman, Vizol, an Angami who explains "a custom [as] a rule which in a particular family, tribe or locality has from long usage obtained the force of law."[3] I will therefore use customary law as it is the term which enjoys greater currency while drawing upon Renteln and Dundes' work on folk law as unwritten, orally transmitted law. In particular, I would like to dwell on their contention that customary law is flexible by virtue of its existence in "more than one place and/or time [and as multiple] versions" (1995: 2). Characterizing this flexibility as "difficulties [and] flaws," Vizol (1976: 2) elaborates that "in certain cases even within one village different customs and different standards exist to correct the faults of their members. This diversity becomes more pronounced when we come to evidence the history of different crimes and infringements."

Here he joins his fellow attendees and speakers[4] at the Seminar on Naga Customary Laws held in Kohima in 1974, in their intent to deliberate upon strategies to capture and fix customary law for posterity through codification and standardization (also in Nagaland Proceedings on Customary Law, Directorate of Art and Culture 1976). Menon (2004: 107) observes the propensity of legal discourse to "fix meaning and create uniform categories out of a multiplicity of possibilities, by suturing open-endedness." She terms this the "paradox of constitutionalism, that is, the tension in which the need to assert various and differing moral visions comes up against the universalizing drive of constitutionality and the language of universal rights" (2004: 2).

Hence any intent to codify and standardize is grossly misplaced and counterproductive to securing more rights for women, in my estimation, because the strength of customary law lies in its suppleness.

This suppleness is what has allowed customary law to accommodate and secure the rights of those who fall outside the purview of patriarchy's protection. For instance, although folklore/law overwhelmingly dictates that ancestral property be passed on to male descendants, there are known accounts of women without brothers who have inherited ancestral property (Kekhrieseno 2002b, 2009; Kelio 2013; Kekhrieseno et al. 2013; Terangpi et al. 2013). Though these are definitely exceptions, they are nevertheless significant because they happened, were witnessed and committed to memory, and live on in lore that is more often passed on furtively almost as afterthoughts. [5] In Angami custom, the personal property of a woman is recognized, even when it comes in the form of land[6] and can be passed on from a woman to her daughters and so on (Kekhrieseno 2002a: 190), thereby constituting a parallel form of ancestral property. It is significant that Kekhrieseno et al. (2013: 39) use both subject pronouns (he or she) in the following passage.

> "Angami traditional law gives absolute rights to the individual owner of land so that he or she can do with it as he or she wishes. He or she may alienate it by sale or gift. He or she may mortgage or rent it to others. He or she may bequeath it to his or her children in the manner he or she wishes...According to customary law only sons can inherit the ancestral house and ancestral land, ***though such restrictions are now sometimes overlooked.***"
>
> (emphasis my own)

The above observations are peculiar to only a few tribes and even among the Angamis, there are some villages where these customary laws and their variations/exceptions would be anathema. Pereira (2009: 269–270) contends,

> giving documented customary law state recognition...has the risk of a romantic and conservative interpretation of customary law by the gerontocratic ruling elite of a community, which may result indiscrimination against certain sections of society. Codification, while bringing about clarity and certainty, may have the chilling effect of freezing the spirit of customary law and converting them into a statutory law system.
>
> It would be much worse if customary laws of several tribes were brought together into a single tribal law as is thought of in Nagaland. Any such leveling of the differences can cut at the very root of diversity and can become an attack on the identity of unique tribal groups. Instead, efforts should be made to evolve a system of recognition that provides for diversity and remains flexible. Flexibility is required because customary laws need to evolve further.

The fluidity of customary laws therefore ought not to be viewed as inconsistencies but as variations devised to maneuver through, without seeming to undermine, patriarchal authority in a society where honor and prestige are key tenets in traditional conflict resolution. In this sense, customary law in praxis is an exercise in subterfuge – at once buttressing patriarchy as well as its gambits.

Precedents threatening the status quo cannot be narrated in the language, space, and time of custom and law. Men who bring them up in public are reprimanded and shamed. Women, already voiceless or in the words of Kuotsu and Walling, "mute beings" (2018: 104), are shown their way back to spaces of silence. The strict segregation of women in the private and men in the public domain in traditional Naga culture has been observed by many scholars (Hümtsoe-Nienü al. 2012; Amer 2018). The scope of folklore straddles both these domains. So while only men may narrate folklore about "the history of village foundations, clan genealogies and history" [in public, formal gatherings], there was no prohibition for women to listen and even participate in private among friends" (Aier 2018: 14). Rather it is in the private domain that both men and women share custody of the folklores of their community, passing it on to the next generation orally. Various facets of folklore, such as myths, legends, and proverbs are connected, in that they often reinforce each other, acting as parts of a whole (Dundes Rentlen & Dundes 1995; Dundes & Bronner 2007). So that a legend may explain a proverb. Or a riddle may either be embedded within a myth (as in the case of Oedipus Rex) or be the point of entry to a folksong. In the same manner, folktales, myths, folksongs, etc. form the basis of many folklaws or customary laws. If much of customary law functions to bolster patriarchy, it would serve us well to trace back their origins to their roots in folklore and investigate if and how consistently the source corresponds to the outcome.

As I am from Chiechama, a northern Angami Village and reside in Kohima, also Northern Angami, most of my work collecting oral histories and narratives is sourced from the people of this area. I will thus be building this paper on the foundations for three folktales, two that come from the Northern Angami villages of Rüsoma and Kohima and one that is common to all Angamis. In Naga culture, as in many other indigenous sister cultures of the North East, orature in the form of folktales has been a narrative domain in which women as well as men have shared equal space and power. Using these folktales as sites of analysis, this paper will examine the rights and power of women within the institution of marriage – that bastion of patriarchal power. Because marriage is the eye of the needle through which ancestry, inheritance and consequently patriarchal authority are threaded and secured. One of our better known storytellers, Easterine Kire, writes in her novel about an Angami family living in Kohima, A Terrible Matriarchy (2007: 273):

> ...people were unkind and mocked those who could not produce male children. The understanding was that a woman without a male heir would be sheltered by her in-laws but her daughters could not inherit

> the father's property. Their best bet would be to marry a man rich enough to have property of his own. Then they would devote the rest of their lives to trying to produce a male heir.

I will attempt to trace the movement of marriage from a relatively loose institutionality in olden times to its transformation, via colonialism and particularly missionization, to its current legal and sacrosanct avatar (Holleman 1995). A transformation that has curtailed what little power women enjoyed within traditional patriarchy and had insidious implications on the modern rights women can claim today.

Let me begin by narrating the first folktale of Sopfünuo[7]:

Sopfünuo was a beautiful woman from Rüsoma village who married a man from another village. She was a loyal wife to her husband. But her husband became cruel and began to ill-treat her. Unable to bear his cruelty, she left her husband and home at night. She carried her child on her back and lit a torch of bitter wormwood to light their way. It is said that the villagers could see the flames of her burning torch as the two moved through the forest. At some point, the fire died out. According to the legend, Sopfünuo was struck by the spear of an evil spirit and died leaving her child behind. Sometime later the child, while crawling over her body, was pierced by one of her rib bones and also died. It is said that their bodies metamorphosed into stones bearing human shape. When her kinsmen learnt of her sad fate, they went looking after them only to find the two stone shapes. When they tried to pull the mother stone, a great wind blew up to prevent them from doing so. Thereafter, Sopfünuo and her child were brought to Rüsora where they continue to remain today.

Another version blames their marital discord to the jealousy of other women who incited him to cast her out of his home. Yet another simply goes that she was unhappy in her marital home and left without specifically pointing to the husband as the source of her unhappiness – leaving one to conjecture if this was a case of post-partum depression, but that is the stuff of another paper.

The narrative conveniently silences Sopfünuo so that as stone, we will never hear her voice and version of what really happened and why she left. And this silence allows for alternative versions where either other women are blamed for her husband's change of heart or he is completely omitted as the cause of her unhappiness.

What is significant for our analysis is that Sopfünuo has and exercises the agency to leave her husband and that too with her child. Further, leaving her marital home does not estrange her from her kinsmen, rather they seek her out and upon finding her and her infant turned to stone, bring them back to the village where they are enshrined. Today, regardless of how terribly and unfairly victimized a divorced woman may have been in her marital home, one will be hardpressed to find a public and communally sanctioned memorial to her – simply by virtue of the stigma attached to her divorced status.

Shame and honor are the foundational moral codes in traditional Angami society. What is significant with this folktale and the way it has been narrated and passed down is the absence of a proscriptive moral at the end. Shame and the loss of honor is attached neither to the act of leaving her marital home nor to Sopfünuo for having left. Rather the dominant tenor of the narrative is sympathetic, the unspoken moral is one that presents the possibility for women to leave an unhappy marriage and without causing shame or diminishing the honor of her kinsmen.

The second folktale about the origin of one of the clans of Kohima village: Tsutuonumia goes that their foremother, originally from the Semoma clan of Khonoma village, fell in love with one of her own clansmen and became pregnant without being married. Overcome by shame, she ran away to Kohima and lived in the house of Rosu, the forefather of one of the founding clans of Kohima village. She gave birth in the fields, wrapped the baby, and returned home. On the way, when asked what she was carrying, she replied that she was carrying a Chüto or cucumber. And hence the name of the clan that descended from this Chüto or cucumber. The Tsutuonuomia form one of the four Khels (or wards) of Kohima village in spite of the fact that their forefather was born out of wedlock and his descendants are today a formidable and equal clan in the village.

Finally the mother, literally, of all our folktales, the story of the supreme being, Ukepenuopfü or the one who birthed us goes that Ukepenuopfü had two sons from a man so fearsome in appearance he hid himself from his children. By chance, the sons found him while playing. Now exposed, he felt he could no longer stay. The younger son chose to leave with him and off they went down from the hills to the plains. The younger son became the forefather of the plains people and the elder son who stayed back with his mother Ukepenuopfübe became our forefather.

It is ironic that a tribe obsessed with patrilineal descent is actually founded on narratives of single mothers and either illegitimate sons or fatherless ones. And this obsession with patrilineal descent is not exclusive only to the Angamis, rather it is one shared with other Naga tribes and even with all patriarchal societies. Temsula Ao (2013: 128) explains

> ...women accepted their subordination to men due to very practical reasons. Physical security being the foremost, there was another reason, equally important: economic exclusivity. Naga society being patriarchal, all landed property belonged to the male. If a man has only daughters, on his death his property reverts to his male siblings and their sons. In the case of a woman too, if she dies a spinster her ornaments and household goods are claimed by the daughters of her male siblings.[8]

Even as tracing and narrating genealogies establish patrilineal descent and consolidate patriarchal authority, the core of these folktales remains immutable. What is noteworthy is that this irony existed and had not been silenced or edited in "olden" times. Colonialism, missionization, and modernity in general have worked together to erase these narratives or to relegate them into the realm of "folktales" – that genre of meaningful but innocuous half-truths.

Fundamentalist, evangelistic American Baptist missionaries looking for a word to stand in for the Christian God in their Bible translations chose the word for our Supreme being who was Ukepenuopfü (Hutton 1969: 181). What this substitution did was to completely erase the gender and therefore story of our mother goddess and supplant it with the male Christian father god (Hümtsoe-Nienü 2012a). In tandem with this symbolic decapitation, Christianity not only proscribed many traditional cultural institutions and practices but also forced out our narrative space but privileging and imposing Judeo-Christian narratives in Sunday school and colonial syllabi in mission schools (Eaton 1894; Hutton 1969; Pruett 1974; Jacobs 1990; Sanyü 1996, 2017; Mills 2003; Lotha 2007). To be Christian meant to be westernized and civilized and this entailed, if not forgetting our indigenous narratives, then enjoying them as entertaining nostalgic fictions while avowing the truth of the story of creation and memorizing scripture and Shakespeare.

Enough has been written about the nature of Judeo-Christian patriarchy and its intransigent position on and control of women. Proselytization brought with it a more rigid and codified (in the form of the Bible) form of Patriarchy. Ellen Phamnei (Konyak) recalls how her aspirations to pursue further education "was frequently thwarted in her efforts by the patriarchal attitude of the Baptist church and the mission" (Gill 2013: 464). As the place and space of the Church became more central to the social life of the community, this form of patriarchy established itself as that sanctioned by God and consolidated traditional patriarchy (Khiamniungan 2018). Nowhere more so that by fortifying and fixing the institution of marriage and yoking the identity and value of women to it (Kikhi & Husca 2015–2016; Thongrü 2015–2016). To the extent that Kharütso (2015: 49) looks to "Christian ideals of partnership between husband and wife" to "correct" the changes brought on the traditional patriarchal marital hierarchy by modernity without a hint of irony.

It is true that within traditional patriarchy too, marriage was an important institution, one upon which a woman's status and value was contingent (Kekhrieseno 2002a; Kharütso 2015). An Angami woman was marked and groomed for marriage. Unmarried girls and women had shaved heads, it was only after marriage that a woman could grow her hair (Savi 2015–2016). And yet, as the folktale of Sopfünuo and many oral accounts illustrate, leaving her husband was not taboo, shameful, or dishonorable unless in the case of infidelity or wrongdoing by the woman (Sakhrie 2018). In the cases of divorce due to infidelity or wrongdoing on the part of the husband, the woman is entitled to a share of the assets they have amassed together after marriage. With Christianity, divorce itself became a sin. Hence regardless of who has done wrong, the names of both the husband and the wife are struck off the church rolls and their names are announced to the congregation. Shame and dishonor now attached to what was earlier an unpleasant but condoned occurrence. The spectacle of excommunication coupled with the social stigma that comes with Christian sin carries such weight in a society that still operates on honor and shame that many choose to suffer marriage rather than divorce.

During the contentious and violent protests against the Women's Reservation Bill in 2017, among other arguments, the moral character of the women fighting for or supporting the bill came into question. Kuotsu and Walling (2018: 106) record an elderly man's use of the word "oversmart" to describe what happens "when we allow our women to go out" and clarify that the word "oversmart" here denotes a negative gesture, implying that women become loose if given freedom. This expression seems in line with the universal sexual description that surrounds women's narratives.

And the prime indicator of the character of women supporting reservation was their marital status. Divorce meant that the public chose to focus on this perceived moral flaw and allow it to undermine any case made for reservation, however coherent or convincing. This is nothing new in, e.g., American politics. But seen in the light of our folklore and oral narratives, it is remarkable to observe how we have moved from enshrinement to ostracization. In oral accounts of legal disputes collected from Northern Angami, there are many cases where women have borne witness, taken oaths,[9] and even participated in passing judgments. The consequence of inserting Christian morality into contemporary legal matters and extending Pauline standards of meekness and modesty of women[10] from the space of the church to the village council results in ossifying what little agency women enjoyed in traditional patriarchal decision-making processes. Kuotsu and Walling (2018: 119) reveal that

> Many women – both educated and uneducated – share that they are being branded as "feminists," "outlaws" or "rebels," as well as of their husbands being looked down upon as "henpecked," whenever they speak for the need of gender justice and equality in Naga society. For such reasons, and more, it has become the "choice" of many women to remain silent, not only in the social and political spheres but even in ecclesiastical affairs of the Nagas…The prevalence of the notions of "good woman"/"bad woman" in Naga society, from a cultural perspective, is not just imagination, but formulate authoritative projections that work to quell women's political ambitions and aspirations.

In this regard, situating our current patriarchal practices is a sort of chicken–egg conundrum. On the one hand, our traditional culture is deeply patriarchal and operates on a strict segregation of female/private and male/public domains. I have argued that there are few exceptions and variations between and within tribes as evidenced by scholarly observations and within folklore. On the other hand, Christianity, modernity, globalization, and the structures and institutions they introduced are also products of patriarchy – often reinforcing or even imposing new modes of oppression and gender inequity. There is a tendency of many scholars of polity, governance, and democracy in Nagaland to stress the amplification of traditional patriarchal mores in modern democratic practice rather than examining the ways in which modernity has fixed and thereby rigidified them to chauvinism. Kuotsu and Walling (2018: 105) concede that "the position of inequality Naga women nevertheless face in church ministries seemingly results from a fusion between the 'patriarchal domain' of Christianity and the 'patriarchal-culture of the Nagas'." Hümtsoe-Nienü is one among few who explores the ways in which the little customary control and power women enjoyed is threatened by modern developmental policies. Given that "the vicious cycle of dependency on the central government" (Kikon 2018: 53) is the economic lifeline of most people in the state, control of bodies from Village Development Boards (VDB) to the Legislative Assembly become crucial.

So also, with lineage and inheritance. Ao (2013), Kuotsu and Walling (2018) among others underscore the relationship between money, lineage, and political power. From the mythical foremother of the Tsutuonuomia clan to many real Angami women, it is not an uncommon practice for a woman to bequeath either her illegitimate children with her paternal clan name or her children to decline her husband's surname (particularly if not an Angami) and take her paternal clan name. The processes for this range from a simple private taking of the mother's surname to elaborate customs of adoption by the woman's father or uncles or clansmen or the adoption of the non-Angami father into one of the other exogamous clans or another village. In the recent furor against the Citizenship Amendment Bill, the chief minister of our state controversially suggested that one possible measure to curb influx of non-Nagas into the state is to deny ST status to any Naga woman married to a non-Naga.[11] Apart from addressing the threat to patriliny posed by marriage to outsiders, this statement was also a jibe at and threat to women who had married non-Nagas thereby undercutting their effectiveness as spokesperson for Naga women as a whole. As with most patriarchies, control of women's sexuality and ownership of her person are perceived as means by which the purity of male lineage and thereby patriarchal power are safeguarded. Khiamniungan (2018: 194) observes that "inheritance is structured exclusively through the male-line, while patrilineal descent and patrilocal residence further strengthen this male-dominated material base of Naga society." Marriage thus becomes the battlefield on which this power struggle between men is waged. On the one hand, the legal system of this country is changing with the times and becoming more gender inclusive and equitable. On the other hand, the quicksand that is the legacy of the colonial legal system means that categories such as Mrs, W/O, D/O, and Father's name have done much damage to those hidden spaces and crevices that allowed women not just to have power over naming their children but also to own property of their own that they can will to their children under customary practices (Kekhrieseno 2002a, 2002b, 2009; Ao 2013; Kelio 2013).

The integrity and development of indigenous societies as desired by the post-colonial Indian state calls for the enfranchisement of women as equal actors in policy formulation and implementation. Yet the violent resistance to the Women's Reservation Bill or scapegoating women for the Citizenship Amendment Bill as well as the conspicuous exclusion of women from significant modern decision-making bodies and spaces calls for an investigation in, among others, the cultural realm. I have attempted to scrutinize the ways in which modernity (and with it Christianity) has brought with it a certain narrative and practice of patriarchy that may be counterproductive to its own project of "development" (also see Hümtsoe-Nienü 2012b). Of course, one needs to take into account the insidious and pervasive culture of violence that has characterized our (the Nagas') entry into and experience of modernity. Speaking about "India," Menon (2004: 8) notes that this encounter with modernity occurred through a political system that was at its core, violent, distinguishes "our" modernity...from modernity as it emerged in Europe. The dislocation caused by modernity in Europe four centuries ago was equally brutal, but in Asia and Africa, there was a double violence involved – the simultaneous disruption caused by modernity and colonialism.

In our case, the violence Nagas endured was triple because of the neo-colonial armed occupation of our lands by India. Freny Maneckshа (Gill 2013: 465) observes about the impact of the Indo-Naga conflict:

"In an environment where the shadow of the gun prevailed and in a society under attack, the patriarchal tradition became more dominant – the woman's voice became even more muted."

In her body of work, Dolly Kikon (2017) repeatedly characterizes Naga society as a militarized one where violence manifests not only in physical but also in structural dimensions. She writes

> ...the male tribal councils and associations in Nagaland... rise to power also needs to be understood against the backdrop of the armed conflict between Naga national groups fighting the government of India since 1947 for their right to a sovereign homeland. Given the long conflict, state organs and public offices in Nagaland are defunct, and Naga society is extremely militarised.[12]

"The ubiquitous conflict and processes of militarisation of the [Naga] region" (Kikon 2018: 52) which has characterized our "modern" culture simply transposes the age-old justification of patriarchy to our current context. Folklores about how Patriarchy came to attribute the allocation of power to war and the demands of surviving natural menaces. One obvious and popular solution is of course the end of militarization and state-sponsored violence – catalyzed (or not) in the public realm at the expense of the private. In fact, this is one of the common arguments used to justify the opposition to Naga women entering the public realm of politics and governance – for the sake of and in the interest of our "national" cause (Kikon 2002). Our local newspapers report each round of talks and negotiations regarding the future of the Naga people with the center with photographs of exclusively male contingents ad nauseum.[13]

If feminisms' victory has been the "displacement of the opposition [of private and public] itself" (Menon 2004: 11), folklore by virtue of its porous quality can accommodate a more inclusive spectrum of participants and possibilities. Rather than only looking to our future (because that space is currently under occupation), I would like to suggest that another possible solution may lie in our past, through decolonizing our notions of indigenous narratives – these range from folklore and dreams to oral accounts and histories. To see them not just as innocent imaginative exercises of a primitive people but to re-legitimize them as serious repositories of cultural meaning that used to and still can significantly inform contemporary legal deliberations. "It is a fiction that customary law is rigorously fixed and unchangeable: on the contrary, it is through customary law that social life adjusts itself more or less consciously to changing conditions" (Jong 1995: 116). The project of third-world and indigenous feminism has been to contest generalizations and reveal exceptions and nuance (Chakravarti 2002; Menon 2004). Some Naga tribes have myths and folktales of a time long ago when stones were soft (Ao 2012). It may not be too late to hope that this ossifying monolith of patriarchy can be soothed back to softness by remembering and retelling folklores from our past.

Notes

1 Virginius Xaxa, Keynote Lecture, International Conference on "Custom, Law and the Colonial State in Northeast India: Dynamics and Challenges for the Postcolonial State," Shillong, 13–14 June 2019.
2 Ironically, this same rationale is given for the origins of the matrilineal system among the Khasis (Esther Syiemin Preeti Gill (ed) *The Peripheral Centre: Voices from India's Northeast*, New Delhi: Zubaan, 2013.
3 Inaugural Address, Seminar on Naga Customary Laws, Kohima, November 21–23, 1974.
4 Not) Ironically, all men.
5 In my experience, these accounts have always been recalled after much prodding and are always shared with disclaimers that subtly and indirectly place the account in the realm of the anecdotal as separate from the official interview. The subjects' awareness that I am a daughter without brothers may also have a bearing on their willingness to rummage around their memories and disclose these exceptional cases.
6 As opposed to some other Naga tribes, Khiamniungan (2018) recounts how she has to obtain land through her brother's name.
7 Though there are many written accounts of these three folktales, I will not be referencing them as these folktales are widely known and disseminated orally. It would be counterintuitive to treat it like an authored narrative.
8 Though this generally holds true for all Naga tribes, it is important to note that the writer belongs to the Ao tribe and hence speaks from her knowledge of Ao customary law.
9 Traditionally oath taking is a form of voting and usually is done by men and that too of good moral standing. Also see Kelio 2013.

10 1Tim 2: 11–12 – "[11] A woman should learn in quietness and full submission. [12] I do not permit a woman to teach or to assume authority over a man; she must be quiet." (New International Version.).

11 https://nagalandpage.com/battle-grounding-naga-women-again. https://www.deccanherald.com/national/nagaland-mulls-law-check-712850.html.

12 https://www.opendemocracy.net/en/5050/nagaland-fight-for-women-quota/.

13 For samples of these photos, see links https://indianexpress.com/article/india/naga-peace-talks-nscn-im-to-reiterate-demand-for-separate-flag-constitution-6601623/ https://nenow.in/north-east-news/nagaland/nscn-im-nagaland-gaon-burhas-resolve-to-strengthen-peace-talks.html

The groups that feature prominently in the "peace talks" – NSCN-IM, Naga National Political Groups (NNPG), Naga Hoho, Nagaland Gaon Bura's Federation (NGBF), etc. are all male.

References

Aier, Anungla. 2018. *Studies on Naga Oral Tradition Vol I: Memories and Telling of Origin Myth and Migration*, Dimapur: Heritage Publishing House.

Amer, Moamenla. 2018. "Engendering Democracy in Nagaland" in Wouters, Jelle JP & Tunyi, Zhoto (eds) *Democracy in Nagaland: Tribes, Traditions, and Tensions*, Kohima: Highlander Books.

Ao, Temsula. 2012.*The Ao-Naga Oral Tradition*, Dimapur: Heritage Publishing House.

Ao, Temsula. 2013. "'Benevolent Subordination': Social Status of Naga Women" in Preeti Gill (ed) *The Peripheral Centre: Voices from India's Northeast*, New Delhi: Zubaan.

Bhattacharya, P.K. 1976. "General Introduction Directorate of Art and Culture Nagaland" in *Proceedings of the Seminar on Naga Customary Laws*, Kohima: Government of Nagaland.

Chakravarti, Uma. 2002. "Persisting Structures, Ideological Manoeuvres, and Everyday Challenges: Reflections on Women's Movements in South in South Asia" in Fernandes, Walter & Borbora, Sanjay (eds) *Changing Women's Status in India: Focus on the Northeast*, Guwahati: North Eastern Social Research Centre.

Directorate of Art and Culture. 1976. Nagaland *Proceedings of the Seminar on Naga Customary Laws*, Kohima: Government of Nagaland

Dundes Renteln, Alison & Bronner, S.J. 2007.*The Meaning of Folklore: The Analytical Essays of Alan Dundes*, Logan: Utah State University Press.

Dundes Renteln, Alison & Dundes, Alan (eds). 1995.*Folk Law: Essays in the Theory and Practice of Lex Non Scripta Vol I & II*, Wisconsin: The University of Wisconsin Press.

Eaton, Richard M. 1894. "Conversion to Christianity among the Nagas, 1876–1971," *Indian Economic Social History Review*, 21(1), 2–44.

Elwin, Verrier. 1969.*The Nagas in the Nineteenth Century*, Bombay: Oxford University Press.

Fernandes, Walter. 2009. "Understanding Angami Today in the Context of Modernisation and Globalisation" in Kikhi R. et al. (eds) *Angami Society at the Beginning of the 21st Century*, New Delhi: Akanksha Publishing House.

Gill, Preeti (ed). 2013. *The Peripheral Centre: Voices from India's Northeast*, New Delhi: Zubaan.

Goswami, Rahul. 2013. "Socio-economic Realities in Nagaland" in Preeti Gill (ed) *The Peripheral Centre: Voices from India's Northeast*, New Delhi: Zubaan.

Hibo, Visakhonu. 2009. "Village Development Board (VDB) and the Role of Angami Women" in Kikhi R. et al. (eds) *Angami Society at the Beginning of the 21st Century*, New Delhi: Akanksha Publishing House.

Holleman, J.F. 1995. "Trouble-Cases and Trouble-less Cases in the Study of Customary Law and Legal Reform" in Dundes, Renteln (ed) *Folk Law: Essays in the Theory and Practice of Lex Non Scripta Vol II*, Wisconsin: The University of Wisconsin Press.

Hümtsoe-Nienü, Eyingbeni. 2012a. "De-Masculinizing God: Reclaiming the Inclusive Meaning of God in Tribal Tradition" in Hümtsoe-Nienü, Eyingbeni, Pimomo, Paul & Tünyi, Venüsa (eds), *Nagas: Essays for Responsible Change*, Dimapur: Heritage Publishing House.

Hümtsoe-Nienü, Eyingbeni. 2012b. "Challenges of Globalization on Naga Women" in Hümtsoe-Nienü, Eyingbeni, Pimomo, Paul & Tünyi, Venüsa (eds), *Nagas: Essays for Responsible Change*, Dimapur: Heritage Publishing House.

Hümtsoe-Nienü, Eyingbeni, Pimomo, Paul & Tünyi, Venüsa (eds). 2012. *Nagas: Essays for Responsible Change*, Dimapur: Heritage Publishing House.

Hutton, J.H. 1965. "The Mixed Culture of the Naga Tribes," *The Journal of the Anthropological Institute of Great Britain and Ireland*, 95(1), 16–43.

Hutton, J.H. 1969. *The Angami Nagas*, London: Macmillan.

Jacobs, Julian. 1990. *The Nagas: Hillpeoples of Northeast India*, Stuttgart: Edition Hansjörg Mayer.

Jong, J.P.B. 1995. "Customary Law: A Confusing Fiction" in Dundes Renteln (ed) *Folk Law: Essays in the Theory and Practice of Lex Non Scripta Vol I*, Wisconsin: The University of Wisconsin Press.

Kelio, Kezhangunuo. 2013. "Customary Laws of the Angami Naga Tribe," *Journal of Northeast Indian Cultures* I(1), 92–99.

Kekhrieseno, Christina. 2002a. "Changing Property Rights and Women's Control over Livelihood in Nagaland" in Fernandes, Walter & Borbora, Sanjay (eds) *Changing Women's Status in India: Focus on the Northeast*, Guwahati: North Eastern Social Research Centre.

Kekhrieseno, Christina. 2002b. "Customary Laws and Women's Development in Nagaland" in Thomas, C. Joshua & Das, Gurudas (eds) *Dimensions of Development in Nagaland*, New Delhi: Regency Publications.

Kekhrieseno, Christina. 2009. "Changing Land Relations and Angami Society" in Kikhi, R. et al. (eds) *Angami Society at the Beginning of the 21st Century*, New Delhi: Akanksha Publishing House.

Kekhrieseno, Christina, Hibo, V. & Kikhi, K. 2013. "Land and Tribal Identity in Contemporary Nagaland: Insights from Micro Level Studies," *Journal on Frontier Studies*, I(s), 35–50.

Kekhrieseno, Christina & Hibo, Viraho. 2014–2015. "Dynamics of Exclusion in an Egalitarian Society: The Case of the Angami Naga," *Journal on Frontier Studies*, 2, 19–31.

Kharütso, Nokhwenu. 2015. "The Angami Family at the Crossroads," in D'Souza, Alphonsus, & Kechu, P. (eds), *Family and Clan in North East India: Reflections by Christian Scholars*, Guwahati: North Eastern Social Research Centre.

Khiamniungan, T. Longkoi. 2018. "Patriarchy as Structural Violence: Resistance Against Women Reservation in Nagaland," in Wouters, Jelle JP & Tunyi, Zhoto (eds) *Democracy in Nagaland: Tribes, Traditions, and Tensions*, Kohima: Highlander Books.

Kikhi, Kedilezo & Husca, A. 2015–2016. "Institution of Marriage and Bride-Price amongst the Sumi Nagas: Change and Continuity," *Journal on Frontier Studies*, 4, 1–27.

Kikon, Dolly. 2002. "Political Mobilisation of Women in Nagaland: A Sociological Background" in Fernandes, Walter & Borbora, Sanjay (eds) *Changing Women's*

Status in India: Focus on the Northeast, Guwahati: North Eastern Social Research Centre.

Kikon, Dolly. 2017. "Women at Work: the Gender, Culture and Customary Law Debate in Nagaland" in Parismita Singh (ed) *Centrepiece: New Writing and Art from Northeast India*, New Delhi: Zubaan.

Kikon, Dolly. 2018. "Engaging Naga Nationalism: Can Democracy Function in Militarised Societies?" in Wouters, Jelle JP & Tunyi, Zhoto (eds) *Democracy in Nagaland: Tribes, Traditions, and Tensions*, Kohima: Highlander Books.

Kire, Easterine. 2007. *A Terrible Matriarchy*, New Delhi: Zubaan.

Kuotsu, Renchumi Kikon & Walling, A. Wati. 2018 "Democratic Values and Traditional Practices: Gendering Electoral Politics in Nagaland" in Wouters, Jelle JP & Tunyi, Zhoto (eds) *Democracy in Nagaland: Tribes, Traditions, and Tensions*, Kohima: Highlander Books.

Lotha, Abraham. 2007. *History of Naga Anthropology (1832–1947)*, Dimapur, Nagaland: Chumpo Museum Press.

Lotha, Abraham. 2013. *The Raging Mithun: Challenges of Naga Nationalism*, Tromso Norway: Barkweaver Publications.

Lotha, Abraham. 2016. *The Hornbill Spirit: Nagas Living Their Nationalism*, Dimapur, Nagaland: Heritage Publishing House.

Menon, Nivedita. 2004. *Recovering Subversion: Feminist Politics Beyond the Law*, New Delhi: Permanent Black.

Mills, J.P. 2003. *The Ao Nagas* (3rd ed), Kohima: Directorate of Art and Culture, Government of Nagaland.

Mohanty, C.T., Ann R, Lourdes T (eds). 1991. *Third World Women and the Politics of Feminism*, Bloomington: Indiana University Press.

Pereira, Melville. 2009. "Codification: A Swansong for Customary Law?" in Kikhi, R. et al. (eds) *Angami Society at the Beginning of the 21st Century*, New Delhi: Akanksha Publishing House.

Pruett, Gordon E. 1974. "Christianity, History, and Culture in Nagaland," *Contributions to Indian Sociology*, 7, 51–65.

Sakhrie, Kevileno, Forward to T. Keditsu. 2018. *Sopfünuo*, Dimapur: Heritage Publishing House.

Sanyü, Visier. 1996. *A History of Nagas and Nagaland: Dynamics of Oral Tradition in Village Formation*. New Delhi: Commonwealth Publishers.

Sanyü, Visier Meyasetsu with Richard Broome. 2017. *A Naga Odyssey: Visier's Long Way Home*, Clayton, Victoria: Monash University Publishing.

Savi, Seyievono. 2015–2016. "Rediscovering the Idea of Purity amongst the Past Angami Women," *Journal on Frontier Studies*, 65, 84–93.

Suzack, Cheryl, Huhndorf, S.M., Barman, J., & Perrault, J. (eds). 2010. *Indigenous Women and Feminism: Politics, Activism, Culture*, Vancouver: UBC Press.

Simpson, Audrey. 2014. *Mohawk Interruptus (Political Life Across the Borders of Settler States)*, Durham: Duke University Press.

Terangpi, Lily Aye, Khieya, K., & Yhoshü, D. 2013. "Land Inheritance among Karbi and Angami Women," *Journal on Frontier Studies*, 45, 51–61.

Thongrü, Samuel. 2015–2016. "Sangtam Traditional Marriage Rituals," *Journal on Frontier Studies*, 4, 71–83.

Vizol. 1976. "Inaugural Address" in Directorate of Art and Culture, Nagaland *Proceedings of the Seminar on Naga Customary Laws*, Kohima: Government of Nagaland.

8 Creating World Heritage at the Margins of the State

Wildlife, Custom, and Culture

Erik de Maaker

The Challenge

For some years now, the Meghalaya Forest Department advocated the creation of UNESCO World Heritage site in Garo Hills, the Garo Hills Conservation Area (GHCA). Garo Hills, the westernmost one-third of the Indian state of Meghalaya, is a biodiversity hotspot (Bera et al., 2006; Chettri et al., 2010). It harbors large numbers of unique plant and animal species, including many that have so far not been documented. In recent decades, due to logging, as well as changes in the usage of the land, the dense forest that once covered much of Garo Hills has thinned, reducing wildlife habitats and eroding the diversity of plant species (Karlsson, 2011). In addition, coal mining creates substantial environmental pollution. The Meghalaya Forest Department manages a number of relatively small forest reserves, nearly all of which have been created in the 1880s, at the time that Garo Hills became included in the colonial state.[1] In addition, in the 1980s, the Nokrek National Park and the Balpakram National Park were established as a major conservation area. As national parks, these are included in a national-wide (i.e., all-India) scheme, while its management is being done by the Meghalaya Forest Department. Quite a few of the forest reserves, as well as both national parks, are located along an east–west axis, running through the southern half of the Garo Hills. Having been created at different moments in time, these various conservation areas are mostly disconnected. The GHCA was – certainly initially – envisioned as a contiguous area, which would encompass existing conservation areas, while also creating corridors among them. This means that the Garo Hills Conservation Area, as initially proposed, would also relate to land managed and held by villages under what I have written about elsewhere as customary communal ownership (*a'king*) (de Maaker, 2018).[2] This could be included either in the core area or (more likely) in a surrounding bufferzone.

Early 2017, I was approached by one of the main advocates of the GHCA initiative, to become involved in the effort. Based on ethnographic fieldwork conducted in Garo Hills over a period of about two decades, I had and have published quite extensively on changing cultural attitudes toward land (de

DOI: 10.4324/9781003539797-9

Maaker, 2013, 2018, 2020, 2021, 2022), also in relation to North East India more generally (de Maaker & Tula, 2020). To gain recognition as a UNESCO World Heritage site, the Garo Hills Conservation Area would be proposed as a site of "outstanding universal value." In such a site, various kinds of heritage combine, involving, e.g., natural, geological, and cultural values. As mentioned in the extensive literature on heritage studies, the distinction between natural and cultural heritage implies a specific (western) ontological perspective, which often has little relevance for the communities whose heritage it is supposed to describe (Geismar, 2015, p. 72; Muzaini & Minca, 2018). Cultural heritage, to fit the framework of UNESCO, typically emphasizes "the magical-supernatural aspect of local belief," to render it compatible with the "secular-rational" conceptual framework it is expected to fit in with (Byrne & Ween, 2015, p. 130). Such a demand can easily result in overlooking aspects of heritage that are locally considered important, yet do not fit this framework.

UNESCO's application procedure entails a long and arduous process, which includes the drafting of a hefty and very detailed dossier, and it was with respect to this bureaucratic exercise that my involvement was sought. I have tried to contribute in this – as of now not completed – effort at various moments in time, throughout 2018 and 2019.[3] I have met face to face with the people who have taken to the GHCA the initiative, engaged in extensive Skype conversations, and, while in Meghalaya, discussed the opportunities the realization of a Garo Hills Conservation Area might create, as well as the challenges it poses to many of the stakeholders. It is evident to me that the thinning of the forest cover of Garo Hills is detrimental to the biodiversity in the region, mining creates severe pollution, and more generally communal land management is under pressure; developments which combined pose a severe threat to people and environment in Garo Hills. While I would like to contribute to efforts to mitigate if not reverse these threats, I am less certain about the trajectories to be followed to arrive at this. Efforts at conservation of the natural environment easily go against the interests of people who are living on and with the land, whereas their support, commitment, and knowledge should be central to any efforts made (Melick et al., 2012). Creating conservation areas has frequently resulted in people being evicted, as in the "hard conservation" that characterizes many national parks worldwide (Redpath et al., 2015). That the Garo Hills Conservation Area is being proposed within the UNESCO category "outstanding universal value" therefore creates an interesting opportunity, since this can potentially foreground the meaning which land has for people who live on it. The GHCA could then call for conservationist's efforts to align with farmer's connections to land. In this chapter,[4] following up on my involvement with the effort, I explore different interpretations of what cultural heritage in relation to the proposed Garo Hills Conservation Area might entail.

The proposed GHCA is located close to the India–Bangladesh border, and in that sense politically at the margins of the Indian state. More significantly, the Garo community, categorized within India as "tribal," is culturally and numerically marginal within the country. The GHCA initiative could thus result in acknowledgment as a UNESCO World Heritage for an area that is at the margins both in a political and in a cultural sense.

The Tentative Listing

The United Nations Educational, Scientific, and Cultural Organization (UNESCO) has created a framework for the recognition of world heritage. This can encompass sites, landscapes, or built environments, or a combination thereof, which are "priceless and irreplaceable assets," "not only of each nation, but of humanity as a whole" (Intergovernmental Committee for the Protection of the World Cultural and Natural Heritage, 2019, p. 9). Such "most prized" assets should be protected against "deterioration or disappearance," since that would constitute "an impoverishment of the heritage of all the peoples of the world" (Intergovernmental Committee for the Protection of the World Cultural and Natural Heritage, 2019, p. 9). For the Garo Hills Conservation Area to be accepted as UNESCO World Heritage, in other words, it should not just constitute an asset of people in Garo Hills, or even of India, but have a unique value for people throughout the world. In other words, for the GHCA to qualify as world heritage, it should really stand out with respect to the qualities which its proponents claim it has.

Most world heritage sites are listed for their either "natural" or "cultural" value, and sites that combine these qualities are relatively rare. In India, UNESCO has so far recognized only one world heritage site of "outstanding universal value," and that is the Khangchendzonga National Park, located in the state of Sikkim. The park has managed to obtain this qualification since its natural assets ("a unique diversity of plains, valleys, lakes, glaciers and spectacular, snow-capped mountains covered with ancient forests") area l so cherished for their cultural value ("Mythological stories (…) associated with [Khangchendzonga] (…) and with (…) caves, rivers, lakes (…) that are the object of worship by the indigenous people of Sikkim") (UNESCO, 2016). The nomination document based on which the "Khangchendzonga National Park" was acknowledged as UNESCO World Heritage details the natural features of the park, but it also specifies how rocks, streams, and forests in the park are important in terms of religious worship (Forest Environment and Wildlife Management Department Government of Sikkim, 2016).

In 2018, the GHCA was accepted by UNESCO for its tentative list. The tentative list contains proposals for world heritage sites which have garnered the support of the national governments within whose jurisdiction they fall, while roughly matching the criteria set by UNESCO. For the Garo Hills Conservation Area, this meant that the proposal supported by the Government of Meghalaya was accepted by the Indian central government in Delhi, and thus also obtained its backing. The proponents of a site thus listed need to prepare a full and very detailed nomination dossier (the Khangchendzonga one counts about 1200 pages). Such a dossier is currently being prepared for the GHCA. The tentative listing presents the Garo Hills Conservation Area as a "mixed site" of "outstanding universal value" (UNESCO, 2018). This claim is substantiated with reference to culture, geology, as well as biodiversity.[5] For the GHCA to match the biodiversity criterion seems to be beyond doubt. The tentative listing mentions many different kinds of mammals, insects and reptiles, and a large number of rare plant species, including the in situ conservation of unique citrus genes.[6] Compliance with the geology criterion also seems rather straightforward, as notably, the Balpakram National Park contains limestone formations which are rich in (among others) rare nano fossils and bears witness of the India-Asia continent collision which occurred some 56–60 Million years ago.[7]

The cultural uniqueness of Garo Hills is motivated foregrounding shifting cultivation (in North East India known as*j hum*). Shifting cultivation involves making temporary fields on forest land. According to the tentative listing, shifting cultivation as practiced in Garo Hills is "one of the classical examples of traditional methods of sustainable land-use for cultivation in the landscape." This is in line with recent policy reports, which emphasize how shifting cultivation can contribute to the sustenance of biodiversity (Aryal & Choudhury, 2015; Pant et al., 2018). The cultural uniqueness of the Garo Hills Conservation Area is further substantiated stating that many people continue to "hold traditional beliefs" located with, or originating from the traditional Garo community religion, even though the vast majority of the Garo have converted to Christianity (UNESCO, 2018).

When I learned about the tentative listing of the GHCA, I was intrigued but also excited about the interlinkage between (notably) biodiversity and culture. In Garo Hills, the traditional Garo community religion has on the whole become culturally marginalized (certain locations exempted – de Maaker, 2018), but even so the linkage of land use to religion and mythology creates a perspective which can accommodate everyday experiences and engagements with the environment which escape a rigid religious categorization. That is, for Christian Garo, land- and agriculture-related knowledge continues to be rooted in carried over traditions. Moreover, the positive references made in the tentative listing to shifting cultivation suggested that the Garo Hills Conservation Area would come to include measures aimed at strengthening this modality of land use. Here, I expected the project to follow in the footsteps of efforts earlier made by the International Fund for Agriculture Development (IFAD) in Garo Hills (International Fund for Agricultural Development, 2006), which were later on followed up by among others the Meghalaya Basin Development Authority (2017). This would be unusual, since the Forest Department has no jurisdiction over land collectively owned by villages. Realizing the Garo Hills Conservation Area thus seemed to call for a dialogue between government officers and the rural areas' residents, which in the best possible case could result in new strategies to value traditional landscape and environment-related knowledge as cultural heritage, also with the intention to sustain or even increase biodiversity.

Elephants in the Room?

When the news broke in Meghalaya that the Garo Hills Conservation Area had been placed by UNESCO on the tentative list, this triggered positive responses in the press. Roopak Goswami, in an article published in The Telegraph, quoted Garo Hills conservator of forests, Meghalaya Forest Department, Mr P.R. Marak:

> (…) the area still has pristine vegetation, with rich biodiversity unique to the area. Nokrek and Balpakram national parks have a unique landscape and geological formation and are associated with lore, custom and belief of the Garos and hence the proposal for world heritage site under the mixed category.
>
> (Goswami, 2018)

Among the reactions, the news triggered was a letter to the editor by Raka Matachisal A. Sangma, published as a special article in The Shillong Times. In the article, she expresses appreciation for the initiative taken but spends a major part wondering how feasible any effort at conservation is, given that poaching and illegal logging are rampant in the state forests managed by the Meghalaya Forest Department in Garo Hills. She mentions "poaching inside the protected areas," "illegal felling of timber," and "illegal coal mining in and around the proposed site," "all with the connivance, consent, ignorance or under the noses of the concerned departments." This resonated with concerns that had been shared with me earlier that year, when I had been invited to participate in Tura in a consultation organized by the Forest Department on the cultural value of land in rural Garo Hills, in the light of the GHCA as a cultural heritage site. Preceding my talk, I received an email from a colleague of the North Eastern Hill University. Being unable to attend in person, she did want to convey her concerns regarding the proposed Garo Hills Conservation Area. In her message, she also mentioned poaching, as well as the "illegal felling of trees, smuggling of timber," which, she specified, would be done by men from across the border

> crossing over illegally to the Balpkaram area to cut mature, valuable trees for timber. The men cut the trees, carve their names/ initials into the bark, timber, and leave the logs on the banks of the river Mahadeo [flowing through the Balpakram area], so that the logs would be carried down across the border during the monsoon.

The international border between India and Bangladesh, which runs immediately south of the Balpakram National Park, thus creates opportunities for illegal logging, since the logs being taken across the border by the river solves the problem of transporting them over land. Moreover, the wood of trees thus logged is illegal in India, but this qualification would not apply to it in Bangladesh.

The scepsis voiced by Raka in her piece in the Shillong Times was not limited to the viability of conserving nature in Garo Hills but extended to the claims to the unique cultural value which the GHCA would represent. Under the sub-header "Disappearing Cultural Heritage – The elephant in the room," she wrote:

> "I'm clothed, yet I still feel naked." This was what one elderly lady from the village of Kemragrein in West Garo Hills had to say. She felt naked in the sense that she missed wearing ornaments like earrings, bangles, necklaces, and other personal adornments that she used to wear before converting to Christianity. (…) Our culture and our indigenous traditional knowledge (…) is disappearing in the fast pace of life and disregarded as folklore. The dominant Christian community has stigmatised the way of life of the Songsareks [the followers of the traditional Garo community religion – EM], which have a history of living intimately with nature. (…) The threat to the cultural heritage of the Garos is not one external but is from within. (…) how can we nominate something that is non-existent? How can we nominate the traditional values that we ourselves do not value?.
>
> (Sangma, 2018)

My colleague, in her email to me, voiced an opposite perspective with reference to the cultural or religious value of the land. Referring to the Balpakram National Park, she wrote:

> The Balpakram area (…) [is] sacred to the indigenous A'chik/Garo beliefs, traditions and folk literature. The A'chiks for ages have left the area untouched, virgin as they found it when they ascended to inhabit the land. They neither cultivated the area, nor did they rob or spoil nature and the natural formations. For them the area was sacred, and continues to be so till today. The A'chiks of today have tremendous reverence for the land and the beliefs associated with the various objects, springs and rock formations, fossils.

Between this last statement and the concerns expressed earlier by Raka Sangma seem to lie a world of difference. The overlap between both positions is that historically at least, Garo would have managed a respectful and sustainable way of living with their environment. My inference is that whereas both authors refer to "the Garo," Raka Sangma refers primarily to the urban Garo middle class, whereas my colleague's remarks relate to people living rural lives in the vicinity of the Balpakram National Park. In that respect, these two assessments reveal the kind of cleavages or disparities that exist among Garo.

My talk at the Forest Department in Tura combined with one given by colleagues from the Wildlife Institute of India (WII, Dehradun), who introduced our audience of about 30 people to the biodiversity of the proposed Garo Hills Conservation Area. The WII, and more specifically the UNESCO C2C (Category 2 Centre) located there, has been a main promoter of the GHCA and is also entrusted with the preparation of the nomination dossier. The people attending were officers from the Forest Department, some senior members of civil society, as well as a number of younger men working in the field of tourism. The colleagues from the Wildlife Institute of India talked about the impressive variety of birds, insects, and plants which they had encountered on their forays through the forests of Garo Hills. As they talked, supported by photographs they had made, I realized that I had never been conscious of this richness in terms of species. It is not unlikely that my talk about the religious significance of land, which followed, similarly covered "new ground" for them. This part of the workshop experience made me realize that conceiving of the GHCA as a mixed site would not necessarily be easy, since it required identifying and acknowledging differences between the various disciplinary perspectives involved.

In my talk,[8] I argued that the cultural heritage of the Garo Hills Conservation Area should not depend solely or even primarily on its relevance for the traditional Garo community religion, considering that it has nowadays only few followers. Rather, I maintained, cultural heritage should be broadened up to encompass knowledge that relate to landscape and environment more generally. These are embedded first and foremost with practices, techniques, and taboos that relate to shifting cultivation, as well as the forest management practices associated with it. These knowledge and practices are "traditional" in the sense that they have been carried over from preceding generations. Yet they are contemporary in that they are enacted in the present, in the process of which these also continue to be reconstituted and redefined. This was somewhat of a departure from the take on cultural heritage presented in the tentative listing, which much more rigidly foregrounded religious ideas and practices.

Following the two talks, we engaged in discussion with the people who attended the consultation. No one doubted the need for the creation of the GHCA, in fact, all who were present seemed positively inclined toward the initiative. The young men involved with tourism thought it was a particularly promising idea, since in their opinion, the realization of the Garo Hills Conservation Area could help to bring tourists to Garo Hills. The Balpakram National Park, which in their eyes has the potential to attract many more tourists than it currently does, is quite difficult to reach. The one-lane road leading there is in a terrible state, full of potholes, with most its bridges in an appalling condition. The creation of the GHCA would certainly result in money for improvement of the infrastructure, they expected. In this sense, the initiative seemed to be pretty much welcomed as another development-oriented intervention by the state. It was noted during the consultation that Garo Hills has seen many such interventions over the past decades, some of these being more successful than others. Unsuccessful interventions were particularly those that were policies that were implemented to put down, without taking the requirements of the people to whom they were meant to apply into account.

When we were concluding the meeting, one of the young men bent on promoting tourism asked when "cultural consultants" would be recruited for the project. I wasn't entirely sure about the role of the latter, and to what degree these were to be recruited at all, but my colleagues from the WII answered that this would be done in a couple of months' time. I inferred that such consultants could be in-betweens between the Wildlife Institute of India team (none of who spoke Garo) and the village environments in which the initiative would need to be explained to Garo speakers, whose cooperation would be required to realize it. It meant, I supposed, that active involvement of the villages would be sought, in line with the idea that the Garo Hills Conservation Area would pertain to both state forest and village lands.

I had in my talk made some rather positive references to how shifting cultivation can foster biodiversity, and expected at least some people to speak out against it, but that did not happen. Also, from the side of the Forest Department, people seemed quite sympathetic to the idea that we should try to incorporate practices and knowledge not exclusively tied to the Songsarek domain into the phrasing of the cultural heritage encompassed by the GHCA. In addition, people suggested including cultural knowledge present in architecture (bamboo and wood based), ethno-medicine (based on the utilization of plants from the forest), as well as the maintenance of "sacred" groves or forests. These practices should be sustainable for the GHCA to achieve – and once awarded live up to – its qualification. While sustainable livelihoods would need to be encouraged, this would also mean that unsustainable practices, such as coal mining, mono-cropping, or deforestation, should be discouraged. Since the state forests as well as the national parks are uninhabited, it would mostly be the land owned and worked by villages that could espouse this kind of cultural heritage.

Something remarkable about the meeting, which I only realized afterwards, was that none of the officers of the Garo Hills Autonomous District Council were present at the talks. The GHADC is an administrative body that has been created under the Sixth Schedule of the Indian constitution, which governs all the land which villages communally hold. This was (in part) my mistake, since the organizers had asked me to suggest names of people who might attend, and I had mostly invited my academic colleagues and friends, but not suggested anyone from the Council. Yet, it seemed odd that none of the others had thought of this either, notably so since the Garo Hills Conservation Area would also relate to village lands, which are administered by the District Council. I will elaborate on this below. For now, it suffices to state that several people noted this absence and also pointed out to me that the GHCA as projected could only become a success if the efforts made by the various administrative bodies would be coordinated.

Local Perspectives

Some days later, I had the opportunity to together travel with a longtime friend through parts of the fringes of the proposed Garo Hills Conservation Area. We started out along the northern slope of the Nokrek range. The ridge of the Nokrek range constitutes Nokrek National Park. The slopes, on both sides of the range, have communally managed village lands. Some of these village lands might according to the sketch map prepared by the Forest Department early on in the application procedure be included in the GHCA, and we set out to get an understanding of how the people living there related to the initiative taken.

We first traveled to Daribokgre, which is a village located more or less on the western extreme of the Nokrek range. The road is steep, and not much more than a dirt track. The tiny village is a popular destination for people from Tura making day trips, and during a couple of hours we spent there, several cars filled with people from Tura town, with some slipping and sliding managed to make the climb. A largish group of youth rode up the hill on trail bikes. They took pictures, with the Nokrek range as a backdrop (Figure 8.1). At Daribokgre, an enterprising couple had made a lodge and offered a delicious hot lunch of rice and curry. The lodge owners had constructed a traditional Garo house (*nokmande*), made of bamboo, cane, and thatch, for the

Figure 8.1 In Garo Hills, Nokrek peak has become a popular spot for local tourism (Courtesy of Erik de Maaker).

visitors to see and experience. I was hanging around when a family from Tura visited it, and I heard the mother say to her 9 or 10-year-old daughter: "This is how Garos used to live." It was an interesting remark, since I could think of many places in Garo Hills where people still live in such houses, yet the mother suggested to her daughter that this was something from the past. To me, it exemplified the somewhat ambiguous perspective from which "urban Garo" perceive their cultural traditions. While these are a reality for many of the rural poor, middle-class town dwellers are rather inclined to associate these with a cultural past, thus disregarding the socio-economic inequalities manifest in the present. Daribokgre is central to the Nokrek biosphere reserve, and people such as the lodge owners clearly welcomed any conservation initiatives taken, presumably since that would increase the attractiveness of the village as a tourist spot.

We traveled further along the northern slope of the Nokrek range for several hours, until we reached Rongkinggre. Rongkinggre is located at a high altitude, not far from the edge of the Nokrek National Park. People here had not heard of the Garo Hills Conservation Area initiative, but when we told them about it they were enthusiastic, welcoming it as another development-oriented initiative. A road to the village had only been constructed some 10 years ago, while electricity reached just about 2 years ago. People here were happy with these developments. Recently, they had also begun to try to grow areca palm trees, since arecanuts (usedaschew) make for steady returns. Until recently, Rongkinggre's winters were too cold for growing arecanuts, but climate change has resulted in much warmer winters at this altitude, rendering this now feasible. Growing arecanuts has elsewhere in Garo Hills resulted in the replacement of biodiverse forests by monocultures, and in my understanding the GHCA initiative could involve stimuli for farmers to make use of the forest for tree-based crops, rather than replacing it by orchards.

People in Rongkinggre had all converted to Christianity, but that did not keep them from respecting the ancestral *a'song-kusi* boulders. These boulders, associated with spirits that are integral to the traditional Garo community religion (Marak, 2019), are located in a small patch of forest central to one of the village's wards and approached with some degree of awe (de Maaker, 2021). Many Garo villages have such patches of – what some literature refers to as – sacred forest (Tiwari et al., 1999). In my understanding, the forest is not so much sacred, but rather these are places of avoidance. The sustained acknowledgment of these patches of forest, also by people who have become Christians, renders these important elements of cultural heritage.

Traveling further east, we passed several places where people were clearing forest, underscoring my assumption that in this part of Garo Hills shifting cultivation continues to be very popular. It requires a lot of dedicated knowledge of trees, animals, and soil, which is crucial to selecting the right patches of forest to be cultivated, how to trim and chop the trees, how to burn the dried up branches, how and when to sow what seeds, when and what to weed out, how to protect the crops from wild animals, and when to harvest. All this knowledge constitutes cultural heritage, and the creation of the Garo Hills Conservation Area might help to underscore its value in relation to the land.

As we traveled onwards, eastwards, and toward Nongalbibra and then Siju, we crossed the "coal belt" of Garo Hills. Here, villagers make land that has coal-bearing layers available to what are often migrant laborers, who under risky conditions dig for coal. The coal sells at a good price, which renders the business attractive. Yet, digging for coal, and storing it until it is being sold, can severely pollute ground and surface water. Coal mining has been rendered illegal for many years (even though it was more recently once again conditionally allowed (Sitlhou, 2019)), but this has never stopped it, since no such prohibition has ever been enforced. The creation of the GHCA, with its emphasis on nature and biodiversity, would be expected to discourage if not stop coal mining. Even though high-ranking officers of the Forest Department indicated that prohibition would certainly be desirable, they at the same time doubted whether it would ever be feasible to enforce it, given the significant commercial interests at stake. Rumors have it that coal mining would also be financed by business men from outside the area and involve local politicians, which would create even more hurdles to control it.

Complementary Governances

As mentioned above, my interest in the Garo Hills Conservation Area project was initially triggered by the proposition for it to encompass both land owned and managed by the Meghalaya Forest Department, as well as land communally held by Garo villages. The communally held land is, as mentioned, under the jurisdiction of the Garo Hills Autonomous District Council. The council was created upon Indian independence, under the Sixth Schedule of the constitution, which rendered Garo Hills an Autonomous District within the state of Assam. According to the constitution of the GHADC, it has full jurisdiction over the communally held village lands, which it enacts through an extensive list of rules and regulations (Garo Hills Autonomous District Council, 2007). The GHADC is governed by an elected council, the largest political fractions of which create governing council.

When the state of Meghalaya was created, in 1972, the entire erstwhile autonomous Garo Hills district became included in that state. While the GHADC continued to be responsible for the governance of the communally held village lands, Meghalaya state became equipped with the departments common to any Indian state, such as a Forest Department. In Garo Hills, this department became practically speaking primarily responsible for the state forests, as well as (once formed) for the national parks. The Forest Department is a strong organization, funded by the state government. The GHADC, on the other hand, receives only piecemeal funding from the state government and is for most of its funding dependent on the payment of rather nominal taxes by the villagers residing under its administration. Since the Meghalaya Forest Department took the initiative for the creation of the GHCA, I expected it to seek cooperation with the GHADC, if only because the latter was itself involved in a variety of efforts to encourage villagers to engage in forest conservation. However, to my surprise such did not happen, and over time I began to understand that the Forest Department was not truly in a position to negotiate with the GHADC.

People living in rural Garo Hills are on the whole poor, and, according to the classification of the Indian state more or less collectively fall Below Poverty Line (BPL – a poverty indicator of the Indian government). This renders them economically vulnerable and creates a certain dependence on development initiatives offered by government organizations, which these organizations used to coax the villagers to buy into the initiatives they are proposing. Meghalaya is a developmentalist state, where administration and governance are being enacted through the handing out of incentives. It runs a great variety of government programs, aimed at achieving rural development. Programs tend to have a relatively short life cycle, or at least they are subject to being updated regularly. This is also since programs seldom prove to be the panacea which they are thought to be at the time of their inception. Ever so often, the proposed recipients of these programs will complain that either the benefits do not – or insufficiently – reach them or whatever it entails does not fulfill their needs, suggesting that many of these programs in practice first and foremost serve to sustain a sizable bureaucracy, which due to its fragmentation as well as what might euphorically be termed "internal weaknesses" has difficulty to deliver. Villagers, in other words, were quite open to not only whatever initiatives were proposed by the state bodies but also weary of what these could deliver for them.

Following my first research trip in January 2019, I was able to make a second trip in June that year. The second visit confirmed my earlier impression, which was that the Meghalaya Forest Department and the GHADC had difficulties to find common ground regarding the development of the GHCA. Again some months later, I received the news that the Forest Department had finalized the borders of the Garo Hills Conservation Area and had decided to shrink the GHCA to the state forests and the national parks, i.e., the areas which were already managed by them. This meant that none of the communally managed forest lands would be included in the Garo Hills Conservation Area, and corridors between disconnected reserves and parks would at least for the time being not be realized. This decision must have made sense from the perspective of the Forest Department, but to me it felt like a lost opportunity. After all, it meant that in principle no land on which people resided, which was actively shaped by the kind of agricultural practices that made the region stand out in terms of cultural heritage, would be included in the initiative.

Conclusion: How Can Cultural Heritage Matter?

There is every reason to be concerned about the condition of forests in Garo Hills. Satellite scans report a deceptively dense forest cover for Garo Hills, but much of this consists of orchards, with only a small part being prime forest (Kurien et al., 2019). Some people told me that with the imposition of the 1995 "timber ban," which made the trade in timber illegal, maintaining forest became economically unviable since this rendered legal trade in timber virtually impossible. I do not consider this a convincing argument also, because major deforestation in Garo Hills seems to have taken place in the 1970s and 1980s (Karlsson, 2011). In addition, Garo Hills once abundant wildlife has become scarce. Colonial era sources talk of herds that were so large, in that easily 300 animals a year could be caught (Stracey, 1963). Now, the entire elephant population of Garo Hills has been reduced to about 50 animals. Given the stress on the environment, there is every reason to try to find ways in which sustainable usage can be encouraged.

From the perspective of the Forest Department, as the government body which is the main propagator of the GHCA, it seems that conservation of wildlife and forest is a prime concern. The proposal for the GHCA being floated as a mixed site is to some degree a strategic choice, since it is likely to improve the chance of success. Yet, given that the project entails a clear agenda oriented toward "nature," it seems almost impossible not to arrive at an objectified if not reified conceptualization of culture. Hence, the suggestion is to focus primarily on the traditional Garo community religion, rather than on everyday practices which may not be identified by people as religious, even though these certainly represent culturally specific knowledge. In order to foreground such knowledge, and encourage the sustainable economic practices associated with it, a much stronger alignment with initiatives taken at the village level would be desirable. This could also create a ground for conversation and cooperation between the various government departments.

From the perspective of villagers who live close to the state forests and national parks, a possible Garo Hills Conservation Area should help them to utilize their knowledge of the environment, resulting in activities that can help them to improve their life. Rural poverty is a serious issue, which will make itself increasingly felt, the more people living in rural areas become dependent on markets, both as sellers and as buyers, and develop a need for cash. It would make sense to try to follow up on strategies that render the forest productive, thus encouraging economically viable sustainable practices. This means that the GHCA, from the perspective of the villagers, should address the challenges they face in this respect, if it is to be an initiative that is supported by the people whose cultural heritage it is meant to represent.

Notes

1 The forest reserves that were initially created are repositories of valuable timber (mostly *sal* trees). The Forest Department has only in recent decades changed over

to forest conservation (Gadgil & Guha, 1993). Today, it runs many programs aimed not only at forest conservation, but also for instance at promoting the cultivation of tree crops, such as rubber. Such programs result in the Forest Department gaining a certain degree of control of the land to which it is applied, which is why people are suspicious of its intentions, which renders it difficult for them to cooperate with villagers that have communally owned land.

2 In the colonial era, Garo Hills obtained a dedicated land tenure system which was premised on existing land rights. These rights were located with village territories (*a'kings*), each territory being governed by the (senior) residents, under the nominal leadership of a village head (*nokma*).

3 The research related to this chapter has been generously supported by the International Centre for Integrated Mountain Development (ICIMOD), Leiden University's profile area Asian Modernities and Traditions (AMT), as well as the Dutch Research Council (NWO) and the Indian Council of Social Science Research (ICSSR).

4 This chapter has grown out of a paper presented at the international conference on "Custom, Law and the Colonial State in Northeast India: Dynamics and Challenges for the Postcolonial State," which was organized in June 2019 by Nandini Bhattacharyya Panda at the North Eastern Hill University in Shillong, with the support of the Nehru Memorial Museum and Library (Delhi).

5 The UNESCO format specifies 10 criteria, the relevance of which depends on the actual features of the site nominated. The heritage value of culture is defined as: "to be an outstanding example of a traditional human settlement, land-use, or sea-use which is representative of a culture (or cultures), or human interaction with the environment especially when it has become vulnerable under the impact of irreversible change" (criterion V) and "to be directly or tangibly associated with events or living traditions, with ideas, or with beliefs, with artistic and literary works of outstanding universal significance" (criterion VI). Geology is a criterion specified as: "representing major stages of earth's history, including the record of life, significant on-going geological processes in the development of landforms, or significant geomorphic or physiographic features" (criterion VIII). Nature is mentioned under criterion X: "to contain the most important and significant natural habitats for in-situ conservation of biological diversity, including those containing threatened species of outstanding universal value from the point of view of science or conservation" (Intergovernmental Committee for the Protection of the World Cultural and Natural Heritage, 2019, pp. 25–26).

6 "The nominated property falls under Biogeographic Zone 8B i.e. North-eastern India, which is one of the biologically most diverse regions of India. (…) Fifty-two species of mammals have been recorded here so far from Balpakram Landscape, of which twenty-one are carnivores. It holds one of the largest and most-threatened populations of Asian Elephant (*Elephas maximus*). (…) The different forest types, hill streams, rivers and caves within the property provide a diversity of habitat for an enormous diversity of species of invertebrates, 298 species of butterflies, 448 species of moths, 26 species of amphibian, 45 species of reptiles and 347 species of birds.

The State has 3331 plant species recorded of which 1319 Angiosperms (around 834 (25.04%) ethnomedicinal species are estimated to be used in healthcare sector). Among which 116 species were either under threatened or endemic. 17 species are endemic to Meghalaya, 113 Pteridophytes, 248 Bryophytes. A recent survey reveals a total of 436 Rare, Endangered and Threatened plant species have been recorded from Meghalaya representing13.09% of the state's flora. (…) The germplasm of Citrus indica is conserved in-situ at the National Citrus Gene Sanctuary in the Nokrek Biosphere Reserve the area is noted for other wild varieties of citrus fruits as well that provide a gene-pool for commercially produced citrus. (...) The cave systems in the property are crucibles of ongoing biological evolution, with species having been isolated for long periods" (UNESCO, 2018).

7 "Northeast India is significant in the study of the India-Asia continent collision, estimated to have happened 56–60 Million Years Ago (mya). This collision precipitated significant upheavals of geology, climatology, oceanography and paleobiology. Sediments are well developed in the eastern Tethyan realm in the Garo, Khasiand Jaintia hills and makes Meghalaya globally significant in the understanding of early foreland basin evolution. (...) In the Mahadeo Formation dominated by sandstone, the Late Cretaceous fossil content includes foraminifera, plant remains, dinosaur bone sand trace fossils" (UNESCO, 2018).

8 *Living Heritage Under Treat? Changing Utilization, Occupation and Appreciation of Land in the Garo Hills*, January 9, 2018, Meghalaya Forest Department, Dakopgre, Tura.

References

Aryal, K., & Choudhury, D. (2015). Climate Change: Adaptation, Mitigation and Transformation of Swidden Landscapes: Are We Throwing the Baby Out With the Bathwater? In M. Cairns (Ed.), *Shifting Cultivation and Environmental Change: Indigenous People, Agriculture and Forest Conservation* (pp. 281–288). London; New York: Routledge.

Bera, S.K., Basumatary, S.K., Agarwal, A., & Ahmed, M. (2006). Conversion of Forest Land in Garo Hills, Meghalaya for Construction of Roads: A Threat to the Environment and Biodiversity. *Current Science*, 91(3), 281–284.

Byrne, D., & Ween, G.B. (2015). Bridging Cultural and Natural Heritage. In L. Meskell (Ed.), *Global Heritage: A Reader* (pp. 125–146). Hoboken: John Wiley & Sons.

Chettri, N., Sharma, E., Shakya, B., Thapa, R., Bajracharya, B., Uddin, K., & Choudhury, D. (2010). *Biodiversity in the Eastern Himalayas: Status, Trends and Vulnerability to Climate Change*. Kathmandu: ICIMOD.

de Maaker, E. (2013). Performing the Garo Nation?: Garo Wangala Dancing between Faithand Folklore. *Asian Ethnology*, 72(2), 221–239.

de Maaker, E. (2018). On the Nature of Indigenous Land: Ownership, Access and Farming in Upland Northeast India. In E. Gerharz, N. Uddin, & P. Chakkarath (Eds.), *Indigeneity on the Move: Varying Manifestations of a Contested Concept* (pp. 29–48). New York: Berghahn.

de Maaker, E. (2020).Who Owns the Hills? Ownership, Inequality and Communal Sharing in the Borderlands of India. *Asian Ethnology*, 79(2), 357–375.

de Maaker, E. (2021). Aloof But Not Abandoned: Relationality and the Exploitation of the Environment in the Garo Hills of India. In D. Smyer Yü & E. de Maaker (Eds.), *Environmental Humanities in the New Himalayas: Symbiotic Indigeneity, Commoning, Sustainability* (pp. 135–151). Abingdon; New York: Routledge.

de Maaker, E. (2022). *Reworking Culture: Relatedness, Rites, and Resources in Garo Hills, North East India*. New Delhi: Oxford University Press.

de Maaker, E., & Tula, M. (2020). *Unequal Land Relations in North East India: Custom, Gender and the Market*. Guwahati: North Eastern Social Research Centre.

Forest Environment and Wildlife Management Department Government of Sikkim. (2016). *Nomination of Khangchendzong a National Park for Inscription on the World Heritage List*. Gangtok: Government of Sikkim.

Gadgil, M., & Guha, R. (1993). *This Fissured Land: An Ecological History of India*. Oakland: University of California Press.

Garo Hills Autonomous District Council. (2007). *Acts, Rules and Regulations with Amendments*. Tura: The Garo Hills Autonomous District Council.

Geismar, H. (2015). Anthropology and Heritage Regimes. *Annual Review of Anthropology*, 44(1), 71–85. doi:10.1146/annurev-anthro-102214-014217

Goswami, R. (2018, September 22). Northeast: Garo hills in queue for world heritage tag. *The Telegraph*. Retrieved from https://www.telegraphindia.com/states/north-east/garo-hills-range-basks-in-queue-for-world-heritage-tag/cid/1669791

Intergovernmental Committee for the Protection of the World Cultural and Natural Heritage. (2019). *Operational Guidelines for the Implementation of the World Heritage Convention*. Paris: UNESCO World Heritage Centre

International Fund for Agricultural Development. (2006). *Interim Evaluation: North Eastern Region Community Resource Management Project for Upland Areas (NERCRMP), Loan No. 444-IN*. Shillong: International Fund for Agricultural Development.

Karlsson, B.G. (2011). *Unruly Hills: A Political Ecology of India's Northeast*. New York: Berghahn Books.

Kurien, A.J., Lele, S., & Nagendra, H. (2019). Farmsor Forests? Understanding and Mapping Shifting Cultivation Using the Case Study of West Garo Hills, India. *Land*, 8(9), 26. Retrieved from https://www.mdpi.com/2073-445X/8/9/133

Marak, Q. (2019). *Megalithic Traditions of North East India*. Delhi: Concept Publishing Company.

Meghalaya Basin Development Authority. (2017). *Atlas for Natural Resource Management in Meghalaya* (1st edn). Shillong: GIS LAB, Meghalaya Basin Development Authority.

Melick, D., Kinch, J., & Govan, H. (2012). How Global Biodiversity Targets Risk Becoming Counterproductive: The Case of Papua New Guinea. *Conservation and Society*, 10(4),344–353. doi:10.4103/0972-4923.105559

Muzaini, H., & Minca, C. (2018). *After Heritage*. Cheltenham: Edward Elgar Publishing.

Pant, R.M., Tiwari, B.K., & Choudhury, D. (2018). *Shifting Cultivation: Towards a Transformational Approach*. New Delhi: NITI AAYOG.

Redpath, S.M., Gutiérrez, R.J., Wood, K.A., & Young, J.C. (2015). *Conflicts in Conservation: Navigating Towards Solutions. Ecological Reviews*. Cambridge; New York: Cambridge University Press.

Sangma, R.M.A. (2018, November 24). "To Beor Not To Be": Mixed Feelings induced by the nominated Mixed Site. *The Shillong Times*. Retrieved from https://theshillongtimes.com/2018/11/24/to-be-or-not-to-be-mixed-feelings-induced-by-the-nominated-mixed-site/

Sitlhou, M. (2019). Return to the Rat Hole. *Foreign Policy (December24)*. Retrieved from https://foreignpolicy.com/2019/12/24/rat-hole-coal-mine-meghalaya-government-protections-workers-environment/

Stracey, P.D. (1963). *Elephant Gold*. London: Weidenfeld and Nicholson.

Tiwari, B.K., Barik, S.K., & Tripathi, R.S. (1999). *Sacred Forests of Meghalaya: Biological and Cultural Diversity*. Shillong: Regional Centre National Afforestation and Eco-Development Board, North Eastern Hill University.

UNESCO. (2016). Khangchendzonga National Park. Retrieved from https://whc.unesco.org/en/list/1513

UNESCO. (2018). Garo Hills Conservation Area (GHCA). Retrieved from https://whc.unesco.org/en/tentativelists/6356/

9 Legislating "Objectionable Content" in the British Indian Empire and the Case of Assam in Northeast India (1910–1950)

Kaushik Thakur Bhuyan[1]

They found it very violent...they found it this, that...What eventually happened was they asked ten feet, two feet, seven feet cut out...they were being fooled, anyway we had kept twenty feet...they don't understand"...**How come you allowed Zeenat Aman to wear a two piece in Raj Kapoor's film?**[2]

(Ganti, 2009, 94)

When you **define obscenity, it is very much relative to the aesthetic sense of society** (emphasis added). Going to beaches with swimming costume is obscene to rural people of India but it is healthy in a western country.[3]

I think some code is necessary...**they should follow the code**...(emphasis added) what is vulgar and not vulgarise an abstract idea.[4]

(Ganti, 2009, 95)

Introduction

Priya Jaikumar has argued in the twentieth century "that The Cinematograph Films Act (or Quota Act) of 1927, was ostensibly initiated to assist British films against Hollywood's prevalence in the domestic British market, which was shaped by imperial aspirations." A trail of letters, petitions to the state, and memoranda archives the efforts of British film producers to extend the ambit of state protectionism to the empire by way of "empire quotas" and "empire film schemes"[5] (Jaikumar, 2006, 5). European and especially American made films were available in India since the first decade of the twentieth century as images of the British Empire had captured the popular imagination in the United States throughout the nineteenth and the early twentieth century[6] (Sinha, 2013, 91). Despite the shared ideology of racial hierarchy, there were differences between the American and British films. While British films manifested a paternalistic attitude toward the natives, American films represented a fraternity with people around the world[7] (Sinha, 2013, 7). Consequently, until the second decade of the twentieth century, the British government did not feel the need to legislate visual content in the Indian colony[8] (Ganti, 2009, 90). Prior to this, there was no legislation to

DOI: 10.4324/9781003539797-10

certify films for public exhibition in British India.[9] However a great deal of suspicion persisted on behalf of the colonial state toward the demoralizing impact of cinematograph spectatorship on native audiences in India.

The British government in India believed some of them were British in origin while others mostly imported from America as American Hollywood cinema was dominant and flourishing at home and elsewhere especially after the Second World War. Subsequently, in addition to revenue, the ethical question of race and Empire was also raised in the British parliament and governor's provinces regarding cinematograph exhibition in India. Such reports usually came from newspapers in England. For instance, Times of India dated 23rd August 1923 read,

> Good deal of dissatisfaction among British residents in our possessions in the Easton account of unsuitable films shown...The native never seems to grow up...To them are exhibited "sex" films made in American studios...in between may be sandwiched a comic film showing a white man carrying out ridiculous antics[10]
>
> (reference to Charlie Chaplain)

Subsequently on 21st March 1933, the government deliberated on the moral certification of films in India. It argued,

> The *examination* (emphasis added) of the question of control of cinema dates back to the secretary of State's letter of March 1932...The question revolves itself into whether the false impression of western civilization which is undoubtedly conveyed by American films has a bad effect on Indian youths and the Indian public. Here too, opinion differs. The Deputy Commissioner...raises the point that it is futile to *suppress features of modern social life which are freely ventilated in the press as illustrated in papers and literature.*[11]

Stephen P. Hughes' work on silent film in colonial South India has addressed the beginnings of "exhibition" policy used by the British as early as 1913 to prevent a certain European lady called Maud Allen to perform at Madras by enforcing the Public Performances Act 1876 (P.P.A.) and The Public Resort Act 1888 (P.R.A.). He justifies what appears to him that "just the threat of live performance at a cinema hall was enough to prompt the government to initiate its first steps in a long history of regulating spaces of cinema[12]" (Hughes, 2002, 42). William Mazzarella and Raminder Kaur have argued that "the 1920's and 1930's witnessed the struggle over erotic's in printed matter to the affective power of the press as a mass medium with an expanding vernacular audience"[13] (Kaurand & Mazzarella, 2009, 14). While Charu Gupta's work[14] (Gupta, 2012) talks about how cultural production was juxtaposed to establish a pure literary Hindi public sphere in the earliest years of the twentieth century to denigration of late medieval overtly eroticized poetic idioms and a booming mass produced sex manuals[15] (Kaurand & Mazzarella, 2009, 14).

One may notice that the obsession with sexuality either in print or performance especially in literature and its implications on native subjects of the Indian empire was one of the earliest concerns of colonial officials in the modernization of Indian society. Hence display of sexuality or obscenity in print especially performance was to be rectified by sanitization efforts as Stephen Hughes argues in places of exhibit and as William Mazzarella and Raminder Kaur emphasize; by reforming the cultural articulation of gender that characterized the larger course of socio-cultural awakening and rise of middle-class consciousness of Indian intelligentsia in the twentieth century in India. Henceforth, contestations between the "progressive western" and "backward Indian society" rhetoric theories legitimized colonial intervention into affairs of the "Indian domestic space." Consequently, while both the colonizer and colonized affirmed this position, it was *believed* disputable only in the manner in which such a cleansing exercise was to be implemented in which women were sought to be claimed and reclaimed in both colonial and traditional debates. The espousals of such contestations also spilled on to print vernacular, a space wherein the educated natives could rearticulate themselves with or without colonial intervention.

While the depiction of violence could be negotiated in literature through social drama, the concern over erotic content was deeply complicated. The proscription of objectionable literature was

> covered under section 18(e) of the Sea Customs Act and167 (8) that rendered confiscation of goods and a penalty not exceeding three times the value of the goods i.e.1000. Section 292 I.P.C. made importation for sale, hire, 293 I.P.C. –possession of such matter for distribution, public exhibition, punishable with imprisonment up to three months with fine or both.

However, the crucial point was that the above rules **"did not touch films objectionable on other grounds than obscenity** e.g. 'Seditious films' and legislation on such films **was awaited** unless proven to be evaded on extensive scale."[16]

Contestations over censorship as argued in scholarship has been raised over American cinema and the naivety of Indian natives whereas archival records and Priya Jaikumar's work indicate, was only gradually beginning to take shape in the early twentieth century in India. The concept of visual spectatorship was initially raised over **controlling** the production of films either British or Indian productions in India. The central purpose of the colonial state was to oversee that no film was to be produced without a license and censorship constituted one of the *modus operandi* of certification. This was also intended to check the export of undesirable films into India. Isn't it significant to note when both the legal and the mechanical apparatus for the production of Indian films are not yet established, how is it possible to exhibit Indian productions to Indian audiences and blame them for objectionable content produced by European or American studios in Britain America or elsewhere in Europe? If and only if Indians were witnessing European or American productions on a substantial scale can the above be true and "the only means of prohibiting export or import of such films was in section 19 of the Sea Customs Act."[17]

From the legal point of view, since the colonial state was already substantially armed to proscribe objectionable literature, censorship was formulated as a corrective to Britain's moral panic over the degrading nature of European especially American cinema in India which was reportedly having a demoralizing effect on native audiences especially the illiterate classes. The recourse to censorship had its genesis in the Indian colony owing to this anxiety of Britain and censorship protocols as part of the Cinematograph Act 1918 that was believed to effectively address both colonial and the Indian traditional concern over safeguarding the ethics and morality of women within the traditional patriarchal home and the outside. The Cinematograph legislations 1918 laid out that,

> Most of the films exhibited in India are certified by the Bombay and Calcutta Board of Censors...A strict application of principles enunciated in the suggestions...and excision of parts of films containing unnecessary exhibition of feminine underclothing, nude figures, offensive vulgarity and impropriety in conduct and dress, excessively passionate lovemaking scenes should improve the position materially. The Cinematograph Committee was fully alive to the importance of the considerations.[18]

However, the matter was slightly more complicated in matters of its legal execution. The government felt the words "objectionable" and "undesirable" were extremely wide terms and it obviously warranted for a variety of opinions on the question whether a particular film should or should not be exhibited and it would no doubt be impossible to get any board of censors which would be able to function so as to avoid the susceptibilities of all classes and sections of people and at the same time refrain from hampering or irritating the legitimate cinema trade.[19]

> The Home Department in British India voiced similar views on the subject. It was of the view that complaints from authoritative quarters that censorship was lax despite reports from local governments on assurance that "all is well" in terms of censorship of visuals in India was a recurring problem.[20] It explicitly voiced out its opinion that "the institution of the system of censorship in India was quite unsatisfactory itself. The department accepted that there were only two methods to effect censorship of films. First, either it was the responsibility for the

> trade to censor films themselves as done in England. This system was proven they felt to be effective when trade was well organised and of good repute. The second alternative was for the government to step in itself and censor by means of an adequately paid stuff sufficient in numbers for the task. It was also confessed that at that point of time, the government censor boards were too large and composed of men who cannot give time to work."[21]

At the political front, deliberations of the administration explicitly pointed out that there was no information as to whether leaders in England made use of cinema in election campaigns, but it was clear that the case was very different in India as pointed out by the government of Bombay. There was no official censorship of cinematograph films. In British India in the matter of films, the law enabled the censorship board to grant or refuse a certificate to any film without assigning the reasons for their decision and the local government was the final authority in the matter. At the same time, it was agreed on principle that the broadcasting of all political speeches on films should be banned. In the case of radio, no statements were to be broadcast on topics of political and industrial controversy and that would extend to election speeches. However there were exceptions that were raised on the degree of what kind of political content was disseminated.

> In 1936, Jawaharlal Nehru expressed in the press that in the forthcoming elections there were only two parties; Congress and the government and that congress supporters will aim at discrediting and misrepresenting government to the fullest extent within the law.[22]
>
> If elections were held between two or three political parties and the government as was the case in England, it would still bore an unexcitable audience. However it was presumed that in the Indian colony, it was not difficult to visualize in which election speech show ever innocuous might lead to an excitable audience in crowded audiences.

It further emphasized that

> in a contest between several political parties the difficulties of the board of censors in deciding what should not be allowed would be even greater than in censoring speeches than in which the Congress admit to be directed against the government. It would be difficult to make anyone believe that the government was giving an unbiased decision in appeal to section 7 (3) of the cinematograph Act. In any case, it seems that the aim of the congress is not the acceptance of office for purpose of working the new constitution but to enter the legislature for wreaking the new constitution and the ultimate object of congress that is independence.[23]

It is clear from the above extract that the aim and purpose for debarring election speeches from the Congress party by the government rested on the old fear colonial fear of popular dissent and rebellion among native subjects of the colony since the Revolt of 1857. However the matter of execution of the deliberated proposition of the colonial government was intricately entwined in a series of legal limitations. The considerations of applying censorship to cinema were not the same as those of broadcasting. While the former was wholly controlled by the government, the latter was in the hands of private productions in which the private proprietor presumably consults the taste of the public and takes responsibility for what the exhibits. In addition, a more pressing issue was that 'if the board of censors were required to distinguish between **what are objectionable** and other speeches, it is very difficult for them to do so as local governments cannot participate in those decisions as it is merely an appellate authority under the Cinematograph Act. The 'weight of the argument thus lies on securing the observance of local governance in such matters for future effective working of the censorship machinery." "While section 126 (2) of the Government of India enables federal government to preserve control, the sub sections merely authorises giving directions to a province to execution of an Act. There is no section in the Cinematograph Act to give any directions to local government and it is not clear if the federal government would have any power If any local government decided to allow political addresses in the future in cinemas."[24]

Subsequently, the matter was further interpreted in the best possible manner by the respective provincial governments.

> Instructions by Bombay board of Film Censors for guidance of its inspectors opined that controversial politics are likely to be objectionable implying that unobjectionable references to politics may be passed. Therefore the Governor General in Council is inclined to the view that the screen should not be used for political purposes of any party. In Central Provinces, the subject was *provisionally accepted* while in Madras the government agreed without zero hesitation that the screen shall not be used for political purposes. The government of Bihar further emphasised on the humongous problem of ascertaining and distinguishing between seditious and nonseditious speeches but accepted the principle that all political speeches be banned so that people would not criticize the government of undue favor to any single party. Chief Commissioner of Ajmer expressed concern that the task of selecting objectionable from non objectionable would be onerous and difficult that would bring accusations of discrimination on the government and in his opinion it was to be subject to suitable censorship than complete disapproval. The Punjab government in the civil secretariat opined that under government service conduct rules 1935, it was the duty of all governments to maintain complete detachment towards various parties…The mere adoption of the creed of independence in itself a matter

of academic interest to most people in the province may not be regarded as sedition...if candidates or parties in pursuance of their election campaign make speeches or issue literature that has the effect of bringing established authority under hatred or contempt, in such circumstances there should be no hesitation in recommending persecution under section 124 (A) of the Indian Penal Code. If election campaigns disturb public peace use of section 107 and 144 of the Criminal Procedure Code can be considered.[25]

Tax Incentives and Accusations of Gullible Public Blamed for Sexual Motives

So far, the central focus on censorship as envisaged in British India had very little to do with sexuality to begin with. The foremost concerns of the British imperial state were to focus on the introduction of legislation to control production and exhibition of films in India. Under the board of censors under the Cinematograph Act, there was no provision for improper films and their private exhibition and exportation.[26] The Home Department instructions were to focus on the registration of all persons or firms producing films, the licensing of such persons and films, *penalties* for omission to register for producing without license, inspection of places of production by a district magistrate or a magistrate empowered by him, prohibition of import of films except under license and inspection of certification by the examining/certifying authority of films imported, and the power to confiscate and destroy improper films. This process involved a certain amount of fees and could be executed legally. Point four posed the central and most vexed problem for the state to execute. This has been unacknowledged and almost absent on scholarship on the subject of censorship.

As early as 1922, the secretary of state was informed about the disparities between what the cinematograph legislation could do and what it could not. While agreeing that the colonial government received complaints about import of objectionable films especially with reference to the presence of Bolshevik and American Cinema in British India since the enactment of the Cinematograph Act 1918, the government laid out that it wasn't the guardian of private morals...The duty to foresee that any improper or objectionable films did not enter India was covered by the already existing section 18 (c) Sea Customs Act. Rather than morality the central focus of the government thought it unworthy to put the trade to inconvenience as it would still be possible to smuggle such films by book, parcel post which in the event of a thorough check by custom officials would still come into the colony by crews of incoming steamers. Hence, the primary concern to legislate and supervise content in cinema was initially tied to commercial profit and customs excise duty rather than what constituted vulgar or unethical content at that point of time. In support of the arguments made in this section, let us look at some of the deliberations made in the Cinematograph Committee 1927–1928.

The constitution of the committee under the chairmanship of Rangachariar was the first of its kind in colonial India even as late as 1927–1928, its principal aim was to understand, organize, and develop production, exhibition, and censorship of Empire films in India. Manashita Dass' work on the mass audience in India has argued that

> spectatorship emerged in colonial India as a site not just of imagining community but also of asserting class difference and social hierarchies wherein cinema introduced a new set of powerful cultural distinctions and a context of consumption that 'were not' particularly conducive to imagining this space as unified and homogeneous or to picturing the audience as a fraternity of equals and a horizontal comradeship.[27]
>
> (Dass, 2009, 77–98)

However, the contention that such a space was not conducive also seems partially true. The Cinematograph Committee although elitist in its composition of its members tried hard to understand the social and class complexities in understanding the politics of cinema exhibition and participation of both the European and Indian audiences. The first few questions asked by the committee to all relevant members of the public and state in the questionnaires sent out to all parts of the country focused on the very nature of the class composition of the audience. It asked,

> In your experience to what extend do Indians (1) educated classes (2) illiterate classes frequent cinemas? To what extent is there increase in attendance? (3)Explain in what area or place your answer refers. Can you give an idea of the average composition of cinema audience in your locality and (4) what percentage of audience consists of children under 14 or adolescence?

Reports from agent[28] (I.C.C. evidences, Vol.I, Central Publication Branch, Calcutta 1927-1928, 23–27) for Universal Pictures Corporation New York, USA in India responded that one-third of attendance for educated classes and two-thirds for the uneducated. There is no increase in attendance for educated classes but an increase in 5 percent for the illiterate classes "in case of Indian productions." In the "fort city" (Bombay), educated Indians and Europeans watched films and in places like Girgaum – mostly educated and uneducated Indians and in Parel and Dadar – Hindus seemed prominent. The average composition was 3 percent and the most popular films with Indian audiences were one that they could easily follow like Indian productions, foreign serials, comedies, drama, and thrilling features of adventure variety. "Successful Indian films like *Krishna Jamuna, Sinhaghad, Gulbakavli, Aladin, Magician of Bengal, At the Clang of Fetters, Sadarba* and *Laila Majnu* were popular." "The educated classes enjoyed topical Indian news, national literature, history and social drama; the illiterate classes history, mythology, folklore and romances"[29] (I.C.C. evidences, 1927, v-24). As Manashita Dass has established, "cinema" played a key role in extending the Indian public sphere beyond the confines of the "lettered city"[30] (2009, 79). My only contention in her argument is that the very "amorphousness of this audience seems to have sparked an almost obsessive interest in determining the precise composition of the audience and in gauging the possible effects of cinema, especially western films, on its different segments"[31] (Dass, The Crowd outside the Lettered City, 84) is partially true because audience composition was heterogeneous in other nations also. The problem in India as the I.C.C. realized as argued so far was in trying to condense Indian educational and cultural diversity into one single standard of law. That is why while obscenity in literature was easily punishable, in cinema censorship ban meant losing finance on certification as well as exhibition of films.

Nonetheless while demand was excess to actual supply, Indian productions couldn't compete with foreign productions for weakness of the industry in India at such a nascent stage for want of better technique and equipment. It was also pointed out that profit depended on several factors and the "chief intention was to make a certain amount of films produced in the British Empire to be compulsorily exhibited in Indian theatres."

> If there is compulsion in adopted Indian films have to compete with films made in other parts of the empire despite the fact that educated class of Indians do not find appeal to Indian produced films at present; in such case they would not appeal much to anybody outside India.[32]

The primary objective of the state was to acquire taxes[33] remitted out of the Amusements tax that was directly related to a certain degree of unease for total prohibition to cinema trade by the colonial government on mere complaints of objectionable content by either government officials or the public in general. That is why the issue of censorship caused a consistent source of perplexity and worry for the colonial state. Further the social susceptibilities of the subject colony needed to be addressed as well.

On questions about the availability of objectionable posters in cinema houses by the C.C. members, the supervisor, Bombay Entertainments Duty Act, in his evidence testified he had seen none. Mr Stenson reiterated that he had seen western pictures shown in India in which English ladies are made to dance on dinner tables some scantily dressed. He supposed such things won't ever happen in any civilized society in Europe and such pictures were shown to uneducated Indians.[34] (Q) But decency is common to both, whether European or Indian? (A) I should say if a man has been to Europe or if he has come out of it, he would not believe these pictures are for real. (Q) I think you exaggerate the importance of the uneducated classes. (A) Yes, but there are boys who have never seen England and they may take it that these things are true. (Q) Is this impression gained from any conversation with Indians or is it a mere guess? (A) I have questioned many boys who frequent cinema shows and believe that a train running at 150 miles speed and a man jumping from a tree are true. (Q) I would like to have your independent view as you are the first European who has come to give evidence...we have heard complaints from European gentleman and ladies that exhibition of western life to an easterner produces a lowering effect on the European. (A) That is not my complaint. I don't think it's a serious thing. (Q) Do you think present censoring is not strict? (A) Censoring is all right.[35]

In another instance, it is interesting to note that objection to complete censorship was voiced by an educated lady member of The Bengal Presidency Council for Women especially at a time when the nationalist struggle was at its formidable years since the Non-Cooperation Movement (1920) and the mass demonstrations and boycott of the Simon commission in the year of publication of the C.C. evidences.

> Q: Has your association at any point of time complained to the board of censors about the nature of films shown here?
> A: No. I am afraid we have not dealt with it at all.
> Q: You do not want to lovemaking scenes?
> A: I do not think it is necessary.
> Q: You do not want to ban kissing scenes?
> A: What the council thought I believe was that it should not be made slow. It should only be a passing incident.
> Q: Almost everybody complained that one has not acquainted himself or herself with the rules which now prevail as regards censorship?
> A: I see the close ups are still in evidence in films.
> Q: Close ups are in evidence everywhere. In England also it is in evidence very largely. How is it that the English society does not revolt against it? It is not we

Who misrepresent them, it is the westerner himself/herself who represents in that light and they do not tap the source of mischief without coming here and putting a stop to it?

> A: They are a totally different people.
> Q: So then, you must have a different class of cinema for the western and a different for the easterner?
> A: No. it would be a good idea to have them censored in England.[36]

Silent Yet Alive: Censorship in Assam in Eastern Periphery of British India

A host of writings are available on the political history of the region since Edward

> Gait's *A History of Assam* (1904) to Sanjib Baruah's *India Against Itself* (1999) in contemporary times. Comparatively very little has been written on the social-cultural history of the region especially with regard to the genesis and development of cinema spectatorship in the region. Starting with Joytiprasad Agarwala's *Joymoti* 1935 and *Indramaloti* (1939), a host of films based on historical figures re-recovered from Ahom Buranjis, focussing on the Ahom dynastic feuds, Ahom Mughal conflict (1616–1682), Maomoria rebellion 1769–1805), Revolt of 1857 to mention a few; Assamese cinema in the vernacular has since colonial times grown out of a strong sense of middle class (Sharma, 1990, 3)[37] consciousness evolving out of cultural interaction with its closest metropolis of Bengal as well as colonial introduction of western education, missionary activity and the least acknowledged aspect i.e. cinematograph legislations and middleclass participation of the regional intelligentsia in visual spectatorship. This section will focus on two major key points. One, when and how were cinematograph legislations enforced in the province and secondly how did Assam respond to censorship contestations being debated in the rest of India as mentioned in the previous sections.

First, almost all scholarship has acknowledged the genesis of cinema in Assam with Joytiprasad Agarwala's *Joymoti*,[38] the first film in the Assamese vernacular based on true events recovered from Ahom *Buranjis* and exhibited at Calcutta in 1935.[39] The question no one has acknowledged is how it was exhibited without the availability of the Cinematograph legislation in the province. Despite the fact that Assam remained outside British India till as late as 1826 and 1838 when upper Assam was wrested from Purander Singha into British dominions, within hundred years, the natives of Assam could witness its indigenous cinema because the film was passed by the censor boards at Calcutta. The cinematograph legislations of 1918 although covered only the major port cities of Bombay, Calcutta, Madras, Burma, and later one at Punjab, the regulations were flexible in allowing any producer from any region to register any film for certification under anyone of the boards. At the same time, *Joymoti's* content focused on women's self-sacrifice for one's husband was used by Jyotiprasad as rhetoric for nation and region. Despite its nationalist overtones, it was passed by the censor board. In this sense, colonial censorship was negotiated through the use of Indian traditional folklore and history as allegories for channeling national and regional awakening which constantly baffled censor board officials in deciding what constituted objectionable propaganda by subjects of the British Indian colony.

Second, there is scarcely any record in general scholarship about cinematograph legislation and the debates surrounding the effectiveness of censorship in Assam. Did censorship debates reach peripheral Assam at all? As early as 1922, 13 years before the first film in North East India is exhibited, the government was well aware of censorship legislations. On the issue of control of production/exhibition of films of an educational value, Government of Assam

> agrees that legislation is required on moral and political grounds and would provide for a license for production of films and their supervision.[40]

It is interesting to note that Assam did not have any film nor censor board at that point, yet it was fully aware of the concerns over safeguarding the moral interests of the Empire.

However cinema exhibition existed owing to import of European films into Assam. As early as September 1920, the Secretary Calcutta Board of Censors writes to the Manager of the Victoria Bioscope, Assam

> Certificates will be issued for films mentioned here in for a sum of rupees 48-/- at a reduced rate of rupee 1 for each film except film "Rebel Russia." In future fees for all films will be rupees 5-/- for every thousand feet or fraction of thousand film examined…Rebel Russia has been refused a certificate by the Deputy Commissioner of Darrang…should not be exhibited under prosecution under Cinematograph Act…copies in your possession must either be destroyed or returned to importers…with the undertaking this would not be hired or exhibited any where in British India.[41]

The All India Women's Conference a few years after *Joymoti* (1935) at meeting held at Shillong (headquarters of undivided Assam in colonial India) brought out the resolution that,

> The conference lodges its emphatic protest against the overt as well as covert of ***obscene literature*** "throughout India." We have cause to believe that such ***obnoxious literature*** is provided by small bookstall holders for younger generation that is to students of schools and colleges of both the sexes. We request authorities to take drastic and immediate steps and stamp out the evil as soon as possible and give encouragement to publication of better literature. We request public and government to ensure that all such journals and newspapers that continue to indulge in the pernicious practice of publishing obscene and outrageous articles and advertisement which insult womanhood in general and violate all laws of decency that cannot be tolerated by any civilized nation.[42]
>
> The Amrit Baazar Patrika[43] in Calcutta in July 1935 in its correspondence reported something similar. "As for the dissemination of vulgar literature Calcutta has acquired notoriety in regard to it. There is an almost endless variety of vulnerable literature from lampoons and satires and sex publications to indecent stories put in periodicals…One

would think that in these days of trade depression the only trade that is thriving is the trade in obscene literature."

The excerpts although silent on the exact detail of what was depicted ascertains with some degree of certainty that much of sexual content came from literature *and not* from cinema as it was still at its infancy and the consistent presumption by scholars that censorship was an ethical question over erotic content is a much later development that becomes critical in post-independence.

However in matters of immediate politics, Assam was in consonance with views expressed by its administrative counterparts in the rest of India. In 1936, the Governor in Council (Assam) opined that

> the only party that could use the cinematograph would be the Congress party to create a deadlock and wreak the constitution and hence it would not be allowed to use films or the press or both for the purpose. However the message implicitly also showed no comments or views on allowing speeches and political campaigning by other parties or associations.[44]
>
> Most of the films exhibited in India are certified by the Bombay and Calcutta Board of Censors...A strict application of principles enunciated in the suggestions...and excision of parts of films containing unnecessary exhibition of feminine underclothing, nude figures, offensive vulgarity and impropriety in conduct and dress, excessively passionate lovemaking scenes should improve the position materially. The Cinematograph Committee was fully alive to the importance of the considerations.[45]

To these recommendations, it was further stressed that,

> Though each local government can censor films, it is difficult for them to reject a film passed by Bombay or Calcutta and I also think it can hardly be held that a different standard should be imposed in Bombay and Calcutta to what is imposed in Lahore and Peshawar.[46]

The apparent complexities of determining obscenity or unsuitable content perplexed officials dealing with censorship in the censor at different provinces. While The Censor Boards under the Cinematograph Act were ***clearly empowered to censor content that might explicitly convey impressions of vulgarity, sexualism propriety, and excessive love scenes, it was rather seen as a question of how much was acceptable than what wasn't.*** Such a paradox of content interpretation vexed the legal power of the Board to first understand what to cut and when to cut. To add, despite the knowledge of American films supposedly affecting moral concerns of the natives, the colonial government did not hesitate to reiterate its strict vigilance on the matter.

In supporting the work done by the censor Boards in India, it also stressed that since the country was huge and its habitants so varied, a particular standard could not be adopted for all regions especially after a certificate was granted by the two most important and powerful provinces of Bombay and Calcutta.

Consequently, the issue of the complicated question of formulating a standard policy for moral control of films is not restricted to the governor general's provinces. In spite of a general stand undertaken at the Deputy Commissioner's level, the matter is referred to the provinces for their opinion as well. For instance, the letter continued that,

> We should impress upon the local governments their own powers of the Cinematograph Act to stop exhibition of films that got a certificate from Bombay or Calcutta boards...It would of course be unpopular with cinema proprietors, but that I should not much mind.[47]

In response to the circulars handed out to local governments on the matter, W.L. Scott, Secretary to Govt. of Assam, Shillong dated 24th October 1923 to the Secretary Home Dept. Govt. of India opined that,

> The Govt of Assam taking into consideration the known difficulties surrounding all censorship efforts are satisfied that the canons of censorship adopted by the censoring boards *are reasonably adequate and that the vast majority of films exhibited do not in any way tend to bring western civilization into contempt*.[48]

One may wonder why history is silent on the absence of participation of Assam and what implications did the legislations of 1918 have on Assamese cinema and censorship in the decades leading up to partition 1947. Literature on Assam in the early twentieth century is replete with instructions to women on cooking, cleaning, motherhood, and self-sacrifice as well as caution toward reading of erotic manuals. This is outside the scope of this chapter and as argued before erotic's in literature was already covered under the press laws for proscription which wasn't the case for cinema. The cinematograph legislations were reworked for the second time in the history of Indian cinema in 1952 to address the changing political and cultural conditions of Independent India that is also outside the purview of the chapter. What is sure is that the government over the years since 1922 was consistently debating the nature of censorship and the Government of India confessed in its correspondence to provinces in 1925 that

> progress in the matter could not be made partially due to depressed condition of cinema **and mainly little *concrete evidence* of existence of evils which it sought to remedy. It remained to be proved in the opinion of His Majesty and Governor in Council there was *sufficient evidence***

of prevalence of any abuse in the indigenous film industry to warrant control over legislation for confiscation of improper films.[49]

Despite the central government itself being at crossroads over the dilemma over censorship in the early twentieth century, peripheral Assam in Northeast India still managed to convey that,

> Government of Assam adheres to the views expressed in letter Pol.450/1711 dated March 1922 and have nothing further to add.[50]

Almost all the films made since 1930–1950 in Assam were based on popular folklore and community history and that is why the intelligentsia in Assam was able to sustain self-assertions of region and nation by deploying its traditional historical narratives onto cinema and that proved successful in negotiating the colonial state's surveillance through censorship in the region for the period discussed.

Conclusion

Therefore, censorship and cinematograph legislations in British India to use Nicholas Dirks' words were part and parcel of "colonial knowledge that enabled conquest and also produced by it"[51] (Cohn, 1996, See Forward). Accordingly, the occidental European view of the Indian Orient was seen as one in which "cultural forms in societies newly classified as traditional were reconstructed and transformed through "such 'forms of knowledge' which in turn produced its own set of categories and oppositions between colonial and the colonized, European and Asian, traditional and modern, East and West."

Therefore politics of censorship and censor boards to restrain or excise portions of films found unsuitable in the exercise of Cinematograph Act 1918, the administration found negotiating this very cultural dichotomy[52] (see Chatterjee, 1994; Nandy, 1998; Prasad, 1998) (between the east and west) unpredictable and contrary to European standards of orchestrating knowledge into governable hierarchies of one standard rule of law (See Metcalf Thomas, 2008). Thus, while on the one hand most of the officials affirmed the suitability of the censoring mechanism in the colony, some accepted the moral dilemma of the colonial state in deciphering the character and nature of morality when it came to the question of cinema. Therefore censorship anxieties as most scholars on cinema have suggested could not be legislated only on presumed threats to Britain's moral prestige, seditious activity, obscenity by performers, or places of exhibit as these spheres were covered by press laws (1878/1835/1908/1910/1930), Indian Penal code (1860), and Dramatic Performances Act (1876) to regulate performances *in places of exhibit* and *not the performance itself*. This dilemma of ascertaining which performances ***may be*** constituted objectionable in the period of study was intricately tied to the larger cultural question wherein ideologies of the west versus east *continued* to be contested between colonial administrators and Indian middle class.

Therefore it may correctly be argued that the contribution of cinematograph and cinematograph act both as a visual space and a piece of legislation regarding censorship respectively played a significant role as major sites of exchange and interchange of sensibilities in what Partha Chatterjee's work on Nation and its Fragments has argued as the "interplay between the colonial and colonized." Such interplay of colonial intentions for acquiring control over cinema production, taxation through certification/exhibition, and most importantly the practice of systematic legislation between Britain and within the British Indian administration in India were major players that defined censorship debates in colonial India including and beyond sexuality of performers/performance in Assam and India.

Notes

1 File No. 147, Political Branch, National Archives, of India, New Delhi, 1922. Henceforth referred to as N.A.I.
2 Ganti, Tejaswini (2009). "The Limits of Decency and Decency of Limits" in *Censorship in South Asia: Cultural Regulation from Sedition to Seduction*, (eds). Kaur Ramindar and William Mazarella. London: Routledge.
3 Ganti, *The Limits of Decency*, 101. Subhas Ghai's views on censorship in India.
4 Ganti, *The Limits of Decency*, 95. Madhuri Dixit's views on censorship in India.
5 Jaikumar, Priya. (2006). "*Cinema at the End of Empire: A Politics of Transition in Britain and India*", Durham: Duke University Press, 5.
6 Sinha, Babli. (2013). *Cinema Transnationalisms and Colonial India, Entertaining the Raj*, London: Routledge, 2.
7 Sinha, Babli. (2013). *Cinema Transnationalisms*, 91.
8 Ganti, Tejaswini. (2009). "The Limits of Decency and the Decency of Limits, Censorship and the Bombay Film Industry" in *Censorship in South Asia: Cultural Regulation from Seduction to Seduction*, (eds). Kaur, Raminder and Mazzarella, William. London: Routledge, 90.
9 Home Political (1922), 147, N.A.I, New Delhi, 2.
10 Home Political (1926), 168-III-26/2-4.
11 Home Political (1932), 16/32, *Report of the Indian Cinematograph Committee Evidence*, National Archives, New Delhi, 15–16. Henceforth, referred to as I.C.C.
12 P. Hughes, Stephen. (2002). 'Policing Silent Exhibition in Colonial India South India' in Vasudevan Ravi. (eds.), *Making Meaning in Indian Cinema*, New Delhi: OUP, 42.
13 Kaur, Ramindar and William Mazzarella (eds). (2009). *Censorship in South Asia: Cultural Regulation from Seduction to Seduction*. London: Routledge, 14.
14 Gupta, Charu. (2012). *Gendering Colonial India, Reforms, Print, Caste and Colonialism*. New Delhi: Orient Blackswan.
15 Kaur, Ramindar and Mazzarella, William, 15.
16 Political (1922), 147, N.A.I., New Delhi, 4.
17 Home Political (1926). Film Censors, 168III/26, N.A.I., New Delhi, 3.
18 Home Political (1932), 8/16/32, Report of the I.C.C., N.A.I., New Delhi, 35–36.
19 Home Political, 168-III/26, 3.
20 Home Political, 9.
21 Home Political, 9.

22 Home 2/16/36, Department Notes, Prohibition in Forthcoming Elections use of Cinematograph Screen, N.A.I., New Delhi, 1.
23 File No. 2/16/36, Home Department Notes, Prohibition in Forthcoming Elections use of Cinematograph Screen, N.A.I., New Delhi, 2.
24 Home. (1936), 2/16/36, Notes, Prohibition in Forthcoming Elections, N.A.I., New Delhi, 2.
25 Home Political, K.W. (1936), 2/16,1936, N.A.I., New Delhi, 1–7.
26 Home Political (1922), 147, N.A.I, New Delhi, 1.
27 Dass, Manishita (2009). The Crowd outside the Lettered City: Imagining the Mass Audience in 1920s India, *Cinema Journal*, Vol. 48, No. 4 (Summer) 77–98.
28 Indian Cinematograph Committee Evidences Vol.I, Central Publication Branch Calcutta, 1927–1928, pp.23 – Written statement of Raosahib Chunilal G. Munim dated 16th November 1927.
29 I.C.C. Evidence (1927–1928), Central Publication Branch, Calcutta, 1928, v-24.
30 Dass, Manashita. The Crowd outside the Lettered City, 79.
31 Dass, Manashita. The Crowd outside the Lettered City, 84.
32 Written statement of Rao sahib Chunilal G. Munim on his views on the question of inclusion of Indian productions for participation in the policy outlined in the Resolutions of the Imperial Conference to encourage empire films.
33 In the fort city of Bombay alone, total tax levied for a duration of 15 years for cinema was roughly 7, 50, 750 rupees.
34 I.C.C. Evidence (1927–1928), Vol. I, 40.
35 I.C.C. Evidence (1927–1928), Vol. I, 41.
36 I.C.C. Evidence (1927–1928), Vol. II, 918–920.
37 Sharma, Manorama. (1990). "*Social and Economic Change in Assam: Middleclass Hegemony*", Delhi: Ajanta Publications, 3.
38 Ishwar Prasad Chowdhury, *opcit*, pp. xxvii-158. Also see Gaurav Rajkhowa, Coming Back to Life: Jyotiprasad's *Joymoti* and Nationalist Politics in Assam, 1890s–1940s in *Bioscope South Asian Screen Studies*, 2nd December, 2015; Anirban K. Baishya, Restore, Revisit, Remember: Reinstating the Region in Three Assamese Films, *Journal of South Asian Studies*, 28th May, 2017, 431–446.
39 *Assamiya*. (9th March, 1935), Nehru Memorial Museum and Library, New Delhi, 4. Bhuyan, Kaushik Thakur. (2024). The Politics of Spectatorship: *Textual Traditions, Cinematograph and the Moral dilemma of the Natives of Assam in British India* (1900–1935) in Parichay Patra and Amitendu Bhattacharya (2024). (eds). Frontiers of South Asian Culture: Nation, Translation and Beyond, New York: Routledge.
40 Political Branch, 147, NAI, New Delhi, 22.
41 Police Department, 824. C.B., Assam State Archives, Guwahati, 16.
42 Political Branch, LIV 55/38, *All India Women's Conference against Obscene Advertisements in literature and Newspapers*, Assam State Archives, Guwahati, 2–3.
43 Amrita Bazar Patrika, *Vulgar Literature*, July 1935, Manuscript Section, National Library, Kolkata, 1–12.
44 Home Political, 2/16/36, 4.
45 Home Political (1936), 12–13.
46 Home Political (1936), 16.
47 Home Political (1936), 18.
48 Home Political (1936), 54.
49 Home 207/25, N.A.I.,1 925, 44. The highlighted portion of the text is reproduced as it in the archival file.
50 Home 207/25, N.A.I., 1925, 44–48.
51 S. Cohn, Bernard. (1996). *Colonialism and Its Forms of Knowledge: The British in India*, New Jersey: Princeton University Press, see Forward.

52 Chatterjee, Partha, "*The Nation and its Fragments*, Princeton: Princeton University Press, 1994; Nandy, Asish. (1998). *The Secret Politics of Our Desires: Innocence, Culpability, and Indian Popular Cinema*, New Delhi: Oxford University Press; Prasad, Madhava. (1998). *Ideology of the Hindi Film: A Historical Construction*, New Delhi: Oxford University Press. Metcalf Thomas. (2008). *The New Cambridge History of India: Ideologies of the Raj*, New Delhi: Cambridge University Press.

References

Amrita Bazar Patrika. (1935). *Vulgar Literature*: Manuscript Section. Kolkata: National Library, 1–12.

Baishya, Anirban K. (2017). Restore, Revisit, Remember: Reinstating the Region in Three Assamese Films, *Journal of South Asian Studies*, 2017, 431–446;

Chatterjee, Partha. (1994). *The Nation and Its Fragments*. Princeton: Princeton University Press.

Cohn, Bernard S. (1996). *Colonialism and its Forms of Knowledge: The British in India*. New Jersey: Princeton University Press, See Forward.

Dass, Manishita.(2009). The Crowd outside the Lettered City: Imagining the Mass Audience in 1920s India, *Cinema Journal*, 48(4), 77–98.

Ganti, Tejaswini. (2009). The Limits of Decency and Decency of Limits. In *Censorship in South Asia: Cultural Regulation from Sedition to Seduction*, (eds). Kaur Ramindar and William Mazzarella London: Routledge.

Gupta, Charu. (2012). *Gendering Colonial India, Reforms, Print, Caste and Colonialism*. New Delhi: Orient Blackswan.

Hughes, Stephen. (2002). Policing Silent Exhibition in Colonial India South India. In *Making Meaning in Indian Cinema*, (ed). Vasudevan Ravi. New Delhi: OUP, 42.

Jaikumar, Priya. (2006). *Cinemaat the End of Empire: A Politics of Transition in Britain and India*. Durham: Duke University Press, 5.

Kaur, Ramindar and William Mazzarella (eds). (2009). *Censorship in South Asia: Cultural Regulation from Sedition to Seduction*. London: Routledge, 14.

Metcalf Thomas. (2008). *The New Cambridge History of India: Ideologies of the Raj*. New Delhi: Cambridge University Press.

Nandy, Asish. (1998). *The Secret Politics of Our Desires: Innocence, Culpability, and Indian Popular Cinema*. New Delhi: Oxford University Press

Prasad, Madhava. (1998). *Ideology of the Hindi Film: A Historical Construction*. New Delhi: Oxford University Press.

Sharma, Manorama. (1990). *Social and Economic Change in Assam: Middleclass Hegemony*. New Delhi: Ajanta Publications, 3.

Sinha, Babli. (2013). *Cinema Transnationalisms and Colonial India, Entertaining the Raj*. London: Routledge, 2.

Index

Pages in *italics* refer to figures, pages in **bold** refer to tables, and pages followed by "n" refer to notes.

For Product Safety Concerns and Information please contact our EU representative GPSR@taylorandfrancis.com
Taylor & Francis Verlag GmbH, Kaufingerstraße 24, 80331 München, Germany

www.ingramcontent.com/pod-product-compliance
Ingram Content Group UK Ltd.
Pitfield, Milton Keynes, MK11 3LW, UK
UKHW020003200926
475702UK00015B/2447
* 9 7 8 1 0 3 2 8 8 8 1 8 7 *